# The Trouble With Authority

a psychological memoir & field guide
on how to survive the maddening erratic
behavior of mankind

in 151 proofs

Volume I

Also by Joseph D. Reich

If I Told You To Jump Off The Brooklyn Bridge
(Flutter Press, 2009)

A Different Sort of Distance
(Skive Magazine Press, 2010)

Pain Diary: Working Methadone & The Life & Times
Of The Man Sawed In Half (Brick Road Poetry Press, 2010)

Drugstore Sushi (Thunderclap Press, 2010)

The Derivation Of Cowboys & Indians (Fomite Press, 2012)

The Housing Market: a comfortable place to jump off
the end of the world (Fomite Press, 2013)

The Hole That Runs Through Utopia (Fomite Press, 2014)

Taking The Fifth And Running With It: a psychological
guide for the hard of hearing and blind (Broadstone Books,
2015)

The Hospitality Business (Valeviel Press, 2015)

Connecting The Dots To Shangrila: A Postmodern Cultural
Hx Of America (Fomite Press, 2016)

A Case Study Of Werewolves (Fomite Press, 2018)

The Rituals Of Mummification (Sagging Meniscus Press,
2017)

Magritte's Missing Murals: Insomniac Episodes
(Sagging Meniscus Press, 2017)

How To Order Chinese During A Hostage Crisis: Dialects,
Existential Essays, A Play, And Other Poems (Hog Press,
2017)

American Existentialism (Tuba Press, 2017)

An Eccentric Urban Guide To Surviving (Analog Submission Press, 2017)

The American Book Of The Dead (Xi Draconis Books, 2018)

From Premonition To Prophecy (Delinkwent Scholar Press, 2018)

Statutes Of David (Pen & Anvil Press, 2018)

I know why old men sit in front of windows all day sighing & crying & living & dying when the sun goes down on the city at night (Kung-Fu Treachery Press, 2020)

Makeshift Press
114 Wild Rose Lane
Winchester, VA 22602

© 2019 by Joseph D. Reich

All rights reserved. This book or parts thereof may not be reproduced in any form, stored in any retrieval system, or transmitted in any form by any means—electronic, mechanical, photocopy, recording, or otherwise—without prior written permission of the publisher, except as provided by United States of America copyright law. For permission requests, write to the publisher.

Cover art © 2019 by P. Forester
"Love or Confusion" is printed here with permission of P. Forester.

ISBN: 978-1-7341558-0-8

October 2019
MakeshiftPress.org

*For
gone
conclusions*

# THE TROUBLE WITH AUTHORITY

"The man that cannot visualize a horse galloping on a tomato is an idiot"

-Andre Breton

Abstract:

Sometimes existence just feels like when you're a little kid with a slight build sitting in the lake teeth chattering shivering water skis crisscrossing which can't keep straight due to fear and anxiety stuck there feeling like forever (them seeming to have a damn good time just gabbing away not appearing to give a damn) mandated against your own will and volition the personification of separation-anxiety not wanting to be there behind that great big intimidating engine leaking all that goddamn disgusting diesel beaten to the bone with absolutely no confidence or conviction in a ridiculous trembling timid tone of hesitance going–"hit it!" suddenly being viciously yanked up like a puppet by an insensitive ventriloquist and in the back of your head thinking–'what the heck! this isn't even fun!' and knock-kneed wobbly having no control barely get up trying to keep your balance (and for that matter self-respect and dignity) and topple over right on your face limbs flying all over the place being dragged like some sadistic nun pulling you by the ear overwhelmed all absurd and weird with all this water shooting up your nose clogging every last single one of your orifices feeling slightly suffocated dazed disoriented and wondering why the hell you're even out there as they tell you you should have just let go the rope…


Specifics:

Testing authority i never really thought
was all that bad considering all the crap
it in fact had put me through in the past



1

For a child lying back on
his back in his plush back
yard looking up at the bright

blue sky and passing clouds
and fading sound of propellers
and dogs dying down at dusk

imagination becomes
his concept of mortality
of death of his time on earth


2

All that time brooding and daydreaming
in the remains of the opaque late day light
within the detail of fluttering falling leaves
savoring the smell of brand new white tee's
like the scent of that thin slice of bubblegum
inside crinkly packs of glossy baseball cards


3

We should go back
to the time of toddlers
to the musicality of language

when words meant nothing
when words meant it all…


4

We always had gi joe with the kung-fu grip
& his buzz haircut in camouflage kneeling
ready for anything in that uncomfortable
split-level in the suburbs with absolutely
no carpeting on the floor and raw popcorn
stucco on the ceiling (as if some symbol
of life for all things incomplete or some

blueprint for pain & suffering) an even
stranger dysfunctional family with all
those deep dark secrets yet this stoic
alpha-male figure of literal object
permanence always made us feel
better & more safe & secure as if pro-
tecting all forms of separation-anxiety
all forms of neglect emptiness & loss
nothing wrong with that absolutely
nothing at all a boy's imagination
& everything he was supposedly
supposed to be getting ready for

proof:

The great thing about action figures
was they were always so malleable
and flexible and always felt like they
were sacrificing themselves for the
greater good like they could some
how make miracles from all those
authority figures trying to keep us
down and allowing us to keep our
imagination just a little bit longer

anti-proof:

There takes a certain amount of naivety and innocence
with rebellion not just all that earned and necessary
built-up anger but also spirit and imagination
while the wise ass delinquent with his under
cover grin practically tap dances to detention

proof:

Real rebellion was all that acting-out (trying to attract attention
for kind and wild and desperate reasons and never malicious)
and crazy shit you did without realizing it in elementary and
all those visits you did to the vice principle's and detention

and should have put this on the list of extracurricular
activities later on for your college application…


5

As kids and adolescents we judged our friends
and the ones we loved by the color of their eyes
like the different variety and subtle shades of crayons

never got laid at any of those keg parties
but sure as heck a hell of a lot went on


6

As kids we were hooked and addicted to statistics
like how many specific hits and doubles and triples
and homers and runs batted in and we relied on
the back of baseball cards and sports columns
on a day by day basis as believe it may have
helped us to naturally escape that grave
impending feeling of gloom and doom
acutely sensitively felt in our fragile spiritual
immune systems and the devastating loss
(emotional desertion and abandonment)
of all those people and things who made
us feel safe and secure which was our
fleeting object-permanent-vision deep
down of what we unconditionally loved
so turned to our sports heroes and childhood
mythological gods like thurman munson and
johnny bench walt clyde frazier and earl "the pearl"
monroe to find out how they did the night before
which was an instinctive and intellectual deflection
(even a mathematical language of substitution) to our neurotic
and nihilistic mortality (of brooding and fixating and obsessing
and worrying) a parallel thought-pattern which allowed us to
live vicariously through our innocent and spirited imagination
of how much longer (days and nights and dusks and dawns;

a proverbial 'bewitching hour' if you will) we had on earth in
this strange rather vague unstable indescribable thing called reality


7

proof 1

I think the best thing
          about boyhood
   was being wild
       with real
           action & adventure
     was the only
type of rebellion
       toothless
           topless
    with goggles
          on exploring
   the deep blue sea
         of the y
not getting home
     till a bike
         was grace
             fully
    flung
& forgotten
   like some holy
        sentimental
             object
 blooming
    right in front
        of the mailbox
            & front lawn
     & sun
        went down
  & the dew
     at dusk
started to form
     filthy
        feening

```
                    reborn
                          with a whole future
                    to look forward to
         for the time
                    being
                          content
                                & comforted
         in a home
                    of cordoroy
                          & secret drawers
                                      of baseball cards
                    with feasts
         of fish sticks
   & sloppy joe
```

proof 2

As boys we'd make sure
to pack brown bag lunches
of bologna sandwiches
on wonder & scooter pies
if we were gonna take off
the next day to china the
moon or the mountains
standing all morning
over the waterfalls
to catch rainbow
fish but it was
the conversation
that really did it
captured our essence
convinced or not
exactly sure of
what we just saw
& what we had not
returning home from
the pond in the forest
when the sun really
started to become
hot racing our
bikes back

somewhere
between our
imaginations
& the other
side of the tracks
taking shortcuts
from the back
of the super-
market through
trails we had
already literally
carved out
trampled
& tread on
for situations
& occasions
just like this
while it's little
details like this
of our footprints
through thicket
which remains
indelibly etched
in our consciousness


proof 3

All that time spent as a kid
    listening to jazzy rock & roll
        over a.m. transistor

  riding your *schwinn* bicycle
     all day after school
        guiltily brooding
          with absolutely

            nothing to do
             & nowhere to go
    a huck finn in the wind
   always on-the-run

from an eternal crime
not sure what had done

    dusk & when the last
          of the day's sun kicked-in
              feeling your deep-down
     empty existential mortality
murdered, missing-in-action

          melancholy
       day
    dreaming

in that great big plot
        of sand at the y
           & pizza joints

  (whole mess of *playboys*
        discovered in the dumpster
           & spending all day trying to recover
                *rc cola* bottlecaps

                    to get
                    15¢ off)

    where 'nice sicilian boys'
          treated you like their first born son


proof 4

You brood
    sitting at the end
        of your porch
  in your blue
      football uniform
          at 7 years old

proof 5

A subliminal obscure sense of belonging
which meant it all with those rituals and
daily activities like milk bottle deliveries
that neighbor always on the roof at the
end of the dead end in the beginning
of the seventies no one ever made
any mention of either peeking in
on the dentist's wife, suicide
ideations, or trying to steal
the cable next door things
seemed so much simpler
and pure so much to look
forward to while everything
true and false were your skinned
knees peeking through ripped cords


proof 6

We learned about the human female anatomy
from those two young jewish sisters who lived
next door who said if we show you ours you
show us yours and had never seen anything
that empty vacant and raw even strangely
scared me a bit about the hidden secrets of
girls; a little later on in elementary at recess
while in the middle of some great muddy football
game just minding our own business suddenly
showed up out of nowhere (some really weird
game of seduction) and asked if they wanted
us to see and witness them strip naked and
literally did so watching their undeveloped
torsos making these dance gyrations we had
never seen before right behind the bare bushes
hidden and hugging the brick facade of the school
named after some unknown president and i swear
all the boys started seething and feening like a wild
pack of pavlov's dogs (and strangely enough felt
bizarre phenomenon of being violated and taken
advantage of) and they said we were always

the ones who were so sick and mischievous
and couldn't keep ourselves out of trouble
but i don't know looking back not so sure




8


A

The slanted windows left slightly open
over the cubbyholes ushering in the first
stray sweet scent of a single blade of grass
sprouting from the mud of mother earth
in the spring triggering the imagination
of a young boy at his classroom desk.
the next time he will experience any
thing of this nature and a similar sensation
will be a couple months later the first couple
days of summer with the heat of the holy season
and has that rare feeling and emotion like some
prisoner after paying his dues being released
from captivity (somewhere between the fine
line of illusion and reality) into the brilliant
and blinding splendor of sunlight and that
schoolboy literally with his heart thumping
wandering home down long languid suburban
roads but also with a sense of brooding and
nihilistic ruminating (not sure but also can't
wait what the season will bring him) like
jean-paul sartre's concept of existentialism
of what to do with all that freedom (and its
consequences). the boy with all that mad
mischief and curiosity and passion will have
a hard time keeping himself out of trouble, but
that's all relative kinda comes along with the territory

B

Wealthy white girls wandering home
still in their wet bikinis and sandals
down those long country roads of

tall husks of corn knowing exactly
what they're doing, starting a life
of seduction and crime of passion

husbands with their wives required
to be perfect gentlemen; some
becoming alcoholic gigolos

and others the walking dead
going back & forth on their lawns
while who's more alive hard to tell

later on at the barbecue all's forgotten
but honestly in more ways than
not the sacrifice of a virgin


C's

I always could never stand those couple times
a girl declared her love for me (and in the back
of my mind thinking you gotta be kidding)
and had to come back with a punch line
just as convincing and never quite sure
who i felt worse for her or for me?


9

In our later-adolescence how closely
was the concept of love and romance
and the female body intertwined while
looking back nothing could have been
more spontaneous, full of spirit, exciting

proof:

My greatest discovery was orgasm
the release of pain and tension and suffering
into pure pleasure and passion with no need
for any sort of language or semantics into clear
lucid instinctive revelation natural ecstatic freedom
indescribable (un)imaginable my first wet dreams first loves
in suburbs of ethereal seasons every city country i've rambled
knocking on the window of the skyline and finally letting me in

10

With first love everything happens in slow-motion and silence
the tranquility of the brilliant abandoned solitary train station
the midnight streams and steeples penetrating the blossoming
keen senses the muffled tones of church bells and foghorns
grandfather clocks and every tick-tock last single flake of snow
falling in front of silhouetted streetlights creaking homes towns
which no longer seem yours holy and haunted foreign strangely
distant but perversely more familiar nursing beers in barrooms
all night with that pure gorgeous angel you love in the flickering
opaque light with very little to say 'cause madly in love while
don't have to and that says it all her stroking your five o'clock
shadow in the early morning hours of the bleary-eyed basement
just lying there naked sacred caressing cradled in some pull-out
sofa in just fishermen sweaters while all is silent as a prayer as
the winter wonderland snows build up in the sill and the chilly
steaming windows turn a glistening crystal while the whole town
will soon at last be still traced by the mercurial ethereal elements
of the season blanketed in that holy surreal miraculous snowdrift
taking on a contemplative and brooding feel and fantasy of simple
geometric shapes and forms as finally at last there's absolutely
not one living soul to think of just you and her and your whispers
and promises and pillow talk while all that peripheral madness
and anxiety and stress from the unnecessary bullshit and
nonsense of existence just suddenly magically vanishes
time stands still and all turns calm and silent…

proof 1

When you used to come out steaming shower
onto those cold morning floors when you were
first in love that phenomenon of a thought-pattern
being so lucid (almost with 'good' racing thoughts)
feeling so alive, yet strangely enough, also at a loss


proof 2

First love never wanes
a matter of fact with time
(and what that does to you)
can even develop a quality
of more nostalgia and
sentimentality...


anti-proof

You lose your first love way before you ever lose your first love
because of your concern of losing your first love and becomes
the ultimate self-fulfilling prophecy of what love (and the fear
of losing it) does to you wondering now where your first love
is her best friend who'd never talk to you told you how much
she was really fond of you and knew that was it and it was
over and long gone while that's the thing about first love


11

I recently hooked up on facebook with an old ole best
friend of mine who used to live next door and of course
we went over all the good times and it felt like it was
just yesterday, actually 35 or 40 years ago, but going
over good times and sentimental memories isn't that
what life's all really about and thus therefore felt just
like yesterday and we talked about our kids and how
in the present day he in fact dances almost every day
with his teenage daughters and thought that's pretty

damn cool and why not just dance every day with
your daughters, as we only go around once and of
course grew up on *meatloaf* and *saturday night fever*
while giving each other advice and wisdom like never
go on one of those cruises, as could actually lose
your soul and then i saw his facebook photo which
showed him in some beach bum hat holding a huge
can of beer in a brown paper bag with a great big smile
right in front of that cruise line and thought man ain't that just
the classic metaphor for mankind so full of contradictions and lies
but i guess a pretty nice guy one of the few who never betrayed
me or maybe just the nature of childhood didn't have the time?


disprove 1:

I have decided i want to spend
the rest of my life on one of those
idiotic cruise lines with no specific
return date or time all bundled up
on deck in one of those comfortable
recliners simply reading all those
leather-bound bios by people like
churchill and lincoln and darwin
"remembrances of things past"
nodding-out from the all-inclusive
all-you-can-eat seafood buffet
and open bar while shuffleboard
shot by fleeting phantom strangers
always most fond of going through
the ritual of reading the obituaries
on a daily basis of dead duchesses
and third cousins from beverly hills

the chaplain and undercover detective
strolling on deck with their casual
and pathetic small talk...

the captain as desperate and down on his luck
as the dope addict and wife asking him for a divorce
who suspects cares more about his fantasies of the girl next door

those well-mannered polite modest and humble
hard-working deck hands returning back to
portholes from polishing shattered chandeliers


disprove 2:

Most people are intimidated by beauty
and don't know what to make of it and
race off frightened like tourists back
to their absurd and safe false reality

there's a strange ridiculous sentimental
lost empty quality in home movies trying
to vainly, futilely, grasp at one's identity

the ice cream man is as sleazy and
threatening as the mean-spirited
idiot thief bullying athlete

the pretty high school girl both
holy and seductive knowing how
to instantly make an intellectual
connection and give the impression

(through flattering expressions, romance
and the possible offering of sex) of rescuing
the lost fathers of the small quaint tourist town


disprove 3:

I keep on sending sentimental videos
to my wife with no reply think i more
so preferred when i used to runaway
as a kid on a *greyhound* cross-country
with a walkman strapped together with
a rubber band or a piece of scotch tape
and listen to tom waits while least it left me
with a tear in my eye when the bus crawled
into reno, portland, san francisco...and had
nothing to look back on and a whole future

ahead and took a room looking out over every last
single sad silent alley in america which was the weather

supper coming in around the corner…


disprove 4:

The philosophers and scholars throughout the ages
have devoted their lives to researching and trying
to figure out the principle and concept (realities
and existence) of love and god what is it? where
is it? how much do we need of it? while in my
estimation don't think we should try so hard
or obsess so much to find out if we got it or
not yet if we really want try just a little harder
as at the end of a long day find it necessary to
be able to just sit back and relax in our recliners
and maybe catch a good game with a rum & coke
and let it all come to you in whatever proportion
and amount you naturally decide to choose


disprove 5:

Dear nietzsche ain't sure if it's me and just a coincidence
but really don't think so while more so a behavioral pattern
as all those supposed 'good church-going, fine upstanding
citizens' i have always found to be so full of hypocrisies and
contradictions even passive-aggressive with see-through morals
and ethics used solely at their own convenience and self-interest
('human all too human') leaving me feeling confused and conflicted


disprove 6:

They ship you off to college and those who were
originally motivated and inspired and expected
to get a well-rounded education (yet due to the
ridiculous, conformist element of prerequisite
fraternities and sororities, what it means to be
a proud follower) otherwise feel totally alienated

(not a part of) feeling like getting your spirit
stolen from you on a daily basis with things
taken can never quite get back, and end up
returning, disenchanted, damaged, confused
conflicted feeling cheated not quite exactly right


disprove 7:

Idiots in the stands in their mob mentality
hollering in unison like at those victims
at the coliseum, thirsting for blood
not a single independent soul around
a bunch of faux posers pretending
to act all scary and tough in the safety
and comfort of their absurd herd; our future
great leaders government officials and judges


disprove 8:

They say when we become parents
we are able to figure out all the games
of children but has it ever been considered
also figuring out all the bullshit of parents?


proof 1:

It is of my sincerest belief and conviction that those
who were spiritually and psychologically subjugated,
taken advantage, brow-beaten, made to feel constantly
guilty (filthy with a sense of self-loathing) conflicted,
tormented (and forced to repress their feelings and
emotions) during that profound and significant period
of adolescent growth and development will have a very
difficult time finding (identifying and recognizing) or
making any sense in their later life of any true form of
happiness (comfort or contentment) because cognitively-
behaviorally are just not 'used to it' or have no real clear
experience (insight or understanding or comprehension)

and when these natural feelings and emotions present
themselves and are manifest and 'come on' experience
the perverse psychological phenomenon (having become
hardwired in the cognitive 'immune system' and physiological
structure) of an exact opposite dynamic through a sudden active
trigger of anxiety and trepidation (which appears to come out
of nowhere) when naturally experiencing any of these selfsame
feelings of intimacy and affection or happiness and 'mental
freedom' with the natural instinct and instant need to flee
(the scene) due to past built-up defense-mechanisms of
coping and survival all originating from a constant inundation
(of the senses) due to emotional spiritual and psychological trauma


proof 2:

In our later-adulthood after feeling a bit defeated,
beaten, cheated, manipulated, betrayed and taken
advantage of by life and mankind through sublime
and subconscious psychodynamics, perversely end
up feeling like the 'ultimate stranger' (of self-loathing)
and sometimes have those necessary, soulful dreams
(of redemption) of old friends and lovers of kindness
and compassion from our distant past in random
safe and secure pleasant areas where good times
happened, and instantly recognize their traits and
characteristics (and expressions) on a mutual, familiar
level from deep in our natural and intuitive, transcendent,
metaphysical/spirited psyche, while ask the operational
question–"don't i know you from somewhere?" (already
knowing exactly how and where you know them) and
hope they say "yeah" and when and if they do (or give
the impression) realize this reaction and mutual feeling
of innocence and happiness is one of those good dreams
which provides the implicit, necessary function of
love and support and validation and empowerment

proof 3:

Here's the shortest myth of all time how an
older wizened man a bit spooked and broken
by life just walks out his room in the middle
of the night and right into the door of a grandfather
clock; closes the clock door as if instinctively
(might even call it symbolic) he's trying to keep
all those ghosts and phantoms and past behind
him and when they search for him he's nowhere
to be found and naturally without telling anyone
simply decide to accept it and live with it and
never gets mentioned again and every time that
clock strikes on the hour have pleasant memories
and dreams about him or those conflicting keen
surreal ones are instantly placated and mollified
and flow like some mellifluous river into the tide.
he used to have this idea and concept or wonder
how you might have that soothsayer or ancient
shaman and thought wouldn't it be better if had
some sort of sacred magician who could sprinkle
some secret elixir right onto the skin (and penetrate
the bloodstream) to heal all that pain and suffering
embedded deep in the subconscious to almost allay
or alleviate all those nightmares of trauma and loneliness
and isolation so you have this myth where this older man
just walks out his room in the middle of the evening and
never seen from or heard from again but provides some
kind of soul sacrifice every time clock strikes the hour


proof 4:

In my middle ages what to say about that striking tall
svelte young doe-eyed red-haired girl perfect pristine
alabaster skin whose innocence like some monument
of angelic madonna-whore feminine beauty in her high
top black sneakers tight jeans and flannel with a simple
and subtle hypnotic smile who could drive all the guys
wild working at the local town hardware like some graceful
ice skater doing figure-eights all around the stagnant state of

stone-faced ice fishermen old timers knowing her natural power
of seduction and putting them all under her spell for the short
while politely asking is there any way she can help (and can't
help but to spend all day in there helpless forgetting why they're
there) and think man this vision and experience is more healing than
practically almost any therapy while the delicate mist like a blanket
starts to slip down the mountain and railroad tracks lead me home
back to town. the pumpkins will start to come out soon and will
close down the dairy cream like a sneaky sleepy vanishing moon


proof 5:

We used to in science lab
in junior high school
always strangely
watch this film
over and over
of eskimo
out on the
frozen tundra
hollering–"car-i-bou!
car-i-bou!" and now
many decades
later find i'm
hungry and
really able to
relate and connect
to for what reason
i'm really not sure
perhaps it's the pure
spirit and solitude of it all
that crie-de-coeur of "caribou!!!"


proof 6:

How to write a letter to a used car salesman
(the classic metaphor for man or plato's parable
on how to handle a madman attacking you with
a weapon) who has no concept of character or

communication while yourself a social worker
forced to self-advocate for your own self-respect
and client's rights and honesty and integrity and
autonomy and self-determination and empowerment
and just like everything else in their ridiculous and
pathetic existence ('cause know no different; how
they were trained and raised) expect no letter back
and got no other choice but to go up the chain of
command to their manager; some little smiling
twerp on the internet (wondering if it will get
any better cause this is where it all started and
made his quota and molded and manipulated
their fucked-up and fragmented character)
like when you used to have to call a d.s.s.
worker to support a client in crisis and never
got a call back ironically experiencing the exact
same sort of neglect and eventually had to leave
a message for the supervisor and out of natural
consequences (classic clinical family dysfunction)
call back the next day like nothing had ever happened


proof 7:

Searching for queen
for queen mattress
& she must be a
real queen & not
one of those of
royal breeding
but someone willing
to go all out & dig deep
& of suffering & seen
something of this life
& her share of living
& been on the brink
& thus of real feeling
& really feel her & be
of spirit & soul & a
soulmate to spoon
& snuggle & sleep
on the other side

of this sighing
scene of me
poor life


proof 8:

We were both such damaged tortured haunted souls
was absolutely no need at all to be told to go down
to the sofa as would both naturally end up there and
mutually spoon and snuggle and soothe each other
and coil naked tearful trembling exchanging past
stories of previous traumatic family experiences
having developed spiritual trust and able to
make a connection and relate to each other
as if beacons guiding one another through
the darkness and similar real-life nightmares
in the silhouetted shadows of wild swaying
branches splashed through the plantation
shutters and bathed by the stray light of
old black & white film noir and felt far more
comfortable there like truth or dare rare familiar
strangers more than they ever could in some
square safe & secure bed and got them to bed


proof 9:

The worst those out-of-touch clueless
and critical ridiculous judgmental parents
who turn the kid hostile and helpless (are so
full of it will even say such shit like why are you
so angry so self-absorbed and clinically narcissistic
just makes one feel instantly lonelier and alienated)
while in american cinema have been brilliant acting
performances and tirades and soliloquies to mimic
these maddening profound feelings such as jason
robards in 'long day's journey' marlon brando
in 'last tango' jimmy dean in "rebel without
a cause" jack nicholson in "five easy pieces"
dustin hoffman in "the graduate" vincent
gallo in "buffalo 66" river phoenix woody

allen in "annie hall" and the list goes on
and get so absorbed no wonder why you
watch them over and over and over again


clinical conclusions:

She was just nice to look at
just enough to get by in this life

who said i ever wanted to get by?

so she was just nice to look at...

When you first meet a guy to try and do a job
you can see what they're all about by all their
bullshit and lies and their expressions and body
language and what they tell you and don't tell you
and almost have to make your decision and choose
based on who you think might get the job done with
doing the least amount of damage or before he has
his psychotic meltdown and demands his money
due to maladaptive thinking or drinking problem

I can see why jesus was a lone sole carpenter and
never hired a crew or outsourced or subcontracted
and thus by philosophical and the logical law of
transitivity it is my belief that civilization is just
made up of a bunch of rogue subcontractors who
don't get the job done take the money and run

You win some you lose some
while strangely enough in the end
end up feeling winsome and lonesome

12

Looking back in retrospect we were all lunatics
in our adolescence literally howling hysterically
leaping off of diving boards in our underwear
pool-hopping in the deepest part of the night
not giving a damn if we got caught or not while
this for us is what freedom was strolling down
warm summery suburban roads in tighty-whities
and sandals soaking studs right before the dawn
reborn, drunk, wasted involved in casual banter
(as if we were the only ones who existed in the
'heat of the moment' might as well have been
just naturally bullshitting the hx of civilization
while in many ways not too far from it) not
thinking nor giving a damn about our future

Looking back in retrospect acting-out in adolescence
and early adulthood was in fact the best act (and
experience and dynamic) of intimacy and affection
and held the most meaning with all those things clearly,
keenly, profoundly believed, and practically became the
'prodromal phase' to my being and identity and later on in life
not by coincidence, my understanding of all things around me

Looking back in retrospect all those supposed
pretty or 'popular' girls in high school (who were
so self-involved and treated themselves like untouchable
goddesses) it almost felt like they were dating themselves
or had such high standards literally i swear were dancing
with their reflection in the mirror until maybe that one
lucky interlude or moment they may have actually been
flirting with you you'd instantly check over your shoulder

Looking back in retrospect all those real romantic
and passionate and intimate even highly-sexualized
relationships made one literally feel 'more alive' or
this strange sense of eternally 'wanted' and 'belonging'
even seemed to almost take on a whole other perspective
of some sort of psychological and spiritual depth & dimension

Looking back in retrospect all those intimate relationships
each had their own intrinsic and kinetic energy and spirit
which concretely became a microcosm and reflection of the
life-cycle and own similar-like stages of growth & development
and thus, along with all those obstacles and challenges and very
profound feelings and emotions concomitant with sudden triggers
of love and loss, as well as one's own mortality, can interestingly
be viewed as well in a rather surreal manner as their own existences

Looking back in retrospect
as long as there were a couple
relationships of love and passion
that's all that can be hoped for...
a wife who gives the impression
she loves you, cleaning out the
bathroom with lovely bleaches
and disinfectants swirling with
the strange scents of the wild
wilderness and drizzle on the
wildflowers, keeping the evening
window open for the blessed croak
and creaking of crooning amphibians

Looking back in retrospect
a woman who has stuck by you
who has not given up on you
is very well worth keeping
always hated expressions
like that if you know
what i'm talking?

proof:

I see ourselves later on in life becoming
something like blind dates not necessarily
recognizing ourselves, our characteristics
and traits (overwhelmed by circumstances
looking for some individual to save our soul)
very tough on ourselves, self-critical almost
to a fault, selling ourselves short, unaware we are
the exact person we've always been looking for

the proofs:

The image of spooning her
on the x-ray table and them
taking close-ups of all your
internal organs your broken
bones and woebegone tissue
real-life beating heart & soul

the nice young blonde girl
helps you off the table and
you make your token small
talk and head back to the
beatdown boxcar diners on
the border in the mountains

you thrive off anonymity
and bleak overcast days
with graying purplish clouds
looming over red brick factories
mills planted along blue babbling

rivers where hills of still-life silent white-
washed libraries & town halls & cathedrals
all look exactly the same and no one around
to speak of in these strange sacred pick-up
stick blissful towns of secrets and shame

13

How many cracked lives i've lived
in this cracked-up life in the shattered
snow globe of a life with all those lowlife
scenarios leaking out and no one seeming
to give a flying which was like the opposite
proof of prove that you exist was this delinquent
kid on the back of a box of cereal tarnished toy
prize constantly full of guilt and acting-out
who couldn't keep himself out of trouble

living a life of a life of crime living outside left
inside the deep down pocket of a fallen angel
making his way through the silhouetted smoke
stack flashing traffic light twilight evenings
of america; dusk was truth or dare and swear
the miracle of her suddenly secretly showing
up out of nowhere wrapping at your door
(finally at last part of some folklore that
someone actually cared) there to save
you and needed it just as bad both being
delivered in the moment (forgotten forgiven)
no matter how long that it might in fact last


14

Beauty frightens me to the core
having to do with mortality
all that raw solitude stuff


proof:

Successes become assholes at very young ages
(the silence & life & times & strange surreal
structures of the affluent slow-death suburbs)


15

In this life, two steps back, one step ahead
leaves you practically dead, barely gasping
for air in the filthy puddle of the movie theater
after futilely, desperately trying to escape reality

proof:

I am refreshed and reborn
by the lightning and thunder
who the hell am i? godzilla
after he stomps through
a mad frantic street in
tokyo? maybe i am
but the air sure as
hell smells fine
the next day


non-proof:

People will travel all
this way just to get to ruins
but never once think to explore
the ruins of their own existence


proof 1

The thing i miss the most about traveling are the leaves
in those ancient cosmopolitan iridescent cities with their
slight fluttering and splashing of keen brilliant transcendent
shadows which brought about a whole other reality and state
of being all that half-crazed mysterious industry heading to
the sea which seemed like all of humanity like clandestine
carnival caravans stuffed with animals and freaks all the
innocent burgeoning beauty of topless teens the brooding
of tormented divorcees fresh mozzarella and shrimp straight
out the shell on a bed of linguine on the sparkling mediterannean
the hustle and bustle and howling and hollering at fresh fish ripe
festive plump bright and beautiful fruit markets of madness and
passion plucked straight from the surrounding mountains where
that whole culture emanated windows full of panini sicilian
and slim bottles of lemon liqueur the modernity of museums
i would never go into but preferred with great vigor to go deep
down the subway to really get to know the people deliberately
getting out in places i didn't know and try and figure out and
explore and find my way home with my take-out vietnamese

couple of beers and writing the day's reflections which would
help me to get to sleep thinking about the following morning
naturally lighting to the train station and drifting out to sea


proof 2

I swear i have fallen in love with certain stretches
of highway (their strange familiarity) quite often
more than their actual destiny like women's bodies
(shapes and forms) at times more than their being;
one cannot sincerely understand these things unless
having truly lived something of a keen solitary life


proof 3

If we are in fact all in god's image
what to say about those soulless
idiots tailing you with a baby
on board bumper sticker on your
way to boston? where's wyoming?
wisconsin? ever see that one with
peter lorre and humphrey bogart
when they were just a bunch of
eccentric expatriate grifters
pleasantly anonymous planning
some jig out in andalucia before
they hitched a ferry out to africa
as kinda put it all in perspective

something to be said
about being a stranger



16

Every time my wife sprays the housespray
ironically makes me feel estranged like
i'm being replicated in a false garden

17

Most women hunger for specific archetypal symbols
(yet how they waver a couple years later in marriage
and rebel against the exact criteria that was required)


18

Sending venus flytraps
to your hoarding mother
in law from the bronx
to get on her good side
like some psychotic kind
of spring cleaning on one of those
fine fall days of revelation & meaning


19

Don't care what you
say american hx was
those first days of school
and the smells of all those
loose leaf notebooks and
new erasers and saying
you were gonna turn over
a new leaf that year and
somewhere in the middle
finding yourself cracking
one-liners in the back of
the class and detention
with all those mad passionate
things you did on the weekend
in the chilly colorful leaves getting
drunk at keg parties and conveniently
forgetting still showing up on monday

20

before:

In the suburbs in the early-sixties my parents always
had like these sophisticated swinger sort of built-in bars
with mirrors (i guess to constantly, obsessively check out
their image & reputation) for entertaining put together straight
from their *time-life* book collection always with spare bottles
of tonic water & spaceship-shaped liqueurs of fancy bourbons
& mouthwash-colored creme-de-mints, creme-de-caramel
& thick & rich cho-co-lat from cha-cha-cha romantic brazil
with all those fine, foggy, gold-gilded, cocktail glasses
and fragile, crystal glass stirrers but nothing ever seemed
to happen and no one ever seemed to use them, like some
absurd, still-life scene of what "leisure" was supposed
to be, or had the potential to be, and would be able to
engage in at their own 'time & leisure' and convenience
just in case that time or scenario ever happened to pre-
sent itself which of course never did and in my opinion
represented some strange safe sense of contentment
or the opposite of crisis, and some classic bizarre
archetypal symbol for the illusion of suburbia


after:

Man some of those commercials from back in the late-sixties
and seventies were so subliminal and crazy like almost trying
to get the whole drinking population stirred-up and feening
and to start drinking like when you think about such jingles
like–"shaeffer is the one beer to have when you're having
more than one…" and then repeating that over and over again–
"shaeffer is the one beer to have when you're having more than one"
or 'how weekends were solely made for michelob' and "i got pabst-
blue ribbon on my mind…i got pabst-blue ribbon on my mind"
or "if you've got the time we got the beer" like when you hear
this, some sort of chemical trigger just automatically kicks in
and would hit your brain and could practically taste that taste
of feeling no pain, as opposed to these days with all these new
made-up man-made disorders and diseases you've never even

heard of (that only a specific psychotropic or pharmaceutical
can cure) and then like showing all these weird middle-aged
couples being safely seductive you cannot even relate to role-
playing these ridiculous unrealistic scenarios (some token
caucasian before & after scene that if you consistently take
this "magic pill" will see your identity change from isolation
and self-deprivation and misery to suddenly feeling liberated
and free, even that just-out-of-reach feeling/instant panacea
of "happy") where you don't even understand what they are
doing or the plot or what they're getting at and the climax is
always that they're living eternally happily ever after but really
actually find yourself situationally-depressed because you know
you never had the leverage or freedom or opportunity like that
to have some upper-middle class privileged and entitled scene
made-up of such things and you're thinking more so of self-
medicating with a couple 6's and how much more you preferred
this country when we were just under-privileged and simply
a bunch of undercover raging and lower-middle class alchies


denouement:

Life-long bureaucrats are buffoons while press their buttons
and you get something worse than being stuck underground
on the subway and hearing over and over again much to your
frustration the terribly patronizing "thank you for your patience"

the greatest fear is becoming a literal statistic
and getting stuck in the system, frightened
that there's no one out there to help you
while what makes it even worse…

is they're supposed to be 'human'
and seeking support and guidance
and being completely mechanical with
their abuse of power and indifference

just shows how much they don't give
a damn, making you feel that much
more hollow, isolated and alienated

the best way to confuse and combat them
is through a good dose of sarcasm and
a taste of their own medicine (almost

imitating them) acting even more matter-
of-fact and didactic, which instantly
disorients them (and if take names)

through 'natural consequences' and fear
of losing their positions (cause these soulless
clones to look in the mirror, maybe even stop

reading straight from the script, losing their
leverage, proving you refuse to be a number
or become disempowered by catatonic tactics)

then suddenly out of nowhere (even a bit scared)
because realize they no longer have the control
or power start to show human characteristics

and believe it or not
might even get them
to actually work for you


21

For someone who has been infinitely unfairly judged their whole
life once they shed that skin of pervasive criticism how suddenly
surreal becomes their existence and something of a revelation


22

We all come from these really fucked-up
dysfunctional families we barely survived
and try to find in our partners something
spontaneous and spiritual (even comical)

in the hopes to try and save and redeem
and more ways than not keep us alive




23

My memories of college was that they were all just so mean
(and couldn't have felt more alienated yet deep down inside
think i really knew it was not me but them) a bunch of rich
kids from the tri-state area coming down to the deep south
thinking the whole world revolved around them, and for me
such a waste of time and disappointment as were so unclever
and uncreative and self-absorbed and self-interested, as just
were going to go into their daddy's business (usually some
where around the diamond or garment district) and couldn't
make a move or exist without their fraternity; the girls all acted
like a bunch of sluts from the sorority and looking back sincerely
and spiritually nothing at all made me feel more lost and lonely




24

A fear of suburbia whose strange deafening artificial silence
and manufactured, manicured "blue" print for happiness
ironically takes on more of a feeling of brooding sadness
and one's own nihilistic existential mortality (and fragile
identity) whose stifling secrets and suppressing (along
with connections and nepotism) eventually always
develops a bizarre dysfunctional mythology while
'the monster from beneath the bed' comes out to
play and the seasons are measured by the stray
fading propellers of the rhythm and cadence of
gardeners, like distant dazed gods, completely
unaware have become a part of our consciousness
because have been subtly out there on the literal and
topographical landscape practically our whole lifetime
with an expectation to make it all look perfect and
the immaculate illusion will heal all our problems

25

They say it might just be the end for the mall in america
and wonder if we'll feel any sense of remorse, collective
trauma, bittersweet reflection or just absolutely nothing
at all like the rise & fall of the roman empire and will
just be left exactly right where we started nursing a
blunt on a pull-out sofa with an episode of insomnia
and midget wrestling muted on our television in some
upper east side condo looking out bleary-eyed to queens
and parts of brooklyn with some aristocratic girlfriend
frigid codependent who claims to be some sort of zionist
able to sniff out all those free samples at *zabars* and always
find yourself sneaking out feeling like some sort of criminal
in the middle of some sweltering summer night in manhattan
with charlton heston ironically simultaneously on the television
in loin cloth on hands & knees haunted howling with the profile
of the statue of liberty and her torch & crown rundown shockingly
still around (like some postmodern shroud) just barely poking out
of the sand and think maybe the infamous swiss psychologist eric
b. erickson was right that we can only move on to our next stage
of growth & development through a period of crisis or state of
flux some sort of psychodrama to sublimate and realize existence
is all just a series of strange sweet phases like childhood or walking
down the aisle, while all the most profound passionate relationships
were the ones in which they needed it the most and were most desperate
and could feel it all on an emotional & spiritual level in their kiss some-
where between prehistoric & pornographic and wonder if will feel
anything at all in the natural extinction of the rise & fall of the mall


26

One has to be secretly just slightly happy to really get mathematics
with something of a troubled constantly misinterpreted childhood
like dissecting the blues and coming up with a partial resolution

anti-proof 1

You are able to figure people out
when you are not trying to figure them out
and will tell you (pretty telling) in everything
they don't tell you as becomes so ridiculous
and ironic 'cause have no idea how much you
actually know about them (their passive-aggressive
expressions without even being aware of it) thinking
they're being so clever and shrewd, but deep down
(through intuition and wisdom and learned behavioral
patterns and body language) so cowardly and crude

most adults just prove pretty poor unconvincing actors…


anti-proof 2

In society & culture those who are the more convincing liars
come off as the most honest climbing that proverbial
ladder of success without even trying…


anti-proof 3

After thievery comes the buffoonery of reality…


anti-proof 4

Everyone lies and when we meet the one man who
might just not, treat him something like the messiah



27

How language just naturally forms and transforms…
blooms and blossoms from sound(s) is like the physical
metamorphosis of bone structure (growth & development

of) body & soul in 'adaptation of species' and 'survival of
the fittest' in all those brilliant and keen stages of evolution

i.e. Overhearing women's whimsical melodic conversation
is like the beat and rhythm (the breadth) of the waves and
their natural cycle and currents echoing on the ocean full
of spirit and passion and when drowsing off between states
of consciousness along the shore hearing their fluid rapport
with perhaps their kids or girlfriends almost in perfect natural
harmony and synchronicity with the symphony of the sea
whose murmurs and musicality without even being aware
of it (and cadences) almost feed off each other taking
on a whole other similar selfsame reality of being

i.e. Nicknames are formed through similar-like machinations
when you have a certain amount of fondness and affection
for that person and make a natural connection through their
personal, physical, and psychological traits and characteristics
and just develops and blossoms from keen everyday observations

i.e. I've always preferred so much more mispronunciations
which always seemed to have far more meaning (and moxie)
far more accurate reflection of that particular culture & society

i.e. Accents i can assure you in no way shape or form
came by coincidence

i.e Where i came from you saw such signs and advertisements
(of an apparently rather low baseline) which read–

*Real Butter…Live Women*


28

Stoicism is good but also in my opinion, believe it or not
need a certain amount of self-respect, self-reflection,
self-pity, and self-sufficiency to survive as well

proof:

The goal towards perfection with all its perfectionistic efforts
becomes more than imperfect when you consider all the rigid,
relentless and ridiculous sacrifices while ironically, paradoxically

more times than not, a shutting-off of the senses
and even at times absurdly losing meaning and
purpose in the attempt towards its attainment


29

I can tell you by how the brain functions (or does not function)
or malfunctions, there is really no such thing as self-destructive
behavior, but really more accurately a machination or manifestation
from some past overwhelming form of constant, overbearing,
emotional abuse, which to a certain extent has cognitively
contaminated the system; a supersaturation if you will, or a
psychological and physiological wearing down and flooding
of the senses (and defenses) until all you got left without even
being aware of it is this (type of behavior). eventually in the
long-run after enough struggle and sorrow and repetition and
damage (through patience and perseverance one can seek a
physical or spiritual redemption) in fact actually step back
(to gain and reframe a whole new perspective) while recog-
nizing and identifying the triggers and patterns of this behavior,
and through the process and dynamics of desensitization (or
externalization) practically (almost by reducing and reversing
instincts and impulses) work their way out of it…


proof 1:

Why is it the trigger often feels more traumatic
and damaging than the actual original violation?
is it that instinctively all those survival and coping
mechanisms kicked in and was purely physical
and later on it has somehow sincerely sunk in

in the spiritual and emotional psyche and the
fragile, vulnerable mind and heart and soul
(shaken to the core) to know a tree actually
needs both the sun and water to grow and
can only last in the darkness for so long


proof 2:

They should make a stamp
for just when you feel sorry
when you feel guilty sealed
with your tear maybe should
just make one for jesus' eye
dripping you just can't win
out here like some camus
parable being found guilty
for eternally feeling guilty
of something deep down
inside you know you are
not and never been guilty
one of those antique dolls
who just looks out to the
twinkling pacific somewhere
between alcatraz and the golden
gate bridge to the pure bleak
lucid madness of freedom


proof 3:

He was just looking for one kind man in his life
perhaps he knew this (maybe not) as always
had been aware of it in himself since he was
a little child so i suppose maybe deep down inside
why searching for just one kind man his whole life


proof 4:

Has it ever been stated that most

critics are simply over-rate-it?
30


It is of my sincerest belief that most guys
have not had enough romance or relationships
(the good and bad kind) before their marriage
and when they walk down the aisle suddenly
start to notice and recognize the bridesmaids
they delusionally believe they might have had


proof:

I think i know why some men turn to drinking...
it's not so much that their women walk out on them
it's that they're around too much and never leave them

                those idiot cliches
              that you'll never find
                  your answer
           at the bottom of a bottle
                  maybe not
              but sure as heck
                   find less
          questions on your way
                     trying
                to solve them


31

In my estimation spiritual and intimate neglect
or the effort not to make a connection
in a relationship may in some ways
be viewed as a 'crime of passion'
even lead to a 'prison sentence'

non-proof:

When people have declared their love for
me i have found myself instantly repulsed
and disgusted by their neediness while this
feeling comes over me of a strange self-loathing

i find myself rather falling
in love with fleeting images
of strangers from a distance


32

Sometimes i swear i just want to go back
and search for old girlfriends in those ole
beatup carrodead copper coalmine towns

try to find them on those backstreet suburban
blocks where their split-level was and go back
to the exact same insane motel on the seashore

and have them whip me raw not too hard
to get some strange sense of closure in front
of the staticky television along with the muffled

rhythmic roar of the ocean beating against the door.
is that bizarre or just some impulsive instinctive idea for
not making things work out even as damaged and fucked-up

and impossible as they were and so smart and to die for?
unload all my pockets for housekeepers whose gigolo
husband childhood sweethearts walked out on them

proof:

It's a strange surreal place
bedrooms made purely out
of jigsaw puzzle pieces
no doors or windows
just the sound of fairies
dancing naked in the rain
all the brothers are simply
half-crazed perverted delinquent
aristocrats always looking to score
with daughters in those vacant summer
country clubs where canals meet the ocean.
at sundown the sunbathing strumpets
have nowhere to go and just casually
hit on by the semi-retired studs just
going through the motions playing
their roles like scavengers going in
for the leftovers and last of the kill.
young vagabond runaways
hitching along the early
evening beach just
grateful to be picked
up and exchange stories
while dropped off a little
further down along the way
parents never around as just
to be found at the masquerade
parties right outside of town
the discos full of hipsters
(actors and politicians)
dancing with no rhythm
while absolutely nothing
to do in this decadent city
and the thinning dusk only
makes this abundantly clear
with the streets deserted and
empty and all alleys lead to the sea
where fateful wars begin and end
in our dreams and imagination.
in the morning all the guilt-ridden

divorcees and kids with drug problems
ditch the sea-stained motels bleary
eyed looking for new beginnings

we always remember where
the sleepy train station is...


33

prologue:

When i pulled off her underwear
and saw that bright red hair
against her pale white skin
it was like nothing i had
ever seen before and
seemed like the person
fuck/action of all things
feminine and demure
nothing looked better
more brilliant and
raw like a miracle
like the 8th wonder
of the world in that
motel up on the hill
on the atlantic ocean


epilogue:

She promised me
a whole weekend
out there but of
course in the morning
just like everything else
said she had to go
and i asked her
if she wanted any
extra soap when she
was in the shower.

she said no thanks
and could see her
through the curtain
peek a tiny little smile


34

I learned about romance and love
from a very tough and handsome
marlon brando with shirt ripped
off revealing his primal muscles
screaming stella at the top of his
lungs at the bottom of the spindles
of the sweltering staircase in the slums
of the french quarter of new orleans
later on as a loner howling under
the el of the metro in 'last tango'
from rhett butler and scarlet o'hara
going back and forth with mind games
and seduction between man and woman
from rocky balboa and talia shire on a very
cold winter's night in the ghetto of philadelphia
after a first date bringing her back to bleak beatdown
hovel and trying to convince this demure frightened
angel to stay with him because he was just as lone
some and both just as isolated and needy for the
companionship with some slow desperate kiss
shedding all their defenses and finally letting
it all go falling in a heap of rags to the floor


35

All those girls
i went out with
all thought i was
a bit crazy but
used to crack

them up and
even made
them happy
for the
short
while

what do
i got to do
to prove myself?

get my
name
written
eternally
in graffiti?


proof #1:

Don't ever take for granted any of those relationships
even the short and passionate ones (especially those)
as the ones upon reflection where you learned the most


proof #2:

You learn at a very young age (even as far back as puberty)
and almost tragic (and a pity) and wish you didn't have to
that even when you do well and work your ass off and remain
modest and humble they ain't gonna necessarily like or love
you; a matter of fact in most cases, i swear, and i guess they
call this human nature (and can see it written all over their face
a genuine disgrace) will turn envious and hate and resent you
and it's up to you to decide at that exact moment to fall for it
from these very serious straight men and stand-ins (a whole
battalion of very little men with napoleonic complexes who
try to turn you lonesome) or got no other option but to thrive
off it (almost positive version of the fight or flight syndrome)
and fall that much more in love with the smoldering blonde
on your shoulder whereas the girl you worked so hard for

proof #3:

You wonder why every used car salesman has the compulsive need to be such a blatant phony and meets every prerequisite and criteria and even stereotype of being a total schmuck while have just become immune and indifferent to them and will do everything humanly possible to sell you the car and will get their whole dishonest crew on board to leave messages (the whole "my name is" without even asking and know exactly what they're doing all a part of their training and schmooze reading straight from the script; she'll even start sending you her pic when she believes the negotiations are running smoothly as if trying to establish some mandated 'finish the deal' sense of intimacy and familiarity and you thinking this is all you got to show me? this bleached-blonde middle-aged lady who looks likes she hasn't gotten it in ages) while in case you should ever have any follow-up questions after the purchase as have one simple and innocent one and give them a call and of course never a call back (real surprise and shocker and believe man puts more time in being a sleazy liar than actually just doing their job) and wonder why mankind just seems like a bunch of boring and obvious opportunistic used car salesmen or that phase in puberty when this all began somewhere around junior high school where they all became like these very sane aloof and arrogant used car salesmen as if establishing a baseline for being aggressive and 'driven' and you thinking most likely missed that lesson


proof #4:

Wouldn't it be great if had a better business bureau
for everyday assholes who have done you wrong?

we used to eat grilled cheese & bacon at boxcar diners
under the stars to forget it all and save our souls

the road will leave you alone…

proof #5:

The masses not so sure what i can
say as these days feels from experience
that infamous real-life collective unconscious
non-existent nauseating and just makes me sick

in unity there's strength to be a coward
and clown and conformist (who lie
and rationalize) to get away with it

how simple murder gets...

the worst thing about indifference
is there's nothing to it; takes absolutely
no personality, character, experience not required

i believe in everything before & after the trigger
when memory didn't play such a big part of it
when wind and the sweet smell of mud and
roses show up to both the wedding and funeral

(if you only knew what
fable and folklore
were made of)

the poor boy hanging out on the corner
at rush hour when the distant twilight trains
race in sparking skinned knees along the river


36

It is of interest how i always find myself far more contented
when i don't know what time it is, when i forget what day
of the week it is, even sometimes the seasons, like when
having one of those real intimate, passionate relationships
and forget all the bullshit around me (all the constant conflicts
and crises that people bring) as time ceases to have any meaning

proof:

Freedom is having the ability (as a kid, adolescent
young adult, or during some period of subjugation
or stagnancy) to actually dream (and fantasize)
and imagine and conceptualize however unrealistic
or inaccurate about all those fine and wild surreal
'good' and 'virtuous' passionate things (all forms
and symbols of what you believe might make you
happy) in your distant and remote 'mature' future
so in the 'here and now' whenever you're feeling
bogged-down or depressed or down in the dumps
in some form or another take a risk or chance at
dreaming big even if a bit out there or delusional
or fantastical; there is a coping mechanism/survival
skill called 'partialization' which implies when you
are completely overwhelmed by the circumstances
and stressors of life to try and just master one simple
minor task and upon its completion often might just
emotionally, naturally open the door (and make more
apparent and aware) to all those others which appear
way beyond your reach or scope of reality while believe
all of these dynamics and things (that has as much to do
with 'state of mind' as anything palpable or tangible) touch
on that often elusive obscure concept of the principle of freedom


37

Has anyone ever measured spirit (all that burgeoning energy
emanating from the soul) but guess that'd be something of
a spiritual contradiction for its selfsame traits and characteristics
of a liberating freedom, romantic and loving feeling and aesthetic,
imagination, ability to be receptive and observant, thoughtful,
generous (intimate, private, contemplative, kind and compassion-
ate) and one's sudden, spontaneous, natural instinct and intuition

proof:

The elements of tangible and palpable natural spirit
involve a certain type of spontaneity and "newness"
(a burgeoning of the senses) and the impression of
the potential for freedom and 'being virtuous'
(whatever form that happens to take on which
is irrelevant because fleeting and ephemeral)
with a natural state of flux allowing for almost
no doubt or conflict worrying nothing about any
thing having to do with the past present or future


38

Sometimes patience for the man of patience
can in fact be his worst enemy because he
forgets his baseline as well as his destiny


39

Be very wary of the man who always has the need & compulsion
to play the role of honest, as 'trust me,' paradoxically, is about as
manipulative (takes advantage) and 'far from the truth' as you can get


proof a:

Likewise, similarly the one playing the role of 'virtuous'
while ironically, perversely, is so full of contradictions,
hyper-critical and passing judgment, believing you are
not worthy enough to be in their very exclusive club
all signs and symptoms of being insecure and not
having a whole heck of a lot of experience in
the world (will even go so far as to get hostile)

proof b:

Being loud and obnoxious and opinionated
and hurling around very pithy generalizations
and accusations does not necessarily make you
'liberal' or what you passive-aggressively believe
to be 'virtuous' but in many ways shows your
complete lack of experience and street knowledge
(some sort of caricature or billboard) while ironically
almost as guilty (judgmental, exclusive, and alienating)

as all those things and people you are so
boisterously, vociferously railing against;
consider reflection, a little more independent
thinking, persistence, making changes from within


proof c:

Why is it the biggest assholes
always have the easiest time
shrugging off and forgetting all
the asshole things they've done?



40

Why is it those people we always
seem to be begging for approval
(in the psychodynamic process
dynamic of overcompensation)
when we really look at it deep
down inside really couldn't care
less what they think about you?

proof:

We even desperately seek approval
in our dreams (and nightmares…)

what ridiculous abused lives we've led!


41

Some of the greatest obstacles and challenges come from
a dysfunctional family unit who was supposed to play the
role of a support system with their subtle abuses of power
and cut-throat mentality, stigmatizing and criminalizing one
with brainwash and lies until cannot help but to fulfill the self-
fulfilling prophecy and thrive off acting-out, in fact, almost
practically (without being aware of it) establish some kind
of insight or sculpt an identity, literally have to physically
divorce themselves and declare something of a spiritual in-
dependence from all that poor (eventual self-destructive
influences) emotional and psychological subjugation and
oppression, while one gets unfairly overly-therapatized and
pathologized by those who do not know a single thing about
them and more profoundly don't know a thing about themselves
(and even appear to sadistically thrive off this psychodynamic)
while clinical words and terms get casually thrown around
like 'fear of intimacy' or 'self-esteem' but gotta be kidding
if ever knew the perverse and overbearing circumstances were
enmeshed in; have we ever once heard the expression of high
self-esteem or even for that matter someone who might have
made the effort to pass a good or kind compassionate rumor?


proof 1

Before family get-togethers it almost seems
like all that thankless work the embalmer does
to make the dead look more realistic and alive

proof 2

I suppose in my life the reason why i've
always looked up at the stars is they're
the only things that haven't let me down


proof 3

The dusty mansion taking on the spirits and seasons
and if know how to appreciate the details of silence
the soul of solitude nostalgia of reminiscing allows
for insightful and positive reflection and revelations



42

I look at life as six degrees of nothingness
somewhere between fate and coincidence
and how we project or process it that's it

you know how we stand forever in front of the refrigerator
while simply staring straight at the item we're searching for?


proof 1:

Every man in the morning gets ready to make a killing
while ironically at the end of the day creeps up his
driveway, looking like one of those slain pieces of
roadkill, shot, stunned, dazed not knowing what hit him


proof 2:

Doesn't life just sometimes seem
like you're never getting
out of the inning?

proof 3:

These days feel like the last one left
in one of those human pyramids
slowly skiing over the precipice


43

You know i think life was just far better when we didn't know
exactly who bazooka joe was with undercover turtleneck over
his mug looking like some sort of double-agent or gangster or
petty thief purse snatcher or for that matter little orphan annie
or the real life and times and sex lives of dagwood and blondie
even for that matter for some reason putting our blind faith and
trust into the president of the united states but now with all this
pathetic social media and news channels where they deliberately
pit one party against the other with their juvenile obnoxious strategy
to not even let the other finish up a sentence we don't even really
know their sincere perspective or what they're saying so how can
they realistically respond i mean even the infamous very conservative
william f. buckley (who now looks like a saint) who they claimed to be
all aloof and snarky gave the impression that he was listening and could
really hear and be interested and intrigued in the opinions and points
of view of people let's say like a norman mailer or woody allen
or jack kerouac and allen ginsberg then come up with your…


proof a:

All those people in american hx who we always thought
were so dangerous and a real threat to the government
(and 'way of life') were not even close to (that type)
those making the original ridiculous paranoid
conspiratorial proclamations and accusations

proof b:

We have learned and been brought up
embedded in our collective unconscious
to worry and watch out for certain states
down in the deep south such as mississippi
alabama south carolina louisiana but when
you look at the subtle southern ones as well
(let's say right on the border) like a kentucky
missouri north carolina and even parts of
virginia and how socially conservative and
insular and the structural racism and politics
and the people who run them in my opinion
becomes even more alarming and reason for
concern; the cultural and economic differences,
understood code and customs (and accepted historical
attitudes and social injustices) as a reflection of the present
day state of affairs in this so-called area we like to call america


proof c:

People would prefer being placated
(manipulated, brainwashed & flattered)
than told the truth (to keep the illusion alive)
as leads to a whole heck of a lot of suspicion
while a reflection of their collective, fragmented,
self-interested character & pathetic insular existence
they will even turn hostile & go on the all-out attack…
(the fight song of the ignorant) a microcosm or personification
of turning defensive then offended going on the all-out offensive
the way they thrive some of the most scheisty criminal shit alive…

43

p,

The editors never get back to you...
but they were the ones who originally
got in touch with you out of the clear
blue sky and told you how much
they really liked and vibed with
your writing and heaped tons
of praise you never were really
asking for in the first place
as never ever really knew
how to react to such things
and when you respectfully
try to get back in touch
they've fallen off the face
of the earth almost nowhere
to be found or treat you
like some sort of burden
act defensive and offended
like some really fucked-up
'hard to get' game of playing
possum or reverse-psychology
like telling you how they've
moved from country to country
or didn't you know i'm planning
for a wedding and you think to
yourself how the heck would
i know you're planning for a
wedding, as you got in touch
with me while do know when
me and my fiance were planning
for ours how we still managed
to hold a miserable 9-5 job and
finish up college for social work
and work with the schizophrenics
all day long and so on so screw you
with your see-through obvious guilt
and you try and reach them when
you're in a good and decent

mood and hope they are too
then,

Whenever i see all these lovely and liberal presses
(those who self-entitle themselves as like non-profit
or progressive or avant-garde or even go so far as to
call themselves "starving artists" even "anarchists")
and will curse or use curse words to try and prove
it; how they're so down to earth and one of us
then hypocritically conveniently charge you like
35 bucks just to read your manuscript for some sort
of contest or award (like winning an all-out hit or miss
lotto) and watch your paycheck go straight out the window
think far more prefer investing like a dollar in the local town
pharmacy on the corner ruminating contemplating on some
fine autumn day right in front of that great big apothecary
window trying to guess just about how many jellybeans

Heck wouldn't surprise me considering the state
of the economy and how obscene things have
gotten like studio apartments in manhattan
starting at $3,000 a month for presses to
jack up their rates and do some crazy shit
for their contests where only the upper-middle
class can afford it and say please include with
your submission something specific like $108
(providing absolutely no reason or logic but
show a very well-groomed photo of some
scholar or supposed guest judge you're
supposed to get all excited about like a
game show host or one of those guest stars
who used to show up on *the love boat*) but
like some subtle form of manipulation or
fucked-up reverse-psychology will think
wow this must mean something like oxford
university or university of iowa and will get
all excited maybe even start breathing a little
harder and justify not putting bread on the table
of your family for like a month or so as sure
this very concrete figure of $108 will make
you famous for like 15 minutes 4 times over

but just like everything else in commercial
reality show america with their bullshit abuses
of power and false advertising will get some
form letter maybe about a year later about
as sincere as some letter of commiseration
from the u.s. army and look just like one of
those old timer alcoholic zombies wandering
wearily staggering aimlessly from the casino
after their adrenaline (liquor and delusions
of grandeur) wear off and real life kicks
in having spent their monthly stipend


q,


## An E-Mail To One Of Those Very Hip And Liberal Editors Who Says Takes No Submissions From Hetero-White Males

i think i'm a white male but i promise you don't necessarily
identify as one if that makes any sense at all? this is really
weird to say and hate talking this way honestly straight-up
but grew up in nyc and my closest buddy from brooklyn
had a 'fear of intimacy' and obsession for drag queens in
the meat market where we'd hang out in a bar in the west
village after working all day and night long at soho books
my roommate who went to columbia university to get his
doctorate in asian studies while myself getting my masters
in social work at yeshiva, bi-sexual; my wife cute jewish
girl from the bronx with a single mom who was a clinical
hoarder; my closest friend and confidante growing up in
nyc, my uncle, eventually died from aids when it was a
death sentence and an actor on off-broadway who used
to cut hair for private clients in their apartments and we
used to have sleepovers at his partner's loft in the east
village and watch russ meyer's films; i pretty much
dropped out of college in the early-eighties, drove
a cab in nyc graveyard shift, worked at video stores,
book stores, clothing stores, ran away from home
more times than i can recall out to port authority
without a penny in my pocket and lived all over
the country, where i had such jobs as installing

cubicles in business parks, driving a truck long-
haul, painting boxcars, removing asbestos, digging
graves, donating blood, working the casinos, and
chasing tourists in hot-air balloons trying to tie them
down in nappa; hustled tenderloin district of san francisco,
portland, and reno, and now pretty much a broke social
worker who used to run the clinical groups for the boy's
shelters in providence, rhode island, as well as work
in a mental health clinic and the school system in
taunton, ma, worked methadone in new bedford
and residences out in plymouth, and a clinician
at montefiore hospital in the bronx; again hopefully
it was ok to write this…just wanted to flesh-out what
i'm about or not about as have never ever identified
with any specific group or culture whose aim it is to
alienate or make feel small any other group or culture
or individual and about as open-minded and welcoming
and receptive and sympathetic as you can get since
i was a kid and know no different, and been all by
my lonesome ever since; also too if interested
please check out a recent epic poem of mine
about 150 pgs. entitled "The American Book
of the Dead" through a press in my literary bio
and if ok am attaching a manuscript in pdf form;
do hope these poems strike a chord and none cross
any boundaries although some might just naturally
as am simply your basic everyday guy who has
had my fare share of meaningful relationships with
women (who i am drawn to and indebted) and consider
them honestly some of the best and most passionate
and substantial moments and interludes of my life
all pretty much coming straight from the gut
and heart; all my best and do hope will dig


proof:

One day i swear i want to just send a message
on a glossy postcard to my editor and tell him
i'm sailing the seven seas and he can get back
to me whenever perhaps by carrier pigeon from
my birthplace of origin alcatraz long island jewish

while up on deck because of episodes of tourettes
the mad scientist with a monocle and chopsticks
operates on me replacing my heart & soul
with a whole brand new funnybone…


45

What was up with the inventor of the scarecrow and how did
he come up with such a novel idea like did he do something
of a seasonal topographical interview with the crow population
or some environmental baseline study or battery of trial and error
empirical tests out of 'quiet desperation' of character and behavior
characterological and behavioral patterns and reactions to certain
threatening foreboding figures where he eventually decided either
instinctively or put a lot of thought into it of taking the extra hay
and stuffing his flannel shirt and dungarees and making something
of a makeshift reality-based face beneath a straw hat and lean it up
casually courageous cautious against a pole and stick it straight
into the fertile soil right there in the center of some cornfield
on some brilliant faded opaque omniscient overcast day?


proof:

God the things did to jesus
trinkets left in a shadowbox
along the ancient walls of civilization

yet still the stray scent of lemon & olive
palm wine swallowed along the tides of
the nile…arab bread in old city jerusalem

the question should not so much be if you
are a believer as that is irrelevant & presumptuous
& made up by man religion a rationalization for things
done to a brother & best friend guilt gets you nowhere
so turn to politics turning a phrase stretching the truth

                                          if you get my drift?

how civilization simply mimics this type of existence
naive & nihilistic; a tragic & pathetic 'might over right'
puppet show with the repetition of impulsive behavioral
patterns, while a microcosm of the origins & machinations

to the traits & characteristics & nature of self-fulfilling prophecy
prophet walking on sea unseen in a sea of false martyrs with savior
complexes & mother with munchausen birthing the "wild child"
who naturally, instinctively, turns reactive & acts-out just to make

sense of himself & sculpt an identity; the pouting hobby horses of
the lit glowing carousel in the brilliant sputtering carnival of carefree
hysterical children brooding bickering parents & strange solemn
widows on the promenade of stunning sirens, modest & humble

minding their own business along the sweeping silhouetted
foothills of flickering fugitive mountains of aristocratic night
clubs & kill or be killed nocturnal creatures nestled in the
thick verdant jungle of rhythmic melancholic chattering
leading up to the winding cobblestone of the kingdom



46

The real poet-philosopher through experience and wisdom
and eventually through keen and perceptive hyper-intuition
is forced to become something of a soothsayer or one of
those ole time traveling medicine men with all those secret
potions and elixirs and true-blue cure-alls in the all-out hope to
heal those who struggle and suffer in his travels along the road



47

Everyone's always leaving hitting the road
horses being transported in caravans
back and forth through the dawn
cats & dogs, poor cubs tipping over

trash cans trying to make their score
butterflies from their cocoons
robins from their sky-blue eggs
nestled in delicate nests hidden
and tucked away in the orchard
wild turkey frightened waddling
like chaplin and then suddenly
taking off into the season
girlfriends you thought
you loved and loved you back
cut-throat salesmen who claim
to be good family men (all
part of the same scam of false
advertising) just to make their quota
bellman into the mist of the mountain
lumberjacks with their loads of split wood
which will be dumped in huge piles on front
lawns at the end of summer and start of autumn
truck drivers rattling up and down narrow hillsides
running for their life literally sliding down slippery
slopes shifting like mad trying to make it home in
one piece alive when the dispatcher on the docks
all he really cares and gives a damn about
that there's absolutely no damaged cargo
tugboat captains and madmen delivering
papers through the bleak darkness of the
deathly silent dawn of the haunted suburbs
right on the border of the flowers and forest
where wild country dogs like werewolves
suddenly lunge out of nowhere either
to protect the crack or cattle or crops
newspaper men setting up their stands
the timekeeper planted in his cage
all day to make sure hotel employees
are entering and exiting and punching in ok
that silhouetted phantom tow bridge operator
who sits in his little box from dawn to dusk
pressing buttons pulling levers and opening
up locks with miraculous erector set industrial
bridges eventually ending up shooting to the stars
for exotic cargo ships, tugs, and garbage barges
bureaucrats, social workers, nerd/old men ushers

embalmers with their drill and makeup
waiters, waitresses smoking their blunts
just to cope and deal with the public
drag queens at dusk who march off
(to the beat of their own drummer
to beat off and blow hasidim and
movers & shakers in publishing)
to cobblestone of the meat market
right where the city meets the sea
the more sophisticated talented
ones who dance at nightclubs
no different than anyone
else all returning back drained
and exhausted with their makeup
off pale as those infamous ghosts
of former selves, silent, reflective
up the elevators of welfare hotels
the old timer bagel & bialy men
who head out at 4 in the morning
in their smocks and aprons full
of yeast and flour with sawdust
on the floors just to make a living
junkie radiologists, female phlebotomists
with bad marriages married to bouncers
a little too alpha and not quite honest
mean-spirited nurses at methadone clinics
zombie-businessmen like mannequins
who are the real madmen taking that
slow-death local back and forth from
the suburbs to the big city to pay off
their mortgages and get that 2 week
vacation to the caribbean during christmas
to give the ridiculous impression of living
gondoliers at the end of the day at sunset
drifting and steering splintered gondolas
back to slums and shutters on the water

48

I have this metaphorical sadistic & cathartic torture
to line up all those freaking lawyers & contractors
against a brick wall (of course with the token gag
and blindfold) and then just leave them exactly
as is for however long, have the phone ringing
off the hook on the hour and keep them abandoned to
know what it really feels like to suffer and be ignored
when needed the most in the midst of existential crisis
when they somehow claimed they were going to provide
all this support & guidance & literally take the money & run


proof 1

Devoid of all that useless made-up political
correct bullshit made up by the liberals
who never once did it i have honestly
sincerely seen bourgeois behavior
in the biggest of 'peasants' while the
affluent for some strange reason always
just seeming to act like a bunch of peasants
all just seeming like stand-ins with very
predictable unconvincing roles of morals
and ethics of what it means to be a success

what happened to the real-life diplomats
traveling actors and slapstick comedians?


proof 2

Why does it always seem like the ones 'testing' you
by the look on their face, insecure, disgraced, and
appearing to somehow have 'failed' in this life
while through this mean-spirited dynamic and
cowardly sacrifice desperately trying to extra-
polate the 'truth' (purpose and meaning) and find

some reason ('beyond belief') to increase identity
proof 3

What it means to be an 'honest, everyday' man
who sticks to the plan and does not take advantage
and find little ways to stray and 'scam' every chance
they get, as have it all rationalized either by greedy
ambition or resentment in their head, and just once
hold true and consistent to their original agreement


49

The playoffs...

sponsored by "american sniper"

up next national anthem

jet fighters zoom overhead
& a wave of fans roaring
ecstatic/orgasmic

where's down-to-earth image of joe dimaggio
kicking the dust after his hit streak got broken?

need a triple-cheese whopper with shot of manishewitz!

clint eastwood's best film in years...
gigantic massive robot which attacks the screen
& kicks in p.t.s.d. indicates it's time for kickoff

1st to get you your weather
can't i just look out the window?
how to avoid death (is how to avoid life)

somewhere between
the ghosts & the moon
a better shade of blue...

always hated that expression don't burn your bridges
as if desperate enough know deep-down inside some
where out there none really out there in the 1st place

me & my delinquent acquaintances used to just climb inside
all the way up the girders to catch a glimpse of midnight skylines
to try & get as close as we could while as far away from the lies

i don't need 6 color-commentators all lined-up in a nice little row
to analyze it all for hours on end before the game even begins

(what happened to sadat & begin?
a dozen salt bagels?)

like talking way too much after sex or loveplay
& going into all the details, all the ins & outs
sort of defeats the purpose no? as wasn't it all
about the spontaneity & trying to forget it all?

(like 1 of those silly little assholes trying to act
all scary & intimidating in the crowd surrounded
by his cookie-cutter herd-mentality for the camera

funny don't seem quite as tough when you
accost them 1 on 1 all by their lonesome
& then look like looking for their
mother, their cellphone, their lawyer)

anti-climactic & want to kill myself in my bowl
of *doritos* & become a sophisticated drunkaholic
without all those very close & intimate pals gathered around
(with 1 token black man all that's allowed) show on commercials

i want to be the 1 designated driver (doing figure 8's)
driving home disoriented with a drinking problem
always liked to challenge authority & even better
myself as they all & it all felt like a slow-death
& what other choice did i really have?

always felt was so much more safe & secure (what'ya call?
cautious) & reflective nursing my buzz & finishing off

kerouac & dostoevsky by pre-dawn window
right around where elijah hides
keeping it open for passover

funny, prayers never answered

senses open, receptive, is the weather...


proof 1

Leaving a broom
under a full moon
blooming on top
of stoop in the
falling leaves
of brooklyn


proof 2

☻ pink buffalo
please show up
to my purply-blue
window in the glowing
snow at dawn to prove
how just as extinct and
alone you are through
the bare blustery news
print forest full of taverns
of ravenous women finally
turning the tables on their
men out on the kill during
the off-season sick of being
taken for granted and no longer
allowing their seductions to remain
dormant; basement freezers now
stocked with unicorn and parlors
not with busts of wild animals
but rather robust flamboyant masks
providing a far more accurate momento

proof 3

Website,
    graveside

spring starts up
right around when
the signs go up
at the tasty cream


proof 4

I have distinct and clear lucid memories
of pre-school how i could never sleep during
nap time worrying wondering about my future

where's my juliette binoche
from "the english patient?"


proof 5

Life just eventually becomes
a leftover fluff & peanut butter
sandwich; a hulk poster ripped
down from the wall of the group
home wondering what it was even
doing up there in the first place?

interesting how mom with munchausen
put him there with a view of the alley and
suburban sluts next door sunbathing in bikinis

## 50

Picasso & shakespeare went through their blue periods...
dare i say plath, hemingway, kafka, nietszche, wittgenstein,
dostoevsky, eugene o'neill, kerouac, burroughs & bukowski
went through theirs too; i find myself these days going through
my own shade of purple which combines the colors of blue and
red for rage for the clueless and those who will never get you
if you ever saw my dreams and what they're doing to me...

proof:

During the holiday season you fall
asleepwasted in your easychair to
the *desi arnez stakes* somewhere
out in the suburbanhillsofkalifornia
over the flashingtelevision all erelvant
who wins with some really cuteclassy
smiling young purewomaninherviewing
all the sexuallyrepressedaristocrats
no mattermakes you feel just a little
bitbetter (like when you used to eat
americancheese&butter sandwiches
on wonderbread on porch inchild
hood) fallingasleep wakingup
to the desi arnaz stakes know
ing hetoo died a brokenman

## 51

I find myself in that phase of life
where i'm yelling back at my tv
such things like—"you conveniently
want us to forget how you scammed
and ripped-off all your customers
and want us to now believe all of a
sudden so sympathetic and supportive?"

america doesn't fucken make movies
anymore; how first you're telling me
you're gonna actually do a remake
of *willie wonka & the chocolate
factory* and now *papillon* with
the brilliant steve mcqueen
& dustin hoffman with what
all your brand-new computer
generated sound effects
& token explosions?
you gotta be kidding
as does seem something
ironically of a crime against man
what next? turning jason robards
& kathryn hepburn in "long days
journey into night" into superheroes?


52

I have never been a particular huge fan of people
who make certain such quasi-like proclamations
like–"i will never forget…" as can tell based on
the delivery of rather disingenuous sincerity (or the
defense-mechanism of 'reactive-formation') have already
forgotten you (or tried to find a way of forgiving themselves
through hyper-sentimentality) while simply providing a built
in excuse or rationalization to try and placate and actually
in fact ironically very conveniently dismiss and forget

often more times than not the real true irony
was you never ever were really thinking
about them and couldn't care less...


proof:

I remember once i ran into a girlfriend of my sister's
from back in high school i used to have a mild crush on
who of course never knew and asked her if she wanted

to grab lunch at the clam bar in grand central station
while she very predictably and practically laid down
the boundaries and rules and regulations and honestly
wasn't even really thinking of that just thought it might
be nice to hang out and have a little decent conversation with
someone from my past and the clams weren't even that great either


proof: letter to a pal overseas

And by the way looking back
why not as god bless and more
power to the "foolish teenagers"
who seem far more worthy than
most people i've encountered
fell in love with my first love
at 19 years old on winter vacation
from college and picked me up while
pondering wandering along the side of
the snowy road with a french friend of hers
pretending they were lost and supposedly
they eventually made a bet whoever i called
first as of course called her first from the train
station all alone under the glow of the lamplight
on the deserted snowswept platform i remember
couldn't have felt any more silent or holy almost
forcing and making a bet with myself to give her
a call as knew in the future if i didn't i would always
end up regretting it and ain't that just a lot of what love is?
this beautiful blonde from germany named andrea to die for
gorgeous as they come and used to roll her own cigarettes
while we'd spend all night i swear gazing into each others
eyes drinking beer in smoky taverns making some of my
pals even my sworn rivals from my hometown jealous
and i fell instantly in love with her first love feeling
almost other worldly a whole other healing reality
and then cuddling all night secretly in the basement
of the home for the family she was babysitting for
with snowdrifts climbing up the crystal gleaming
window in something of a winter wonderland which
helped me to instantly forget it all all the bullshit and

worries and concerns naked in our fishermen sweaters
almost impossible to forget so don't know when
i think about it god bless the foolish teenagers...

proof:

They say when you die
id you should just folk
us on one or two items
& as such i've been go
wing with blt's & tuna
fish on matzoh good
cheap red wine from
the aisle of *super
stop & shop* &
the fresh young high
school girls always
with a smile & big
heart asking if i
need help with
my bags to the car as
i usually just laugh a
little & say no that'll
be alright but maybe
should stop always
being so nice & polite
while probably could
use the small talk with
those bright eyes & fine
bedside manner; they say
when you diet you should
kind of focus on one type


anti-proof:

I never got the concept
        of people racing to work
                prefer tube socks
                        & green *converses*

53


-1

I remember one time picking up this fare very late at night
somewhere in brooklyn at this nightclub and were these
wild puerto girls with mad heart hanging out with these
guys they grew up with slightly intoxicated so alive
getting the most out of life and having a damn fun
time declaring while laughing—"i did some dance
moves i didn't even know i had!" and was so
casual and comical and them all just cracking
up and suddenly realized right there and then
it's all just really about the moment cuz that's
all you really got when you stop to think about
it but urge you not to if you really think about it


0

I remember when driving my yellow taxi
graveyard shift in new york city and there
was usually some point during the night
when i was completely wiped-out drained
(emotionally, physically, spiritually which
to me really the best place to be not thinking
too much about things and just going on my
raw instincts) zombied-out, running on empty
when the streets for the most part were cleared
out like some good ole haunted ghost town
all empty and abandoned and looking around
for that one final fare maybe like some pretty
young party girl usually who for the most part
staggering silly returning from some nightclub
to see if i might be able to take her all the way
out to the long-lost borough of queens which
to me was always something like a whole other
reality or fantasy whose streets and neighborhoods
never made any sense at all and were impossible

to understand or follow but the final destination
with all its strange haunted bridges definately
worth it, while groggy, bloodshot, said why
not as put me right over my quota and of
course always asked me advice about guys
with all their romance problems and seeking
guidance (and the answers were always so clear
and obvious as were the biggest assholes of all
time and think deep down inside already knew
that and just needed someone to talk to to confirm
that, and was happy to as most likely i needed
to too) so remember just cruising cool and casual
looking around 'cause sort of found out how in life
in general if tried too hard just not gonna find it
and was coming around the corner on lexington
around the 30's where no one really hangs out
anyway and pretty residential and the avenue
gleaming and glazed in like a purple drizzle
and suddenly saw this image wasn't sure if
i had seen it or not or if it was just my mind
playing tricks on me and bugging-out being
so tired and all but it was ronald mcdonald
just sitting there all casual all by his lonesome
on some bench right in front of the restaurant
in his clown outfit with his head ripped-off
and was caught between my desire to totally
laugh aloud and crack up or just on a whole
other nihilistic level thought isn't this simply
what life was all about ronald mcdonald
just sitting there in his clown outfit with
his head ripped-off at about 3:45 in the
morning on the corner of 37$^{th}$ & lexington


1


Dozing-off in cab at the end
of my graveyard around 5:04
in the morning around l'arc
de triumph of washington
square park; one only knows
true silence after all the madness

& chaos & cut-throat drama
of them constantly trying
to tear everything apart
like little punks with
napoleonic complexes
making a fuss in a cracked
snowglobe oozing out in
constant revolt with the
same insane draining 24-7
state of flux raw hardcore
hustle of man at his worst
desperate sleazy ridiculous
somewhere between the
haves and have nots the bums
and fake aristocrats while all
just seem like angry drunks never
once having been sober-minded
(a fine line between wino
and debauchery and can
tell you who's more civil)
and like at the end of some
absurd battle like anarchy
in a bottle that should
have never happened
at last not a single soul
around except for the back
of a big white bread truck
which simply reads "eat
fink bread" and think why
not? that just about sums it up


anti-proof:

When you get married they start taking
your sense of humor very seriously
while it was the exact same delivery
and payoff during that period of wooing

anti-proof:

The greatest mistake that couples make is not remembering
or just naturally forgetting all those things that originally
attracted them to each other in the first place...


anti-proof :

Charm is all those slight brilliant remains
of everything they tried to steal from you


anti-proof:

I always had very poor results for some reason
or another with those (who felt the need
to show off) with very good manners



54

From the anti-tourist guide:


1,

Beware young man and please heed my word
you can try so hard and work your ass off and
even end up doing it well and may in fact end
up hating you for that exact selfsame reason
(you initially will feel confused and cheated
and will wonder what you did to deserve this
and with your innocent identity may even take
it out on yourself) and the only thing i can tell
you the only thing i beg of you is to please not
internalize (these jealous and petty aggressive
lies) and simply take it as a distorted form of
flattery while proudly (as difficult as it may very

well seem) move on with your life and your dreams
2,


I always loathed those old timers you never
were asking for advice and always offering it
would quite often start off their lectures with
such cliches like–"young people these days…"
as felt like they were never young, while always
hated and resented being put in the boring obvious
category of 'young people' and ironically in the
end always ended up feeling pretty damn old


3,

Almost every man i have ever met has
felt the need and compulsion to tell me
such grandiose stories and unbelievable
bullshit (with a weak and fragile identity)
as if desperately trying to impress me
yet i still have out of a certain kind
of comradery always provided a sense
of support and positive reinforcement
while have always considered myself
to be a pretty decent acquaintance and
even better friend. when they finally left
i found myself instantly forgetting about
them (possibly through the natural defense
mechanism of 'compartmentalization') or just
overwhelmed and drained (and having that physical
need) and that psychological phenomenon of empty
and vacant due to the common trait and characteristic
(of man) being of such rampant and repetitive self-
absorption (as if taking advantage of my kindness
and willingness to listen and be receptive) while never
once himself having ever considered asking any questions
too busy with tiny tall tales of lies and exaggeration...

4,

Those who do the best to survive suburbia
are those who can keep the secret and play
the role better but then perversely you got
a real-life comedy of errors and you're just
a star or more accurately stand-in in one of
those really bad shows or poor performances


5,

They'll try to steal everything from you
what else do they want? they already
got wife's wedding ring, the shovel
from our barn what next? decorative
soaps? yarn? while one thing they seem
consistent at (this race of self-advocating
adults) is built-in excuses and being unre-
liable and now got a program on television
devoted purely to just hunting and killing
animals; you wonder why they never ever
once tried the formula of one of those drive-
by shootings on all of america dancing and
call it a mercy killing, and be far better off
and you think you'd like to create a connect
the dot book made up of girls you fantasized
to; boys and girls in high school used to just
kiss in cars and make out and do some rather
perverted things and call it things like lookout
point and look out over the lights of the city
which to me seems to be the real american dream…
i used to jerk-off to wonder woman, chrissy from three's
company, what happened to disco? bowling for dollars?


6,

This country has become an all-you-can-eat feast
of false advertising just as long as you come with

your clipped-out coupon at very specific hours
with the watered-down sangria which gives you
an instant hangover and platters of endless shrimp
knowing exactly how to devein all its tiny little legs
with an ambiance of very petty patrons who always
for some godforsaken reason appear jealous and angry
without getting the chance to know a single thing about you


7,

White man too often mistakes the concept of class
pretending like nothing ever effects them, acting
aloof and arrogant, privileged and entitled, self-
righteous and self-important, trying so desperately
to give the impression for some strange, ridiculous
and competitive, insecure reason (and with a mean-
spirited effort and conviction that you do not exist)
of the illusion of their status of living 'happily ever
after' what they delusionally believe (or trying so hard
to convince everybody else) with their adopted snobbery
to mistakenly be something of what it means to be classy


8,

These days we rely way too heavily and put way
too much significance on one-dimensional statistics
to represent and provide a finite criteria and conclusion
for a random arbitrary context as logically philosophically
would be far more interested (perhaps even more accurate)
in hypothetically and conversely just analyzing and assessing
that context without the statistic(s) which in my opinion is
way too shallow and superficial a gauge (that can be man-
ipulated and played) for something so subjective
and intimate in-depth, determined, and destined

9,

I believe those psychologists who thrive
(and therapatize) and so casually decry
such clinical terms like 'passive-aggressive'
'at risk' even 'fear of intimacy' are ironically
the ones containing these selfsame symptoms
and criteria; trust me if you only got to really
know them (how they keep their distance and
omniscience and elements of 'counter-transference')
and not by coincidence exhibit the persistent pattern
traits and characteristics of constantly being a trigger
to such profound, reactive, self-fulfilling dynamics


10,

The key is to always question your unconfidence
(to never give up and be persistent) because there
might just be something right around the corner
which may very well prove the opposite (as you
just pick up the behavioral patterns of sheisty
assholes with very poor character) while
be every reason in the world to in fact be
confident or at least not give up quite yet


55

It is my estimation that politics is simply an extension
to man's poor behavior and character; all of the blatant
contradictions of human nature all the abuses of power

I.

We live in a culture they refer to as a democracy
where the best we can hope for are plea bargains
deconstruct and break down the semantics of that

statement, plea bargain! plea bargain! plea bargain!
products who are scared and won't even cross the aisle
and exhibit absolutely no effort or conviction of independent
thinking sorry that's what you call a functioning democracy?
these lovely senators all need to pile back on the school bus
take a field trip and head back to the city of brotherly love

## II.

All of these politicians indicted being whisked in & out
of those gold revolving doors of downtown manhattan
while over the tv camera the only thing that really matters
is that old black man in bellman outfit who suddenly shows
up with a rag to scrub down the lobby windows to make sure
we historically dramatically see everything that's happening
(like some backwards porthole or portal or aperture) who
of course goes unnoticed and then vanishes which is the
classic clandestine cinemagraphic cultural hx of amerika

## III.

Thus follows the proverbial revolving door policy
if spill the beans (and exhibit the proper amount
of contrition and humility) and manage to stay
out of prison will make their rounds on talk
shows or write bestsellers (the sell-outs that
they are and sell-outs purchasing it) and be
come infamous multi-millionaires again

Dreams are substitutes of substitutes of substitutes
(very similar to the defense-mechanism of substitution)
meaning it's a surreal representative image of something
we have been repressing from the original core source
because it was just way too difficult or traumatic in real
life to try (or have any desire) to make any clear sense of

(the concept and dynamic of desertion and abandonment,
emotional pain, self-loathing, moral conflict, even keen
separation-anxiety made animated and actively manifest
in the effort to process everything in our consciousness
so fragile, for example, like the image amplified
distorted, shattered, and made taboo, or primitive
and fantastic in a house of mirrors with certain parts
deconstructed, then disproportionately exaggerated)
while all of those repressed emotions and desires
as well as morals and ethics get superimposed onto
past symbolic and surreal characters and scenarios
already somehow known or experienced in the subconscious
and played out in images like the pure light from a projector
suddenly lucidly splashed onto the screen in a dark theater

Contrary though, it may also possibly be considered and since
so surreal (and clear and lucid) the process (and reality) of
dreaming is all that stuff (all those images and forms) without
all the armor and everyday disguises, all those established defenses
and defense-mechanisms, absolutely no filters at all; the core nucleus,
would even go so far as to say 'the object or figure' before symbolism
so in fact not really empirically symbolism at all (more so a surreal
manifestation and keen 'projection') of those present day emotions
(of fear or hope) and deep-rooted repressed feelings (of guilt and
anger and conflict) or before felt the clinical need and compulsion
to linguistically entitle it as symbolism (for the sole expressed
reason and function to ascribe it a language or medium for pur-
poses of trying to connect meaning and make sense of it all...)
because so primitive and exposed and raw while in fact really a fine
line between the physiological (the primitive) and psychological
(complex and intellectual) systems to make any fluid linear
interpretative effort simply and solely necessarily towards
reasoning and comprehension, but again its (cognitive, spiritual
and physiological) makeup (properties) and configuration very much
the same (and far closer than you think 'in being') when consistently
just trying to deconstruct, digging towards the source 'of meaning'

An essay on the spirit & psychodynamics of dreaming:
a fictional letter (based on truth and fact)


My Dear Sig:

How are you and do hope you are well and good and thriving out there in Vienna and how I miss our exchanges and psychoanalytic conversations along The Danube, now being stationed out here temporarily during the summer in the brilliant solitude of the brooding Alps. There was a recent bewildering, yet benign dynamic and phenomenon I wanted to discuss and share with you and bring to your attention, and thought perhaps some of your neuroscience experience and scientific studies at the university might provide some insight or shed light on the subject. Over the last couple of decades or so, you know I have been living alone as an avid student and scholar of the human mind, studying as well the hysteria and neuroses of mankind. My dear Sigmund, something I have never shared with you, as upon reflection, perhaps I may have even been reluctant or feared your keen intellect or acute critical judgment and what it meant, while I must confess having had to become very much a stoic or survivor during those rough and rugged years of my existence, as never once during my sleep-cycle (upon my natural awakening) did I have any recall of ever dreaming at all, and think maybe even secretly kept it to myself, while in a strange, perverse, and paradoxical way, savored this, as perhaps thought this is what it meant (or represented) to be strong, or finally, at long-last (through a sense of desensitization) lost all that existential angst and dread which permeated my days, and came on most unexpectedly and profoundly at dusk, nigh the very late evening spending my nights close to sleep-walking, fixating and perseverating in my domicile like something of a phantom; well here my dear Sigmund is what I wanted to bring to your attention! Ever since my beloved has made me aware of the status of her impending blessed pregnancy after lo and behold those aforementioned twenty years or so, I have once more started dreaming again about my childhood and adolescence with the sensation of a bizarre, spiritual re-visitation (might even call it something of an existential, proverbial rebirth) as if my subconscious suddenly been penetrated by some other keen and lucid spirit, fragile and delicate, completely 'holy and haunted,' coming out of hibernation, of which I have no control over, bringing back all those feelings and emotions of fear and guilt and conflict and trepidation along with an element admittedly of nihilism; of the very solitary and surreal, or some sort of real-life bittersweet memory I can't quite seem to get rid of; how strange it is as well to suddenly meet up again with those friends and acquaintances (more times than not archetypes of hesitance or even betrayal) I had apparently after so many years of struggle and suffering so conveniently forgotten, as if this representative significance of a profound life-transition (or even sentimental and traumatic moments and events of my own personal growth and development) somehow became the catalyst to re-open those shutdown chambers of coping and survival mechanisms and once more motivate that stagnated state and chemical equilibrium (of dreaming?) similar perhaps to the parable and image of what a full moon does to the tides and currents of an ocean (one often colloquially speaks of that "phantom pain;" well in this case it seems like something of a triangulation where it gets transferred from the womb to the psyche and back to the womb again). Sigmund, I respectfully wanted to share with you these recent happenstances as feel you are one of the few acquaintances who holds true to their word and who I intimately trust. Please take these thoughts into your confidence and do with it what you will, as believe touches so much on the crux of physiology and the subconscious, or something even finer and deeper, something of a spiritual trigger, which subliminally makes sensitive and receptive that subtle "sixth sense" and metaphysics and parapsychology you know I have taken such recent interest in and put credence; I clearly of course know and respect our intellectual differences but am still very eager with these presenting features and symptoms to gain your insight and take in with an open and willing heart and soul your ideas to the source, as well as those forces with which you believe may be playing a role in recently influencing my new-found sudden phenomenological penchant towards a robust sort of dreaming and those theories which may lead to your beliefs and psychodynamic clinical conclusions of my present day reality. My dear Sigmund, I am eagerly looking forward in hearing back from you and please send my love and affection to the family and the city of which I miss so dearly…

proof 1

If there is so much we repress and thus forget
then to a certain extent is not dreaming the effort to try
and make sense or even go through the process of forgiveness?


proof 2

We also dream from a heck of a lot
of repressed guilt and conflict and
pent-up anger (we could not otherwise
for one reason or another express in our
everyday existence) while the characters
take on all those traits and characteristics
(expressions, body language, personality)
from those selfsame feelings and emotions


proof 3

In our dreams we are the real-life fugitive
on-the-run; the high-expressed emotion
of the raw exposed soul, constantly
searching for that illusory happiness
peace and quiet and long-lost home


proof 4

Dreams are not how you pictured it and everything
you imagined; all those repressed feelings and emotions
(for purposes of coping and survival) turning into a real-life
exacerbated 'spirit' (of a surreal) beyond belief and comrehension


proof 5

Your spirit and soul get superimposed
onto your character(s) and roles
in dreams and nightmares

proof 6

Dreams are a mockery
without the humor
spying through
the keyhole
of a ridiculous
reality & existence


proof 7

The human mind
is like clothes
dripping drying
on the clothesline


proof 8

I like to look at dreams (and nightmares)
as like secret undercover surprise parties
from periods and phases of our life
we forgot and left us feeling empty
vacant and abandoned (unresolved)

likewise can we not kind of view life
as something of a cycle or series
of recurring dreams?


proof 9

Our dreams become something of a picasso painting
deconstructed with primitive forms and images
representative of self-esteem, self-pity, self-
loathing; fixations and phobias, moral and
ethical struggles from real-life surreal fugitives
fragile, fragmented, desperately searching
for some sense of resolution and closure

proof 10

Dreams are the lingering spirit(s) of the subconscious…

proof 11

Dreams during a stable period in which
we are feeling emotions of acceptance
(or belonging) are manifest in surreal images
of sudden and explicit intimacy and affection
whose feeling is of an 'eternal saving,' while
during a phase of rejection or low self-esteem
that of a stagnant and acute isolation and alienating

proof 12

Those vivid and vague dreams which tell me
everything about her and absolutely nothing at all

proof 13

Dreams analyze *me* and when i wake up feel something
of a strange, keen revelation even a bit maddening, disoriented
like those feelings you're not supposed to have for a third cousin

proof 14

The birds wake up at 4:43 in the morning and just naturally start
chirping outside your window putting an end to your dreamworld
proving there's a fine line between wildlife and the spirit of the soul

proof 15

One day you'll just stop having
those bad dreams and be home free…

57

*

I still somehow strangely feel punished by childhood

*

I have always been very tough on myself
then all of a sudden thought as a cognitive-
behavioral role play and exercise who else
would i rather be and thought i'm a pretty
damn decent guy and absolutely no one
else and even felt something of a revelation

*

There's an absurd paradox
that those who we are so
desperately searching for
the most approval are those
in fact should be seeking the
least as by nature and psychological
dynamics are the ones who originally
forced that disproportionate
excessive need to please

*

Too often it is the routine & ritual that we frequently mimic & parrot
as opposed to the source & spirit where this superstition emanated

\*

Advice seems like all that leftover shit
they never quite finished and now
try to live it through you vicariously

\*

If advice was only asked for
while one wonders if it was returned
would that individual in fact be receptive?

\*

Too much advice lacks the true insight of wisdom

\*

Only listen to the advice of a simple man
and may very well find out it's not
advice but straight-up wisdom

\*

Too much politeness turns awfully obnoxious

\*

When the father can take the advice of a son
he eventually becomes humble
and a complete man…

58

I cannot be a bigot or prejudiced
(never have been never will as
can't afford to and too much
experience and always been
pretty damn down to earth)
as well as simply do not
understand half of those
groups or can't translate
their acronyms that
exist for purposes of
justice but too often
contradict themselves

as often come off insular and exclusive
unto themselves (of which i ironically
feel ostracized and alienated) by their
exact selfsame function and definition


proof:

i.e. quite often the definition does not describe the word
because it is devoid of context, state of mind, and mood

i.e. "that's just water under the bridge..."
i never got these kinds of convoluted proverbs
as always just felt too indifferent and insensitive

i.e. like nonchalant, passive-aggressive
statements of–"i'm sure i don't know"

i.e. like–"you know it's something that would take me a couple
hours to explain but you know now that i think about it probably
only a couple minutes" which only goes to prove language
not always the most relevant and reliable medium of lucid
comprehension, and sometimes, just from experience
(and behavioral patterns) more so what you naturally know
and feel through learned and developed instinct and intuition

anti-proof:

Signs and symbols become sentimental triggers
from our youth and adolescence. does not perhaps
the same dynamic exist with language and images

eliciting the same meaning and feelings
and emotions without necessarily needing
to know the exact source or definition?



59

What's up with all those ridiculous fictitious inaccurate expressions
like–'my past seems to have caught up to me.' i'd love my past
to catch up with me especially my remote (not recent) before
all that bullshit and nonsense which just happened previously
that i know clearly was just about the phonies and hypocrisies
of human nature, and had absolutely nothing to do with me...



&

When we get older we appear to existentially, nihilistically
be counting down the days of our mortality, while looking back
at our childhood seemed fleeting, fluidly not thinking of such things



&

The best advice a father can give his son
is don't be like me and then is free
to be whoever he wants to be

&

The child of a clinical narcissist will always end up confused
and conflicted (ending up trying to kill oneself in some form
or another without even consciously being aware of it) with
aspects of pervasive guilt, little to no identity, no clear or
lucid comprehension of a code of ethics, or falsehoods
and truths, while this emotional, psychological, and
spiritual abuse and continual neglect evident (as that
necessary and specific support and guidance never
existed because did not have the ability or empathy
to be sensitive, while everything always came back
to be about him in reference to all instances of the past and
present) on a day by day basis even when in need during crisis

&

One might even say that during that period of adolescence
in that significant stage of growth and development, feels
profoundly 'lost and lonesome,' intrinsically 'haunted'
because is forced to be instinctively defensive, detached,
even disassociating because everything again, in a tormenting
and impossible, overbearing way, always revolves around him
feeling an acute and intense sense of resentment and rejection,
emptiness, hollowness, hurt, pain, loss, and abandonment

&

In my opinion never found it to be of good judgment
certain such cliche expressions like–'you never
get a second chance to make a first impression'
because in looking back in making all that
effort so much time was wasted with all
that brainwash and bullshit and people
honestly who just weren't worth it

        &

"Better late than never"
could never stand expressions
like that as always just seemed

like a simple and convenient rationalization
to really poor morals and ethics while honestly
ironically really didn't give a damn about any of it



        &

They make such infamous noble proclamations
like –"i'm just trying to keep this family together"
these devils of obvious predictable manipulation
who were the exact ones who drew them apart
(in the first place) and never around when emotionally
spiritually and psychologically needed them most
almost causing them to become like angry fugitives
on-the-run searching for whole new realities and identities
but always have that convenient saying hidden up their
sleeve to keep that most necessary reputation going
while those kids underestimated and pathologized
which is almost as criminal as the original lies



        &

"This is gonna hurt me more than it's gonna hurt you"
i never really bought that and seemed like it was
something they just got used to and immune

&

"You're your own worst enemy…"
i always hated people who said shit like this
as felt far more like they were my worst enemy


&

What sounds more crazy & nauseating?
temporary insanity? permanent sanity?
temporary insanity? permanent sanity?
temporary insanity? permanent sanity?
temporary insanity? permanent sanity?
a crime of passion? fashion statement?


&

The tourist is always blessed
with this lovely contradiction
of quasi-curiosity (but constantly
appears to present as helpless with

expressions and episodes of confusion and conflict)
and due to their ridiculous need for co-dependence and
conformity wouldn't even know what it was once they saw it


&

"Are you kidding?"
i always hated those obvious
and dubious rhetorical statement

&

"Open to debate…"
is that just another one of those oxymorons
passive-aggressive paroxysms or play of words?

&

I remember once all of a sudden getting stopped
by some cop whose car literally sped out from behind
the brush, hiding out on some college campus. when
i very respectfully asked him what he had stopped me
for he very defensively went on the attack and  roared
"i run the show!" then proceeded to ask me what i had
in the back of my car which were roses i had just picked
up at the *home depot* and thorny and hostile and red-faced
told me he was gonna let me off this time with just a warning
and to this day still do not know what i had been stopped for and
like the perfect metaphor for what it means to cope and survive in
american culture and what life does to you angrily planted my roses

&

All those boys who go marching off to useless endless wars
seem more like the image of dried-up dead flowers in a vase

&

Trauma and forms of abuse
is the gift which keeps on taking
being suddenly snatched from you
right when start enjoying never getting
the opportunity to ever put to good use

&

And so thus please don't kid yourself…
how deliberate and inflicted persistent guilt
*is* emotional, spiritual and psychological abuse
(engaging one in clinical dysfunction, forms of
'gaslighting' and munchausen, and the vicious
abuse cycle) and does such profound hurt and
damage to the growing developing heart & soul

matter of fact often will stop you dead in your tracks…

&

When you start to get those faraway eyes
trying to make sense & figure out
& stare through all those lies

&

All those people confident they have me down
perfect are the exact ones i lose instant interest

&

Sometimes you wish they'd just cheat on you
so much better than taking everything so literal
being so miserable something i got absolutely
nothing to do with and so what we landed a man
on the moon think about everything that happened
thereafter; watergate, vietnam, inflation so says
the late-great marvin gaye and gil-scott heron

&

I always like watching women observing other womens'
seductions as if this is what they're supposed to be doing
all part of the grand scheme of female growth and develop
meant natural inclination imitation of a daughter after
her mother passed down from generation to generation
scientific scholar sister goddess apprentice subtle
expression and body language lovely non-reaction
(the silent solitude of culture) and mysterious
cryptic thing which makes them women

&

How much we fall in love with the concept of falling in love
all its rituals & routines & traditions & ceremonies; an instant
panacea/savior to the condition (worrying & brooding; eternal
emptiness & loneliness) we too frequently find ourselves in
a certain kind of romantic spirit where they can no longer
hurt or harm you while simultaneously the keen sensation
of being 'eternally spontaneous and improvisational…'

&

It is far less dangerous to fall out of love than to fall into it

&

That very strange and needy literal question of–
"do you love me?" which almost seems to require a direct
answer yet ironically whose configuration feels rhetorical

60

They say behind every great man stands a great woman…
one wonders why not more monuments 'devoted' to them?

                angels
              bend over
             in the field
                 like
             beautiful
              fragile
             bouquets
             of flowers
             gracefully
             scurrying
              around
              between
           the summer
          and autumn
     when the first red leaf
comes sailing in from the mountain


proof:

That deserted feeling not always so bad
if you know how to take it in (with a loved
one) during the mercurial change of seasons
one of those chilly toasty bed & breakfasts
and hidden anonymous motels on the ocean

some misty morning diner tucked
into the cobblestone alley washing
it all down with hashbrowns lobster
omelette and massive mug of coffee

61

Those of religion always seem
to be just a little bit dishonest


proof:

Who invented religion which just seems
like a convenient rationalization
or some sort of man-made sin

those who've i've known in particular
were so passive-aggressive and full of
it and if just once looked in the mirror

(i swear i have met more honest
drug dealers while trust me
even more reliable)

        suppose the exact reason they got into…


62

For the thief he takes so much pride and even places more value on
all those things which have been stolen as has literally and spiritually
had things stolen his whole life (usually from some form of 'poverty'
or spiritual abuse and neglect from an overbearing, impossible-to-
please, brow-beating authority figure) and when taking back from
that selfsame figure of authority (sometimes even completely unaware
of it; 'acting-out' and 'self-fulfilling prophecy' would be a general-
ization or understatement) the ritual and routine even takes on
something of a religious quality with the phenomenon of something
of an instant-panacea, instant-gratification and healing, even for the
time being, helping to empower and to sculpt a new identity, while
interesting, and not by coincidence, exhibits the capability of being
more empathetic and making a connection, kind and compassionate
to perhaps those in desperate need, like stray animals, those hitching

on the side of the road, or poor souls being taken advantage of.
eventually when he happens to look back at that new-found 'hot'
transitional-object (without that profound sense of guilt or remorse
from what life has done to him) it's almost as if it provides a new
spirit or 'trigger' to reignite, recharge, reawake, and redeem
the senses and reality (standing in society 'there for the taking')
and state of being emanating from a life of a crime from
what too often feels like the crime of living…

Hx: remember in growing up and some of those kids
who got tagged with that title of juvenile delinquent
and used to think what did they have to do to earn
such a reputation and upon reflection think i was
even maybe something like in a conflicted state
between impressed and intimidated and heard
that some of them had to actually carry around
with them this identification which was called
a j.d. card (never sure if that was true or not)
and was like what did they have to do or in
what context and scenario were they required
to have to show their jd card like were they
so difficult and hard to handle had to have
it with them at all times for when some cop or
authority figure decided to just randomly stop
and harass them as they identified or instantly
pinned on them for whatever ridiculous reason
they were being threatening or dangerous and
thus therefore put in the unenviable category
of juvenile delinquent and forced them to show
them their jd cards and now living in a bizarre
bullshit day and age of political correctness
where they attribute practically everything
virtue and vice and morals and ethics on
the pathetic basis of knowing all the exact
prerequisite and prepackaged language
you're supposed to appropriately use
and expected like for the record all
soldiers are heroes and how we are
mandated to thank them for their service
yet think i was able to connect and felt far
more sympathetic and even in my opinion
saw them much more as martyrs and mildly

heroic those kids who earned the title of juvenile
delinquent based on something crazy they did and
forced to carry around with them jd cards to prove it

Any and all of that rebellion i did as a kid
made far more sense and of far more spirit
than any of that bullshit and methodical routines
and rituals and going through the motions (what
they refer to as 'daily activities' and 'functioning')
when you supposedly grow up and become one
of those upstanding members of the community

We learn from this life that man is unreliable
(of this he is rather consistent) and the only
time this equation is proven different when
a dollar bill is dangled and thrown in the mix


clinical conclusions:

Never let them say you didn't make it
because you were lazy and didn't make
the effort when the whole time it was really
there right in front of you without even being
aware of it, as most likely just buried deep
within your subconscious (stored and saved)
due to some previous built-up profound
pain and damage, laid dormant for lord
knows how long, while just worn (and beat)
down and just didn't want to take the chance
anymore, as would be tragic of the greatest
proportions (while in fact might just not have
taken that much) and things and life maybe just
for the time being having gotten the better of you
and truths (and non-truths) become distorted on a
cognitive, behavioral, emotional, psychological level

## 63

Man! people place such absurd labels on you
when they don't know a single thing about you
and in truth seems like they really don't know
a thing about themselves, almost as if they're
trying to sculpt an identity from these paroxysms,
impulsivity, and absurd sweeping generalizations


proof 1:

They hate you cause couldn't get something over on you
while able to pick up their moves before they even knew


proof 2:

Some of them so much violate and contaminate
the psyche and soul (for purposes of sanity and
self-preservation) only thing can do is move on


proof 3:

With all of these schmucks who you just cannot trust
and feeling like you constantly have to explain yourself
(knowing they're the scheisters with no soul and straight
up just not doing their job) beware in the long-run (how
they drain you) not to take it out on the ones you love


anti-proof:

Everything they now praise you for is the exact thing
they used to condemn and crucify you for, and thus
experience the psychological phenomenon of feeling
just as skeptical and alone, coming from those phonies
with their convenient amnesia while flattery just makes
you want to drink and be left alone and put a bullet in

your brain, as praise comes a dime a dozen and end up
feeling acutely and profoundly that much more lonely

64

If you keep on proving all the doubters wrong
mathematically, existentially, did they
ever really exist at all?

65

I'm still looking for a role-model
or at least a role or model
to roam or be idle?

66

Freedom is having the ability
to survive and thrive and explore
both your dreams and nightmares

67

What is the opposite of paranoia?
pretty much literally geometrically
coming around full circle and being
hyper-intuitive and sensitive and having
a sixth sense and the exact same traits
and characteristics and results and
symptoms of awfully lonesome

68

For the good and decent writer
one pretty much tries to
rewrite their childhood


proof:

It seems to me that most great philosophers
started their philosophies right in midstream
and where they went with it (the difference
between ideology and actual practice) was
open to interpretation and meaning which
was not always exactly quite really
what they meant and believed



69

They always call them such tragic characters
after they bite the dust but how come they never
made an effort to reach out when they were with us?



70

Has the notion and concept
ever been explored that jesus
was a carpenter and got
nailed to the cross?



71

I don't get most people...they struggle and slave all their lives
just to take these vacations to stand on top of mountainsides
to all view the exact same scene which to me i just find

pathetically depressing and empty and eventually loses
all its meaning. i'd prefer rather hearing the distant clang
of donkeys with heads down, demure, well-mannered, single-
minded accepting their duty and fate slowly, making their way
up the winding staircase hugging the hillside at the end of the day


proof:

Most people just care about getting close to the impression
of the illusion; take for example how we envision or view what
we believe to be the image and reality and true concept of love or
perversely on a parallel plane how people abstractly care to be judged


proof:

The ultimate expatriate cares as much about
where he dies as where he lives while there are
reasons for everything (mostly aesthetic, cultural,
political and instinctive) and why he did what he did


proof:

True punk is not to know
you're punk cuz so out there
and just trying to make it and
can't afford it and can only afford
the clothes on your back and that
secret glance she gives you across
the barroom and grew up with her
and turned out to be real hot that
older sister but useless as know
can only appreciate the moment
just long enough to hold onto it

72

I believe the reason why man who has been
spiritually or emotionally or psychologically
abused keeps on going back to that original
abuse is that in fact their cognitive (and
physiological) baseline has actually slightly
shifted and decompensated or turned stagnated
right around 'that baseline' where that original
trauma happened (even become profoundly
damaged and hardwired) and the only
thing now can psychologically and
spiritually relate to, while at the same
time simultaneously and instinctively
trying to figure out and deconstruct
and reconstruct, even unconsciously
repair and ameliorate that original cause
and all that loss and troubling perplexing
dynamic (and phenomenon) of abuse


73

Charm often proves to be something of a false virtue
when simply used to try and gain an advantage…


74

Everything breaks my heart these days
classically-trained actors passing away
way too young from drug overdoses
slapstick comedians caught thieving
pharmacies in the early evening
romantic bad boys getting familiar
with nymphomaniac virgins by the twilight river
newspaper boys who refuse to leave their foyers
having developed social phobias hurt and humiliated
from something they had absolutely nothing to do with

school teachers found hanging beneath morning bridges
due to guilt and conflict and arrested stage of development
bottled-up passions having gotten the better of them
pig roasts behind the barber with soldiers in alleys
whispering sweet-nothings to budding ballerinas
buddhists in alphabetical order escorting dalai
lamas in limos to puppet shows and lectures
about being an individual while herds of hermits
on cellphones huddle on hillsides in robes & sandals
crabapples fallen in gutters by the schoolyards
and cathedrals whose stray aromas smell
like mystical holy fermenting cider of
phantom boy-bum-broke-billionaires
bastard kids taking off in their getaway cars
from the small city big town where black tulips
blossom by haunted houses in the hills at sundown
you sharing grilled cheese sandwiches with angels
in bleak boxcar diners getting it all out in leftover
conversation beneath the stars in a mass of sacred
silhouetted mountains which will never leave you
and never abandon and next time see them these
spirited seraphim skeleton ghosts of former selves
having made the completely wrong choice in men
kind of feeling deep down inside know you warned
them and now just drive through town like a funeral
procession silent and contemplative hollow and haunted
hearing just the darkened nocturnal brooks hypnotic natural
cadences and rhythms like some solemn hymn palpitating and
babbling beneath the same bridges and ancient wraparound porches
muffled paroxysms of distant throbbing train horn brings you back
to life again back through the labyrinths and tunnels and secret
creaking trap door of the broken heart eternal glowing soul
like that beacon of brilliant light from the cinema splashed
out in a pool of pastels refusing to die down or grow old

proof:

Suburbanization also brought about a certain cultural nihilism, existential angst, and vague, self-fulfilling disassociative-fugue which clinically, psychologically gets defined as reaching one's destination and having absolutely no idea how they got there…

75

Sketch artist gets arrested and put in handcuffs
unaware being passive-aggressive and projecting
and doing sketches straight from her subconscious

The convicted is found innocent based on the philosophical
concept that he's been existentially 'convicted'
almost every day of his existence

The prosecutor gets prosecuted and punitively put in pathological
prison (of his own making) and gets prosecuted himself by other
prosecutors brow-beaten and badgered, trying to break his spirit
(his self-respect and dignity) and make him second-guess
and doubt his existence and identity

The defense attorney's 'offensive' and insulting in minimizing
and deflecting clinically obnoxious with grandiose episodes turning
to the wink-wink defense-mechanism of nepotism and who you know

The judge guilty for never once ever feeling
(the feeling of feeling) guilty

[It becomes challenging to cross-examine 'the dishonest man'
and almost have to be something of an illusionist and escape
artist (even a better con-artist) without him even knowing it
being extra-honest, as deep down inside know how profoundly
dishonest he truly is, while not by coincidence, the original selfsame
reason or reflection of his poor and pathetic character and behavior
and watch his demeanor and disguises unravel right in front of you

His defensive and hostile nature and traits and characteristics
become the evidence (the tell-all and smoking gun) and even
proof (and truth) and course of events, while at the same time
root and results and source even cause for the scene of the crime]

All those (false) witnesses and (innocent) bystanders for appearing
to just persistently stand by and thrive off this suffering (criminalizing)

And the jury held in contempt of court for being so easily 'courted'
by the 'contemptuous' having no real life experience (or experience
with conflict or crisis) and thus the potential to be insightful
and empathetic not having the cognitive nor for that matter
spiritual ability to be fair or objective

The courtroom is just like an auction and only those
who can afford it and affluent are proven innocent
(and deemed virtuous); the auctioneer pounds his gavel
and yells out how only old money is capable of–"Sold!"


76

Mock apple pie: it's my deepest & strongest belief
& conviction that for the next presidential election
should run the *kool-aid* pitcher guy who'll suddenly
show up out of nowhere & crash right through the
sheetrock & all the rubble of your kitchen when
you least expect it (& the p.t.s.d. really kicks in
or leaves you as always completely catatonic) for
as the statistics & demographics seem to indicate
america loves constant action, thrives off carnage
& violence, impulsivity, has practically no span
of attention & lives for constant drama & crisis
while as the present day records & approval rating
proves (for very specific brainwashed groups) you
need to have practically no historical or political
background or experience to run for office so there
he'll be on the campaign trail breaking right through
the walls of the tv studio & debate platform straight into
your living room judo-chopping right through smoke & mortar
flying all around–"o yeah! kool-aid's here and it's time to have fun!

Clean-Up:

Wow, guess i really am like every other freaking guy
when i got nothing else to talk about, how i always rely
and fall back on legends and martyrs like bruce lee when

i got alchies in my kitchen without pigment in their skin
because of all the drugs they claim are no longer doing
and if not casing the joint to steal your wife's wedding
ring along with bonds they cannot exchange and other
memories know in the middle of the job of course are
going to break their agreement (and everything they
swore on most likely based on their chemical depend
ency) and are going to ask for half of their pay and
claim they have earned it after ridiculously dropping
every can of paint and literally every nut and bolt and
tchtochke and every glass animal in the glass animal
collection and of course consistently like every last
one of them because they never learned to listen and
ironically the exact reason why they're in the condition
that they're in when told them please if had any questions
to feel free to come on in, but they have too much of that
stubborn idiotic male pride and passive-aggressive and
resent the position that they're in (are too much men)
and paint everything you didn't ask them and have to
send my wife the angel that she is back into town to
pick up a whole other gallon and want to get paid extra
for the time they put in; i swear ain't making any of this
up (i guess minus what we have to spend to pick up a whole
other gallon of paint and gallons for the gas and a gallon for
our time and patience) so i guess i just always fall back on
bruce lee for all the obvious reasons and most necessary
and desperate subconscious of meaning of just wanting
to murder every last single one of them and tell them how
he didn't have an ounce of fat on him and clearly the quickest
reflexes, and no one ever defeated him even when they all
in real life leaped from dark alleys to try and challenge him
and was just trying to get on in his everyday existence from
the mayhem of murdering madmen who were trying to do
him in and when they pick up their drop cloths all of course
just for effect and hand you their cards as if to suggest
if we should ever happen to know anyone please
don't ever hesitate to think about them…

77

There is a fine line between the porn star and politician
only ironically, paradoxically, one is far
more sincere and less sleazy


proof:

After advice i perversely find myself
needing more advice (guidance and insight)
to get me out of (the confusion of) that advice



78

You wouldn't want to know where
the slapstick comedian got his start
eventually very much resembling noir

proof a:

There has always been a real fine line between
that of the very dry (or even slapstick) comedian
and that of tragedy or suffering or nihilism of the
madness of everyday living 'beyond belief' a sort
of crying or howling if you will if i don't get all this
bullshit and hypocrisy out i swear i tell you it'll kill…

proof b:

Marriage at times can look something like a murder mystery…
(even a proverbial life sentence) where in the long-run everyone
becomes a victim (a hostage crisis of bickering; some pathetic
domestic version with all the petty lies of way too 'organized'
of a crime) constantly having to prove ones innocence always
with the best of intentions  (always going all out for them just
to try and make them content) and always made to feel guilty
(something of a strange mistaken identity) with false accusations

put on the stand to defend your honor and self-respect locked down
in an existential prison if always on the defensive and make absolutely
no effort to show any intimacy or affection while no real witnesses
and all circumstantial evidence conveniently taken out of context


proof c:

fantasy mode…

He could never ever really get in
to any of that sleazy sexting shit

just seemed way too obvious
and lacking in imagination

while developed this natural rapport with an operator
who he had spoken to a number times over the phone

and decided to eventually meet half-
way between brooklyn and philadelphia.

for some strange reason they chose
the boardwalk out in atlantic city

while that whole weekend at last sincerely became familiar
pulling back the filthy poverty-stricken curtains of lonely reality.

she had mentioned to him how her and her girlfriends had said
if they hadn't done it in like a year they were virgins once again

and was happy to make the connection receptive to opening up
this vacant stranger mutually pleasantly violating each other

and agreed if after a year hadn't met someone
would hook up again to meet their quota

as when it came down to the nitty-gritty
innocence a terminally lonely business

79

I. Nomadic Geometric Proofs:
a surreal hx of western civilization
something of a slight intermission


1. a hallway ticking in a clock
2. a shadow of a juggler but no juggler
3. a shadow of a skyline but nothing inside
4. a mouse swallowing a piece of wax fruit
   metamorphosizing into a pear-shaped tuba
5. a whole family wrapped in vacuum-tight safety-proof
   furniture wrap to keep all memories & facts intact
6. a whole swath of sunflowers which squirt
   slapstick liquid made to trigger laughter
   planted in the tuxedo of toot shores
   sprouting from robe of dolly llama
7. a sputtering electric candelabra
   in some lone solitary caravan on
   the distant & splintered fugitive ocean
8. a shipwreck with long lines of tourists
   lined-up at the buffet, old timers in dark
   spats playing shuffleboard, aloof obnoxious
   women playing cards on deck & the schmaltzy
   balding middle-aged band still bent over instruments
9. the shrill sound of a lady suddenly shrieking on the train
   as discovers much to her dismay her husband's still living
   & must continue on in this masquerade called reality
10. a lone deer which just shows up late at night to
    the window of *the jack london* with its beat-up
    blinking lights strung-up for the holiday season
    & all the bums & madmen & drag queens
    passed-out in the lobby, while before you
    know it just vanishes into thin air into the brilliant
    vacant emptiness of the season not sure if this image
    was reality or simply an illusion yet when it really
    comes down to it not sure if any of that matters
11. one of those deep dark dives with dusty
    trophies lined in the bleary-eyed window
    composed of nodding-out veterans, drug
    dealers & wealthy daughter starving artists

12. a cracked snow globe which just feels like the here
    & now she-loves-me she-loves-me-not stagnant future
13. laughing sisters strolling down the avenue at dusk
    spitting sunflower seeds into each other's scalp
    unaware making it all that much more hysterical
14. the palm reader's sons bawling her out in the window
    for stretching the truth & being out of touch focusing
    too much on the future & not enough on the past
15. that perfectly square park in portland, oregon
    where it always seemed to just rain enough
    to make the grass perfectly green & plush
    & made just enough installing cubicles
    in business parks in the biotech hills
    & drove a truck to pay off your rent
    & catch a flik at a movie theater perched
    right over that park bathed in purple light
    at dusk with escalators rising up to the stars
    & feel like a new man heading home in your
    black polished pawnshop shoes to melancholia
    & true-blue solitude hovel over at *the jack london*
16. a mote drying-out on a clothesline outside a castle
    while a pervert with binoculars watches the king's
    slut virginal daughter dancing naked & whimsical
    after she comes out the shower preparing for
    a life of seduction & turning young boys wild
    a wild child feeling persistently brow-beaten
    & taken advantage of by an overbearing
    impossible to please father & without
    even being aware of it turns to a life
    of crime constantly running away
    to carnivals & battles; a battering
    ram & batons left in the tool shed
    of the gardener pretty much responsible
    for raising both children; the court jester
    & king's fool building card castles in the
    courtyard out of tarot cards which predict
    the future ironically tipsy beneath the moon
17. in the end it will just be an old pensive man
    roaming the burnt-out grounds of the palace
    as just over the hedgerow a brokedown vision
    of some silhouetted apocalyptic ferris wheel
    in the distance whose image provides sentimental

triggers of past romantic lovers & all those warm
smoky pubs & taverns of chilly winters he adoringly
stared into her gorgeous eyes all evening & fell in
love with which seemed to last a whole lifetime
while the origami hot-air balloons ready to take
off on a whim with a widow in the grand parlor
providing words of wisdom to her grand daughter
& finally fading away in the lap of some tender
nurturing sister as in the end it does all become
doestoevskian searching for just one simple soul
even long-lost stranger to at last trust & believe in
18. the girl next door spying on you through a keyhole
peeking through sycamores to the plush prison on shore
19. a general store made up of trap doors & folklore trampling
in like some vagabond who's seen too much of the world
engaging in a natural stimulating rapport with a wholesome
wife with flowing red hair & walking out feeling like a new
man finally at last content not having a single plan returning
to your hole in the wall in the hall of the holy mountains
20. a porcelain pagoda with thimbles on the sill filled with
drizzle for the chameleons & hummingbirds in the hills
21. a lumber truck loaded up with timber just to build secret cabins
next to taverns in the forest for long-lost lovers & companions
22. starting to clean out the pools of off-season haunted
motels & put halloween candy up on the shelves
23. plates pasted to the wall glued & pieced together
with shattered expressions of elvis & the queen of
england due to a hx of dysfunction & domestic violence
24. an all-you-can-eat feast for the stoning at the dinner theater
putting on performances by moliere & tennessee williams
the actors & actresses skinnydipping in midnight mountains
which means so much more than any of the broken promises
from so-called businessmen backers old money philanthropists
25. those sweltering summers used to sit inside childhood matinees
watching westerns where you swear it felt like it was raining all
day hearing the faraway tremulous distant echoes of holy thunder
not sure if a part of the movie or something between the heavens
& down under & when you exited the theater back to the remains
of the strange insane blinding sun all that was leftover were those
still & sacred puddles pristine immaculate not exactly sure where
they had come from glistening reflecting wondering what
had happened with a sense of rebirth & redemption

26. those brown paper lunch bags stuffed
with moon pies & boloney sandwiches
27. trucks stuffed with ex-convicts & slapstick comedians
rambling over bridges to move grand pianos for miserable
widows in their victorians up on the tippy-top of mountains
forced to tippy-toe in their socks up winding staircases
everyone always cussing & threatening each other
runaway kids returning home from the circus
28. the haunted blinking radiotower up on the pinnacle of the precipice
& island of deaf children always heard howling through the forest
29. an old black dope addict nodding-out over the beat & buzzing
of his buffing machine unknowingly & unconsciously doing
figure-eights in the lobby of an ice skating rink while some
zombie-zamboni-freak with multiple personalities gets
stimulated by the ritual & routine of his repetitive reality
both placated by the stray olfactory scents spewing from
their contraptions like some hustler-thief in a midnight
garden of overwhelming exotic wild orchid & magnolia
30. wind chimes with their mad rollicking improvisational
symphony before a storm and wind fluttering through
the leaves like a stadium full of monks collectively
chanting in robes not caring at all about the score.
after the rain falls shattered flowers like violent
swans with necks bent over on the prowl
31. horses like holy hearses being transported in
caravans in the mad clandestine rainy nighttime
32. a little wicker basket pushed down the mad river of tears
a little later on a silhouette in loin cloth nailed to the cross
suffering alone shedding the selfsame tears shedding his skin
wondering what he did to deserve this somewhere between
the pyramids & pillars & watering hole & river blues traveler
bob dylan (neil young solo) playing long mean harmonica
*heart brings you back*
33. taking shots coming off shotgun bus on-the-run at dusk
in a long-lost sunken barroom behind the musty mustard
curtains beneath the stars of the bars of a lace curtain
lounge of an asylum of a rising skeleton skyscraper
glowing phosphorescent & foreign in the smog
of a radiant ghost town of historic cobblestone
34. a convention of spies followed by slow ballroom dancing
in a schmaltzy hotel in the heart of a heartless city
all stuffed in the breast pocket of a tweed jacket

reeking of pipe smoke & after-dinner brandy
all around that industrial area where they print
counterfeit money & old puppeteer getting
evicted for refusing to go condominium
. a modest flamboyant waiter who shuffles
through the brilliant darkness bringing
a lit candelabra & dagger & the funnies
& bifocals knowing the starving artist
does not want to be bothered  by the
buffet of all-inclusive exclusive tourists
35. a steam shovel which pushes a whole skyline
right into the ocean where mutant seahorses are
giving birth to stand-in monsters, rebbes in togas
caught with their pants down getting blown by drag
queens in the meat market & the wives of investment
bankers who claim asylum due to husbands who no longer
pay attention to them & to get back at them have affairs
with much younger men willing to give them their first
orgasm & final memories of paris which they claimed
was promised & owed to them in the form of a 20 year
mutual bond in the institution of marriage & never given
the chance or opportunity due to spiteful family members,
absentee father figures & soulless sluts from the suburbs
& now build brand-new kingdoms straight from the shag
carpet used parts of that part of the imagination & innocent
studs they picked up simply minding their own business
not knowing what hit them willing to go all out for them
from the other side of the  tracks on their way to grand
central station & will get them all back at ribbon-cutting
ceremonies, ventriloquist conventions, high school reunions,
mafia weddings & fellow divorcees & bums at bar-mitzvahs
36. who opens & closes the blinds in the steeple to get a view
of the poisonous roses along the overflowing river where
the mob changes wastebaskets without even asking &
charges you even if you don't want it in a neighbor/hood
where gigolos stroll hand in hand with saintly girls cause
don't know if they're gonna be there tomorrow through
the aftermath & sorrow of the broken glass schoolyard
to tugs on the river only place where they keep promises
37. the aristocrat in his top hat is finally passed over the shoulders
by the hands of the monochromatic masses who determine his
final destination which is to see how the other half lives where

holy down-to-earth delinquents & their greaser girlfriends smoke
cigarettes behind the *7-11* & the muddy river & trains come in
& all the promise rings have been lifted replaced by spinning
carousels of pie right by the boardwalk of bleak eternal seasons
where citizens who live at the end of the universe full of faceless
ancient immigrants their babushkas black boys backflipping off
the steps onto the beach & freak intellects fated to remain their
forever cause that's all they know unknown content not to be
known fading into the skeleton soul of the unknown some
where between the mobster barrooms bums blind men
caravan of grotesques from the carnival & ocean

38. the hysterical daredevil alchemist fugitive with a great big
rebellious smile grasping onto the ladder of a burning rice
paper hot-air balloon lets out a dramatic wave for the ages
to the half-crazed crowd of spectators who have no other choice
but to tip their caps and lower their faces like some madman
mechanical mantra from those who couldn't make it going
through the motions looking up to this false god savior magician
like marilyn monroe blowing a million kisses to the constellations

39. ex-convict becomes an exhibitionist wandering naked through
penthouse with a pair of binoculars religiously strung around
neck like some transitional-object he hopes to never forget
while across the street in florescence a bible club meets
along with alcoholic's anonymous & dog obedience;
studs hanging-out outside with pool sticks in silhouette

40. lady in fur coat standing on top of tv in motel
trying to get the mobster started who with his
toughness & damage just ignores her & reads
the comics & bible; birdman of alcatraz sends
a carrier pigeon postcard to joe buck & ratso
rizzo reaching out in a last desperate act of
redemption; the hx of america lies somewhere
between the little rascals, orson welles & edward
g. robinson, woolworth's, wannamaker's & the windy
hideout of the thugs in the forest beneath the blinking
radiotower; at least jimmy cagney always went down
swinging with mad heart while defending his honor

41. strolling around the central park reservoir always imagine
those muted howling faces in the glowing faded autumn
of wealthy widows' tarnished chandeliers whose wise
ass sons take on a life of crime behind the blinds
of beautiful bleak boo-joie balustrade buildings

while deep inside the mind lies those glowing grimy
skyscrapers & gorgeous ghettos lining the seaside
42. first thing the astronauts saw when they
took that fateful walk on the moon was
a staticy transistor tuned to the blues
43. jesus crucified on a box of *wheaties*
which just reads "breakfast of champions"
44. a mayor on top of float in top hat with bullet holes
waving ith porn queen to all those pimps & prostitutes
who voted or him in an incestuous town made up of mimes
& clowns, young ladies who have been betrayed & cheated
on by their men hollering like a nightmare in front of real
estate agencies on the curb, librarians mutely wailing in
the porthole windows of victorians in drizzle
45. the golden dome of the capitol sprouting from the woods;
curious boys after school on a mission wandering through
exploring bookstores & drugstores & hardware stores
for fedoras, flashlights, hatchets & waterproof watches
46. a bizarre suburban yard sale which just shows up out
of nowhere, not sure if it's the kid or the parents who
have just given up on existence & packed it all in with
a whole table full of *playboys* & *national geographics*,
a catcher's mitt, used bongs, a bite plate, nightbrace,
mess of unused prophylactics, pair of binoculars for
spying on the cute girl across the block & the crib
notes for all of shakespeare's tragedies & dramas
47. drunken-chaperone-single-mothers whispering
at the school dance in the thunder of gymnasiums
48. coyotes sleepwalk past the cathedral, past the cinema,
past the corner diner & disappear down the alley
into the valley of moonshine mountains
49. gorgeous red-haired waitresses working at boxcar diners
next door to bridal shops always with the spirit of
phantoms in flowing silk dresses
50. the profile of a cat burglar scaling the side of a building
with suction cups & secret potion to knock out
residents & rip off diamonds & pearls
51. waiters on strike demanding respect from tourists & coquettish
older women obnoxiously passive-aggressively flirting with them
52. a feast of aristocrats & madmen at the afternoon chinese buffet
53. dogs tied up to corner in the lightning & thunder during a matinee

54. a drizzle falls on the village bringing bear down from the mountain
& old timers with their wagons dragging cases of *pabst blue ribbon*
a crow flies through the purple mist of the peppermint wilderness…
55. wealthy white women with kleptomania problems taking off in
tears & tiaras in long gold *cadillacs* their husbands purchased
for them exactly like treating them like just another possession
a glass animal collection suspiciously shattered on mantle
56. daughters with nymphomaniac problems spreading open
alabaster legs in front of smart phones in bathroom stalls
their fathers from vaudeville with drinking problems
& napoleonic complexes on line at unemployment.
when they both get home they'll try to put their
split-level in the suburbs out with buckets of fire
firemen arrive whispering gossip & rumors…
57. young girls from the block with no life in their
eyes mechanically hula-hooping for their lives
58. a full house which rises up above the moonshine
59. a teacher making out with his student right in front
of the courthouse with smoke from the pig roast
60. a white trash cop in leather boots & ten-gallon
not man enough to give a ticket to a devil on a
motorcycle acting like a wannabe rebel peeling
through town but will pull over a housewife going
a couple miles over (most likely for issues he does
not have control over) & then give her his infamous
ridiculous passive-aggressive male chauvinist lecture
not too dissimilar than those affluent industrialists
from columbia in white tuxedos with handlebar
moustaches & straw hats who used to come over
in riverboats to do business in an area so dense
& thick & verdant couldn't even get a shovel
through the jungle & where the pan-american
highway ended with endless twisting rivers
& jesus christ lizards dancing over lilypads
giving the impression that they're walking
on water & water hippos & white monkeys
swinging from the tree line in the distance
61. the bloated human cannonball & tall thin
strung-out giant dragging his pair of pawn
shop stilts returning home through the chop
stick alley of the movie theater to weather-

worn wraparound porches in a land of hippies
& lawyers with chemical dependency problems
62. the old perverted usher wanders
down cobblestone in the thunder
63. rest are swingers who act elitist & bourgeois
mowing their lawns with ascots on & preach
& pass judgment on their first born expecting
the best of manners who only end up eventually
parroting poor behavior or turning overly-formal
64. a church woman in the choir with a diagnosis
of munchausen disorder condemns all the liars
(while brainwashing bewildered children) but has never
done one honest thing in her higher-than-holy existence
65. an old timer with his stubby cigar & *coke* bottle bifocals
meticulously maneuvering tweezers like some grownup
version of the game *operation* in his dim basement repairing
his ship in a bottle as contented as this bizarre american
phenomenon of suburban freedom & escapism
66. a wax museum full of martyrs who've been brutally assassinated
67. a country who blindly worships & gives omniscient status
to doctors & politicians & talk show hosts & soldiers
68. a real true-blue wanderer the son of a senator blowing his shofar
in the shadows of decadent cobblestone alleys of foreign cities
69. a chain gang still cuffed around wrists & ankles sharing
triple scoops with sprinkles cracking-up at the creamery
70. the mistress still dressed-up in whips & leather
taking measured sips of her tea at the coffee shop
71. in the not too far distance in the man-made canals
acrobats on gondolas swallowing swords & fire
72. a lighthouse whimsically winking for lost
romantics like a brooding bird on a wire
73. sighing crying dolphins serenading all the secret
melancholy lovers outcast on-the-run in the off-
season; fugitives of fate from the cities way up
north just making it over the mason-dixon &
their call like some bellowing beacon suddenly
reminding them to simply never give up on living
74. a pristine beach which overlooks a smoggy
polluted skyline full of silhouetted fire escapes
& spires from the beginning to the end of time
75. how you find yourself still fixated & infatuated
with mythological borders when they desperately

slipped out & escaped in the middle of the night
   downriver on rafts out of sight to different palms
   to different psalms to the land of figs; the land
   of milk & honey & fields of wine & women
   while smokestack steeples where they used to keep
   the orphanages shoot past your window from *gare
   de lyon* down to the decadent palm trees of the
   mediterannean on the border of france & italy
   where the railway workers from the union are
   always on strike, as up to your own devices
   to figure out what they're saying over the intercom
   & have to switch trains to make it down to naples
   all the way to the boot of the hustle & bustle
   of southern italy where old barbers will literally
   wrap you up in a warm terrycloth towel, lather
   you up & shave your skull with shots of espresso & opera
   before you take the ferry over to the misty shores of sicily
76. this was the exact same strange sleepy fleeting feeling
   you had when you used to take those long slow trains
   from the big easy crawling through the sacred stamen
   of the sweating seeping magnolia & crepe-myrtle-
   swamp-lagoons of the deep south that couldn't help
   but to penetrate every pour of your being physically
   mystically spiritually & transcendentally through
   brick alley bible belt country up to mason-dixon
   slums of old black richmond, virginia, washington
   d.c. finally at last making it to patterson, new jersey
   & grand central station, a delinquent still on-the-run
   being met by your older sister who appeared to have
   a modicum of a sense of humor compassion & sympathy
77. images of prisoners like parrots keeping secrets
   in large oversized cages on a field trip once
   a year during the change of seasons along
   the siene while aristocratic angelic parochial
   school girls in their plaid dresses & the key
   to the lock around their necks involved in
   sadistic slapstick seduction on the parapet
   with donkeys tied up to the lamplight for
   purposes of transport guidance & insight
78. the poets & philosophers the only ones
   who have survived living a life of crime
   having risen above all the betrayals & lies

79. on the ferry to sicily crazy candelabra calamari buffets
along with corny cabaret & asian men in sequin jumpsuit
crooning half-crazed opera to a very tough audience of old
timers nodding-out fantasizing about neighbor's daughters
80. upon arrival the carcass bones of the belly of the beast
suddenly swing open & out waddles morbidly-obese
gigantic twin dwarf bullies & men in their *mercedes*
with their miserable aloof wives mourning behind
sunglasses single-minded shooting to the suburbs
81. stud-gigolo-soldiers well-groomed & neatly
dressed in uniform looking to make a killing
82. dead dogs passed out from the humidity
out on the steamy lawn of polizia
83. your taxi driver in fishermen cap snapping
his fingers to some ridiculous outdated disco
literally running over the bones of strays not
seeming to give a damn on your way to palermo
surrounded by the majestic mafia mountains
& miraculous fertile fruit & fish markets
84. street urchins & wild dogs bum-rushing tourists
with peach baskets mashed over snouts, while
blood-thirsty hags sit on stoops laughing aloud
& wind-up bride & groom walk proudly down
alleys to the the holy mouth of the savage sea
85. you make it back to your dimly-lit porthole
with saints & crucifixes over your headboard
behind windswept weather-worn warped shutters
in one piece, but really not sure, to commercials
where housewives just to please their men & stay
slim strap vibrating belts around their mid-section
86. you sit bronzed & contented on the pensive promenade
along the mediterannean eating a slice of sicilian with fresh
olives straight from the mountains watching the gorgeous
olive-skinned siren-goddesses stroll in seductive sundresses
87. fall fast asleep to the continual sound of wailing
of young hustler merchants in maddening alleys
what it means to be completely anonymous & alone
(lone!son soulful stranger) literal definition missing-in-action
88. at dawn right around where all the great ancient explorers
come from somewhere between valencia & barcelona
the cobblestone starts to get hosed down along with
tourist stands & postcard carousels outside the bull

fighting coliseum; the gypsies & petty thieves
get conveniently shipped in for the ceremony
with saltwater taffy & tee shirts & posters
of matadors, glassblowers & flamenco
dancers; the origins of folklore & civilization
89. a chimpanzee somehow having made it across
the strait of gibraltar from africa to andalucia
in the evening becoming something of a relentless
scavenger panhandling for polenta & slice of pizza
90. a catacomb of siamese cats & stray dogs
staggering from heatstroke which leads
to the lush verdant banana leaf courtyard
where in the morning they serve champagne
& cream puffs & honey cake & *pompadour tea*
91. a strange sleazy old man in goggles swims
beneath where they keep the morning buffet
92. a drained old lady like a jigsaw puzzle
which has broken down into a number
of pieces parasitically scowls in the lobby
93. in the brilliant clean cobblestone alleys
of shadowy cafes sitting on top of stools
at the bar in front of beaming mirrors criminals
& gigolos & pastors take their morning coffee
before a day of hustling & seducing & saving
94. a seductive madonna-whore mother daughter
in their tight chords pick up their morning paper
from the magazine stand just outside the square
95. classically beautiful bronzed chiseled wives bide
their time in sophisticated shoe shops still wanting
to attract & turn on their brand-new banker husbands
both looking at it as something of a mutual investment
96. later on with the rest of the townsmen they will
gather around the flaming carousel at sundown
keeping an eye out on their creatures somewhere
between the beach & mountains of lemons & olives
97. vultures huddle up on top of palm trees in the morning
of costa-del-sol minding their own business harmlessly
looking down on the tourists who are the real vultures
98. a bird on a wire hiding behind the blue mist mountains
that house missions & madmen & martyrs & fountains
99. you bid farewell from the aromatic train station in the ancient
jewish quarter of sevilla hit with the heat of africa & andalucia

100. somewhere between the posh hotels & policia multi-colored
parrots conspiratorially crouch way atop telephone wires
in the glowing fading iridescent twilight of barcelona
101. it rains so much in the summer bicycles get
stolen & magically reappear in the autumn
102. girlfriends take off & just doesn't matter
mailbox casually full of arrest warrants
103. what else can you do but make a name for yourself
& take off from the lake back to the poverty-stricken
wealth thinking up schemes to keep yourself out of trouble
104. you get into the luxury hotel business...
105. dogs on leashes getting familiar in private parks
while prudish men & women not getting it look
off to the horizon in areas so unfamiliar don't
even have neighborhoods named after them
106. monuments of madmen in drowsy closed-down abandoned
red brick smokestack rundown town always glazed in the
radiating dim glowing sun of autumnal alleys & windswept
phantoms right around the cannons of pick-up stick pine forest
factories with mischievous boys snickering like mad scientists
bent over with magnifying glasses trying to burn the whole damn
thing down & drizzle falling on the jack-o-lanterns at sundown
107. soft silent suburban roads which go on forever with gigantic leaf
piles stacked on each & every corner when the nocturnal dew of
brisk early evening seeps into the anatomy of blissful deserted
nightfall & all turns to guilt & loss & thoughtful reflection
silhouetted right before the bewitching hour steaming soulful
showers curfews & curtains & time for all kids to enter slumber
108. a long sleek immaculate white *cadillac* with bat lights on
which simply vanishes into the bleak purply night, while
young pretty girls sweep up the donut shop in silhouetted
whispering nocturnal whoops-johnny-whoops mountains
like brilliant beacons beneath beaming flickering starlight
109. a foghorn in a bundle delivered to a stoop
a whole group of storks shuffling through
solstice thieving streets back to the river
where all broken hearts at last finally
meet like lingering spirits somewhere
on the brink of nightmares & dreams
110. buddha with a fishing pole nodding-out in the fog
111. the banana pudding man shows up from burntdown
stadium to deliver his elixir to the old puerto ricans

112. we all end up at the bleak diner on the border of madness
 & freedom like a buffet of leftovers & bouquet of plastic
 flowers wasted & half-crazed & disoriented & contented
 with the hustlers & drug dealers & drag queens & ancestors
113. you take great pride in playing the part of stranger & trickster


II. Certain Like-Minded Stanzas Of Proof Of Reality
 Having Something To Do With G. Stein & Alice B.


I.

on self-
deprivation,
celebration
(same as self-
mutilation &
self-preservation)
or how
to prepare
to prepare
to prepare
to cook a goose
with your down
time way after
the holidays
on a fine raw
drizzly over-
cast day
not too far
from monmartre
when you finally
feel comfortable
in your own
smock
like
jambon
et fromage
croissants
pouffing

hair & doing
her makeup
in her switch
blade jack
knife fine
ally content
being an ex-
patriot
with 4 chiens
named after
the surrealists
& french
symbolists
forecast
for 4 cats
with a ticket
in back
pocket
of apron
for gare
de lyon
& thee
south of france
knowing all
the twists
& turns
& palm
trees
bye
heart


II.

italy.
friday.
don't respond
s'il-vous plait.
how much
for the ballet?
the chalet
on the lake?

that one much
closer to thee
dusk-dawn
of heaven
when look
king from
the train
window
coming
frum venice
where those
old men hold up
traffic with their
mob of sheep
as opposed
to those
little bo
peeping
wannabe
aristocrats
whose silly
little seething
just feels
obvious
& mean
cruel
& cheap
& might
be nice
to have
access
to row
boats
&
kind
women
in sun
dresses
whose
small
talk
keeps

you
afloat


III.

when you
were young
she was so
young she
used to take
her stuffed
animal
with her
every
where
we went
as some
transitional-
object (d'art)
every place
we traveled
all over
europe
venice,
lake lugana,
emerald isle,
nice,
santorini,
sevilla,
sicilia,
valencia,
barcelona
& used
to get
a kick out
of how all
the young
housekeepers
sometimes
seductive
sisters

who felt
even younger
would place
& prop it up
in different parts
of our hotel room


IV.

first time
you tried
a nectarine
bowl of farina
blood orange
fresh lemon
from the sill
from the hill
side of sicily
slim svelte
bottles of
limon liquor
right from
that neat
brilliant
beaming
dusk window
after all day
wandering
bronzed
handsome
contented
through
alleys
& aqua
ducts
an ex
patriate
next to the
ancient winding
steps of the
cathedral

leaned up
against
the hill
& preferred
just getting
away from
all the wealthy
townies & tourists
widows & gigolos
who always ironically
just made you feel
hollow like the history
of civilization staggering
back down the cobble
stone to the take it
or leave it bones
of the ocean


V.

you substitute
all the bullshit
& madness
of amerika
like the d.c. killer
& hx of constantly
corrupt chicago
literally trying to
sell off obama's
vacant seat
in the senate
for your imagination
of local news out of barcelona
2 banditos chased down avenue
with a stolen picasso followed
onto local bus taking it hostage
at gunpoint but constables back
off due to a sense of spanish pride
& fear of harming portrait while end
up hijacking bus all the way down
to cordoba in andalucia region

where apparently waiting for a
ferry to cross strait of gibralter
apprehended at cafe table
having passed-out with
an empty coca-cola bottle
'seated woman with green shawl'
gaggle of panhandling gypsies
tourists and stray dogs


VI.

the fact is before
you were ready
to finally take off
to your long-lost
gypsy vagabond
haunt in portugal
most specifically
the azures
had to figure
out what to do
with that sky-
blue mandolin
you had purchased
from that pharmacy
window in washington
heights, manhattan
triggering sweltering
summer evenings
& remembrances
of cloisters
contemplative
strolls over
the george
washington
& the brilliant
mists of
the hudson
so it wasn't
even so much
missing any

specific human
but most of all
what to do
with that
sky-blue
mandolin
from that
pharmacy
window
which
never
let you
down
& kept
you from
feeling
blue


VII.

on blue
gloom
& doom
days you
take time
out to spit
shine thee
furniture
& hope
the deer
& ant
elope
are
doing
fine
& sir
viving
thee
wintry
season

VIII.

when thee
snows calm
down might
as well
be thee
lower
east
side
might
as well
might
be A
bodega
& see
ing eye
dog a-
long thee
tinkling
wind-
chime
East
river
might
as well
be an ole
polish
widow
brooding
in her moo
moo might
as well
might
as well
might
as well
finally
be right
over might
those long
sighing fog

horns right
up along thee
hudson inn
side sleepy
holler wit
nothing
& every
thing to
look for
ward to


IX.

look back
wards too
to all those
model glue
airplane
instructions
encyclopedias
sports statistics
manuals of
etiquette
suburban
yellow
pages
where
would
call up
bridal shops
& ask them
to marry me
in my child
hood voice
of mockery
& hear these
young ladies
giggling (prob
ably the exact
same i'd see
naked in

the ladies
lockeroom
when my
mom
would
take me
swimming
at the y)
thee alice
b. toklas
cookbook
boxcar diner
menus &
chinese
menus
which
read
like the
egyptian
& tibetan
book of
the dead
how to
conjugate
irregular
verbs which
led absolutely
nowhere &
would only
use until
decades
later on-
the-run
frum
amerika


X.

when all
my report
cards read

was a class
clown with
great potential
didn't know
how to
take that
took that for
a compliment
& questioned
potential for
what matter
of fact even
felt resent
full while
perhaps
in my
hard
of hearts
felt they
were
sexually-
repressed
& passive-
aggressive
& just did
end get it
& had mad
heart & spirit
& really sin
searly was
contributing
something
positive to
the environ
meant thee
only way i
knew how in
the true-blue
ambiance of
thar here
& now

XI.

child
hood
wuz
the
con-
fusion
between
suicide
notes
& love letters
nodding-out
in the class-
room & upon
awakening
not sure if
out of just
anger
or anxiety
folding it
into the
perfect
paper
airplane
& tossing
it out the
window
into the bleak
loose change
of seasons


XII.

in retro
spec
when
it came
down
to it i got
deceived

by all the
people they
referred to
as honest
(the mean
& wicked
typewriting
teacher
the old hag
french professor
just hanging around
to collect a pension
making nice all-
american football
player break down
weeping in hallway
a punitive principal
& his best friend
gym teacher)
when it came
down to it why
i had to go it alone
when it came
down to it
why i turned
towards the
companionship
arms & bosoms
of one-night stand
long-lost girlfriends
& gained all my
wisdom & rev-
elations
in thee
rhythm
of pil-
low talk

XIII.

my first love
was a very
removed
cousin
who i
had
heard
had a
mad
crush
on me
from
3,000
miles
away
out in
los angeles
& decided
to just become
pen pals & first
she would just
end it with hugs
& kisses until
in the end it
all ended up
looking like
some hard
core score
card of xx
oooxxooxx


XIV.

that girl
from yeshiva
university wurz
weiler school of
social work who
got pissed at her

best friend from
the island for outing
her as being a republican
but actually was a real
life nymphomaniac &
in the middle of class
confessed to me she
was wearing no under
wear & what was
i supposed to do
with that follow
up with some
real clever
fine pithy
punchline
like prove
it or meet
me in the
bathroom
anywhich
way it'd
all end up
sleazy &
what end
up guilty
asking her
to leave
social
policy
to relieve
all stressors
& tensions
when was
just simply
following
up with
her offer
ending up
poverty-
stricken
on pro-
bation?

XV.

mary poppins
floating past
my window
with umbrella
in the thunder
with mascara
running down
her punum who's
become ophelia
who's become
southern belle
i used to know
& live with in
the west village
on horatio & man
left her for a much
younger woman
who's become
blanche dubois
& ended up
having sudden
temper-tantrums
& meltdowns
taking it all
out on me
when she
thought
i reminded
her of him
or that
gorgeous
thin red-
haired
girl
i used
to know
who went
off to college
& artist boy-
friend ended

up abusing her
tying her to chair
& taking pictures
of her naked
that rich girl
from michigan
who refused to
kiss me but when
coming out of shower
in sweltering new york
city summer wood
be a cocktease show
me everything beneath
girl on the lake who picked
me up at the general store
& much older woman at the
movie theater on the weekend
when i was already abandoned
& she pleasantly took advantage
back to her ranch mansion
on perfectly manicured
cemetery dead end
literally dumped
me off after i had
served & satisfied
all her needs like
some gigolo scene
& puked on the tracks
before my shift working
on the docks loading
furniture for a bunch
of yuppie schmucks
& thought about all
these women as
long as they just
had air-conditioner
& provided shelter
& allowed me to
dream for just that
little short while

XVI.

or maybe all i require
is that flying nun
& she'll just pick
me up on my porch
in the morning dew
in my businessman suit
clutching onto briefcase
as perhaps all i need
is an aerial view to
get away from it all
her habit whipping
wildly in the wind
while our hearts
beat as one
soaring over
the pig farms
& steeples
& gigantic swirling
ice cream cone
& thimble-like
oil refineries
& those horrible
flashing flags
from used
car lots
& casinos
& smokestacks
& slaughterhouses
& silhouetted mountains
& broke down shacks
along the boardwalk
& when we're
all done not
having said
a single thing
to each other
will just drop
me off once more
on my porch right
around the rolling

thunder of nightfall
like some obscure
forbidden erotic dream
of guilt & liberation
& just wave at her
as i see her gradually
getting smaller & smaller
like some black balloon
from a carnival
disappearing
to the horizon


XVII.

o the mirageomarriage!
joey you got a whole
creamer behind thee
pomegranate lemon
aid! i had no idea!
i told you! i am
so sorry! you
should be
dancing
yeah!
yeah
yeah
can you
pick up
lox &
cream
cheese
olive oil
bread
& brie
been
a long
mad
den
ning
winter
& thee

birds
finally
out of
nowhere
returning
to the wire
which just
naturally
teaches
you to
take
absolutely
nothing
for granted
as soon will
be changing
back our tires
& opening
up again
the dairy
cream
a right
of spring
passage
right on
that holy
river
gurgling
swollen
into thee
sacred
thawing
passage
far end
mistycall
mountains

XVIII.

last wish
before i go
a creamsicle
fresh brewed
cup of joe
chopped liver
half sour pickle
before i escape
up into the fall
foliage foothills
hearing
the spirit
& murmurs
& whispers
of her pillow
talk assures me
i was once loved
& always a natural
rapport whenever
the cops come
to get me always
able to charm them
with a modicum
of small talk
even a little guffaw
to break up their day
& realize they're just
as lost & lonesome
(maybe experience
of years of always
getting into trouble
as a teenager)
before they lock
me up & alas
some down
time on the top
of rock bottom

## XIX.

claiming the best you
can do which seems
something of a lame
leftover proverb is
to live something
of a happy
healthy life
got no idea
what that
would look
like…like
the closest i
ever got was
my beating
heart waiting
for the plane
to take off
from la
guardia
to charles
degualle
with a couple
bucks in my
pocket knowing
all the things
i was gonna do
when i got picked
up by that little mad
man dwarf taxidriver
snapping his fingers
to some really
strange out
dated disco
i guess digging
it cuz thought i was
something of a hipster
wired wasted gangster
from amerika whizzing
with tears in my eyes
sentimental reflective

past le tour d'eiffel
wheeling & winding
wild up the cobble
stone hills of mo
mart just like
g. stein
alice b.
toklas


XX.

still can't
make the
exact ole
factory
distinction
(& wonder if
any that'd matter)
from the brilliant
aromatic trigger
of cocoa butter
or is it the distant
self-soothing hypnotic
aqua pristine ocean
of the caribbean
or simply some
beautiful exotic
puerto rican girl
spread out with her
ravaging rubenesque
figure like some miraculous
mermaid solitary sophisticated
her long seductive silky hair
flowing down her olive skin
bosom at some wild chaotic
blissful insane city pool
right below the sweltering
lower east side clothesline
tenements unsung getting no
attention should be getting

like some sonia braga
seraphim of the ages


XXI.

i don't mean no disrespect
but don't know what the big
deal about marilyn monroe
was & yeah she had that
wonderful wave with that
will to save you smile
all that flesh & bone
& seduction but isn't
that usually the shit
that drives guys off
the deep end & if all
of them are getting off
to her tony curtis & jack
lemmon & arthur miller
& joe dimaggio & both
of the kennedy brothers
doesn't that sort of make
us all ho's & if one day
get up the guts to ask
her to become your
betrothed maybe just
maybe might for the first
6 months get all that real
down home lovin during
the infamous honeymoon
period but eventually just
like everything else proves
to be high maintenance
on the borderline of
compassionate & craziness
constantly confused by the
concept of love & the need
& will to want to save her &
be damned if you do damned
if you don't & doomed with
all her blue gloom & doom

moods she loves me she
loves me not & drinking
& pills wondering what
did i get myself into?


XXII.

liberal loose laid-back
was digging my mad
smart neurotic borderline
jewish girlfriend who spoke
fluent russian from riverdale
go to lesbian nightclubs with
her classmates from social work
school on the weekend in manhattan
or stroll hand in hand (just coming off
a bad marriage) with pal out in p-town
'cause they were simply friends while
cool with it as i literally knocked out
5 papers over the weekend which
were due & her later on complaining
about & had to come back with don't
get mad at me you spent all weekend
walking hand in hand with lenore am
sure i want to die in monmartre with
a view of sacre-couer & suicide love
letter of do not disturb like some fold
up collapsible version of le tour d'eiffel
(like baudelaire said when they fucked
up the translation of *le fleur du mal*
hope they can find someone just as
good to translate it back) to know
with the true expatriate tries to get
back all that original love & passion
which has gone bad (what does it mean
to be a real romantic?) looking back at
my bittersweet childhood knowing
i was right to challenge authority
on a daily basis ending up contented
with a wise ass smirk in detention

XXIII.

fantasy
of 1st
frau line
bewtiful
blonde
german
girlfriend
30 years
later petaling
her red bicycle
still with that bun
of golden straw
blowing sundress
returning home
like some goddess
from the garden
simply turning
her head
looking
into the
dregs
of my
ghetto
mansion
what else
can i do but
reciprocate
to prove i'm
still existing?


XXIV.

never got
too much
into any
that part
ying snorting
first line of d
first line of c

washing
it down
wash
ington
dc
going
down
town
copping
it from
aband
done
buildings
on avenue c
& avenue d
did about
as much
for me
as fluff
& peanut
butter
preferred
½ a tab
of speed
chased
with ½ a
cup of coffee
winding up
winding down
up on top
rooftops
of harlem
convent
& 135th
with black
girls & ex-
convicts
my best friend
from elementary
found 86th having
od'd on the surface
of the deep blue

sea at the city
pool on pitt st.


XXV.

if only
had a
seeing
eyed
dog
to see
thru
awe
these
awful
things
had a
sawed-off
machine gun
for every one
of these god
damn triggers
false father
figures
& did a literal
volley back
& forth
connected
to the source
of the original
rape & violation
sorry but there
was no better
feeling when
i ended up
marrying a
much better
bride (who
i casually
paraded
right by)

than that
girl who
thought
she'd
make
me
lose
my
mind
non
shall
lant
lee
break
my heart
but came
out the
ven-
tril-
o-
quest
having
swallowed
my dummy
with a
sarcastic
grin on
the other
side of the
disappearing
act amen
of wis
dom


XXVI.

looking back
to childhood
what color
crayon do you
think you'd be?

when you look
back do you
remember the
exact colorful
name on the side
& what made
your heart leap?
this to me
has so much
to do with being
& personality
release & lay
them all out
on the kitchen
table & finally
figure out things
& reality & your
thought pattern
what you're all
in fact really about
& range of emotions
& feelings & moods
& tone & shades
& way of being


XXVII.

a rose
by any
other
name
be pink
in a white vase
like those stunning
scarred red brick
row of gorgeous
monochromatic
buildings on
23rd street
across from
the infamous

chelsea little
further down
towards 8th
& 9th avenue
on the westside
when the sun
hits it just
right right
around
twilight
going
down
over
palisades
in jersey
where
they
keep
the holy
flowing
hudson
streaming
vast & open
transcendently
leaving room
open for the
imagination


XXVIII.

how to eat flan
with that leftover
beer from a keg
you keep on
forgetting
to return
on the roof
in the west
village &
that southern
belle who works

at *pierre-deux*
looking for
some hoodlum
younger man
to save her
belting mad
karaoke hymns
tipsy & tearful
to some lost
& forgotten
savior in fallen
leaf cobblestone
alley somewhere
between midnight
& change of seasons


XXIX.

let's say our childhood prayers
& make our promises & pinky
swears over tuna fish & matzoh
in junior high school cafeterias
over ham & cheese sandwiches
that have been blessed by rabbis
& older brothers we looked up to
'cause sneaky-eyed spied through
basement windows having heroically
gotten laid for the very first time
over milk & cookies like a fine
cheap wine for the solitary boy
who has decided to hide behind
the melancholy midnight moon
over leftover crab rangoon &
chicken wings & fries with
hot sauce from the bleary
eyed refrigerator from the
night before & only make
raw proclamations during
the pensive chilly season of
autumn with dew dappled
scarlet & golden leaves

scattered all around in
the sheltered shadows
of riverside park along
the hudson right below
the ragged shattered
sputtering chandelier
skies & our favorite
faded flannel & our
buddhist bible & no
bread in our pocket
or booze on the table
(not even nuts left out
on suicide sills as an
offering for the pigeons)
with absolutely nothing
& nowhere to go nothing
to look forward to but the
here & now & the pure
empty vacant future of
a distant purring prowl


XXX.

just a place that
feels like home
just a pillow that
feels like home
just the shadows
just the storms
just warm with the snow
falling down your window
just that simple impoverished
room in new orleans listening
to that transistor radio & ole
ragtime the only thing that kept
you going a real-life starving artist
surviving off *hotel bar* bread & butter
sandwiches just one of those slim
clean immaculate neat & tidy
milkmen with a bow tie on
getting ready to operate

on you in the back of
the ambulance with
your bullet-proof
glance & hand
stuck in there
resting eternally
on broken heart
him thinking it's
a gun or got some
sort of napoleonic
complex but really
one of those ticking
little golden watches
to hypnotize the
masses having
tried to break
out & escape
on a gigantic harp
from the jagged cliffs
of lockup when all
you really wanted to
do was keep yourself
out of trouble & busy
with something meaningful
directions for how to tango
for how to rumble for how
to play cowboys & indians
for how to overthrow some
government for how to read
your haf-torah to become
a man in the jewish religion
& start jerking-off religiously
to chrissie from *three's company*
still searching for that pristine
kingdom to be eternally happy
& safe & secure & let it all
go & finally forget it all

## XXXI.

all those symbolic
archetypal myth
ological dream
like beasts &
creatures which
now just co
habitate &
physically
show up
to your window
what if in (f)act
without even
being aware
of it have done
something of
a role-reversal
touching on the
notion in your
later stages
of growth &
development
have become
them in mind
body spirit
& soul
solitary
contemplative
with a heart
of gold always
having a little
fear of yourself
& deep down inside
knowing your some
thing of a primal
gentle giant
as well

XXXII.

how to
live alone
how to
listen to
classical
radio
french
rap &
staticy
jazz
from
n'orleans
how to
make
petite
fois
faux
gras
& a
new
sense
of yer
self in
chinese
rest o
rant
how
to eat
a pear
dipped
inn A
kettle
of
car-
amel
all by
yer
lone
some
by a

map
filled
out on
your kit
chin island
by your child
of the united
states of amerika


XXXIII.

while still
searching
for that lit
illuminated
beacon of
the batmobile
with those pimp
clattering chandeliers
zooming through the
deep dark desolate
evening up through
some transcendent
trapdoor to the stars
that lone solitary
midnight tug
or imaginary
caboose chugging
past your home to
the great unknown
to know that death
will really be
just one simple
soft punchline
with absolutely
no explanation
no stories to tell
nothing political
& no bullshit at all
starting from the middle
going back to the original

spirit where it all began
the core desperate
maddening call
of seagulls
& hypnotic
soothing rhythm
of waves rolling
back & forth
in their natural
contemplative
chorus from
the ocean
to sands


III. The Old Country

i could never stand that expression which always
seemed to glamorize neglect or even a bit of an
abuse of power from those relatives from the old
country–"better to be seen and not heard" often
even referring to their own kids, while honestly
would prefer hearing from them. i was the original
chaplin. many of my acquaintances were the ones
who ran away to the circus. i had women whose men
were the barkers and ringmasters in the middle
of messy divorces. when i got a little older i
became one of those cabana boys who opened
up those chairs and cleaned out the cottages
and was compensated by affluent aristocratic
women whose men were always missing-
in-action feeding me whisky and chinese
in their suburban bathtubs. my best friends
were those acrobats who stood on each other's
shoulders with elastic ear to ear smiles while
waterskiing and entering the time capsule of
home movie cameras. the wounded widows
who used to wander the boardwalk at dusk
and put up their laundry on the line on the
horizon resembled the walking dead as if
reenacting their lives as violated housewives.
large ladies staking their claim at the hog races

while state cops in their muscle-clad uniforms and ten-
gallons as if becoming their own monuments of what
it means to be self-made men of unmistaken machismo.
young slut-seductresses of the country club and carnival
with their seething delinquents (really the romantics)
who eventually will be taken advantage 'cause can't
keep up with them. the soldiers always in sunglasses
with their shirtsleeves rolled up playing the role of studs
shuffling on and off the ferry at dawn with the half-crazed
out-of-work actors taking minor pathetic slapstick parts
doing vaudeville in foreign accents, morbidly-obese dwarf
twin bully brothers and wind-up geriatrics waddling down
the ramp to the land of corruption and redemption. the poor
sicilian girls from the slums returning home having worked
the french summer resorts while pimps and preachers
making small talk in immaculate shadowy cafes
taking their morning coffee. old men who eternally
hang out on the corner pretending to hit each other
over the head with fold-up chairs outside of ol'
time barbers who still serve shots of espresso
while blasting opera. scorned lovers like
myself bleary-eyed and battered ready to
jump into taxis driven by little madmen
past sleepy melancholic mansions in
the dewy luxurious palms of the suburbs
nodding-out from exhaustion to ancient cities
of cobblestone and not caring if i ever make it
home dead or alive from the petty crime of life
deriving from that population otherwise known
as the sticks and stones of better to be seen
and not heard. the donkeys and dead
dogs coming around the curb...


IV. Surreal Stanzas (the nature of noir)

:: we move like silent film stars through the night

:: a pained grin on the dripping soaking milkman

:: the leftover forgotten pretty girls from vaudeville

:: a parasol left in the gutter of a southern belle

:: burlesque dancer with her hourglass figure who instantly
triggers all the businessmen in their plume of smoke to start
howling and feening and seething and drooling like a pack
of pavlov's dogs (increase their libido and fantasy worlds)
and instantly automatically ameliorates and heals all their
conflicts and problems and helps them to get on with
miserable menial realities and stagger off drunken on
7 & 7's to improve their daily functioning and meet
their quotas and dream of their long-term targeted
goal of that quintessential corner office in heaven

:: the sailor in his all-white uniform in broken bamboo
night will fall in love with strangers; a girl he thinks he
might love, while simultaneously falls out of love with
his mortality and will never ever really quite return home

:: rain falls on the rickshaw

:: we are all absurd strangers in a dark
movie theater obscurely watching our lives
flashing right in front of us on some chaotic screen

:: the combustive, churning wheels of the train
exact same as the built-up collapsible waves

:: idiotic strangers brooding, worrying having a difficult
time making the distinction between work and play

:: our childhood was like some brilliant keen
surreal freakshow of a haunted holy life of leisure

:: when we get older we slow dance
in the stirring echoes of a conch shell

:: naked incestuous cousins eavesdropping
like kettles seething through the keyhole

:: through the rainy portholes they lift
the blinds to the sunny deck of the
splendid cruise ship on the ocean

:: dreams are the isolated imagistic division
of visions and the exact dynamic as well as
opposite deconstruction of the imagination
leaving one to question deep down the
meaning and purpose of their existence

:: i love for the most part how trains and buses
just creep through the deep dark haunted evening
and then suddenly just show up like some saintly dream
coming out a nightmare in the milky dawn, bleary-eyed, reborn

:: i love when they spoon you
forks & knives not included

:: it seems like in all of those ole time black & white
hollywood films they were having a damn good time
(actually had clever quips) like the first exhibitionists
(what i had heard too were pretty wild & promiscuous)

:: werewolves dancing with werewolves

:: politics involves a certain amount of addiction

:: the vietnamese and portuguese fisher-
men return for their bundle of heroin

:: it's not so much that you care that they steal from you
(as have simply gotten used to) it's the trigger to that
violation and original betrayal of trust and truth

:: do we ever really recover from the open
wounds of betrayal or just become a bit more
calloused, cautious looking out for the deal of devils?

:: dogs prove to be man's best friend
(with their protective look of sympathy
and compassion) during thick and thin

:: those true-blue troubled youth were spiritually neglected
and abused way before any of those clinical conclusions

:: nothing equals the power of a child's imagination
almost making a spiritual connection with the
transcendent gods and spirits around them

:: often those who don't get your sense of humor
turn paranoid, defensive, and hostile while ironically you
were coming from a place of mad spirit kindness and compassion

:: when you deconstruct and break down language
often it runs parallel and consistent with the
contradictions of human nature and behavior

:: women know their exact influence over men

:: an instant panacea to all the emptiness of living


V. Your Local Manifesto

1,the matadors have all been locked up
and their token roses neatly placed in plastic
vases in boxcar diners along the off-season ocean
2,all the actors are overpaid and don't act anymore
3,the same holds true for ballplayers and get paid more
than most third world countries always on injured reserve
4,sailors still come in and we are required to refer to them
all as heroes no matter what they did and don't know what
country or war they're returning home from because be-
come a government policy to keep it all on the downlow
and neat and tidy and clandestine and show absolutely
no clips (blood or gore) on television so as to avoid any
sort of backlash or protest or possible real-life rebellion
5,(which can potentially be captured by innocent bystanders
on their smart phones as everyone these days has become
some sort of self-important aloof and arrogant film director
bunch of brainwashed blind followers with very little to offer)
6,all the legitimate idealistic candidates of honesty and integrity
are forced to bow out early because don't have the backing of
big money pacs and can't afford to go on the all-out attack
to distort the facts  and keep their campaign intact

7,all the suburban white women (apparently a significant
demographic) are miserable and angry as maybe
might not be able to get granite for their kitchen
8,the same holds true for their children disappointed can't
stand the size of the water parks and no wifi for their apps
9,we can now confess our sins and be instantly forgiven
over one of those screens at a drive-thru cathedral then
get food delivered to our car window of wings and tater
skins and zoom off to the horizon a brand-new man
10,rich kids whose parents are all workaholics (famous
for their emotional and spiritual neglect with their
connections to children's psychiatrists and anger
management) head down the highway at dawn
for their early morning dose of liquid methadone
11,cruise ships religiously stranded
out on the high seas with botulism
and food poisoning and get escorted
back to shore by tugs where no longer
are there ceremonies of confetti but tongue
depressors and toilet paper and the tourists
all laid-out on stretchers for their final destination
12,lucy ricardo has given up on her dream of making
it big in show business and is on her third marriage
and has married a very driven and competitive
safe and secure gravestone salesman
13,alfred hitchcock's silhouette has gone on a crash diet
now on one of those before & after infomercials down in florida
14,every three months the patient is required to show up to their
primary to sign some sort of legal form due to an all-knowing
know-it-all orwellian directive mandated from the medical
community even if they have absolutely no history of drug
abuse or chemical dependency or addictive personality
15,(the doors all read something like "please do not bring
your firearms in" with a diagram of a primitive
weapon or gun with a slash through them)
16,quick and clever one-liners do not exist anymore and it is all
some choreographed very practical joke which must contain some
sort of punch line or slapstick element or staged set-up blooper of
violence (as this is what's deemed to be hip and hysterical for the
adolescents) like very obvious and predictable neatly-packaged
shrink-wrapped fortune cookies with their pre-manufactured
proverbs made in the factory so as to avoid any leftover crumbs

or getting sued for wisdom taken too literally and all
those promised dreams not meeting expectations


VI. Mortality: or the murder rate


version #1

The tow trucks and horses
rattling past my window
somehow make me feel
more safe and secure

a little later on will turn on that channel
to purchase one of those real-life glass
cubic-zirconium promise rings to prove
to my wife how much she means to me

those sad saintly broken-hearted hygienists
spend half their paychecks on in the wee
hours of the night with tears in their eyes

(think what might even be more apropos are one
of those ol' time mood rings that go back & forth
flickering between the shades of black & white
to prove how much i am a martyr but don't
know how much that will really accomplish)

apparently marie osmond's going
to play her last show in vegas

didn't even know she was playing vegas

which strangely enough triggers
and touches on the concept of
one's mortality in amerika

version #2

I can't stand when
those singers such as
billie joel & the bee-gees
& even barry manilow got
big & they actually did write
some great lyrics and then
it was cool to just trash
them like you never
even liked them
or they never
even existed

it's shit like that that
i can't stand about man


version #3

Those days when
all that mattered
were those long
overgrown blades
of grass sheltered
by the shadows
and the brilliant
madness of over
flowing brooks
through patches
of pachysandra
whose simple
quiet sound of
gurgling always
seemed to stream
through the keen
senses and seasons

version #4

I always
had a dream
of having
an affair
with
royalty
with my
burning
mattress
on the floor
in the poor
part of
n'orleans
jelly roll
morton
jimmy
rogers
ol' satchmo
crooning
on the radio
while had
so much
to offer
as sure
ragtime
saved my
ragged soul


version #5

Living in that ole
broken down hotel
in the tenderloin district
of san francisco so alone
not knowing a living
breathing soul while
the only thing that
got me to sleep
was oldies radio

from that transistor
on my night table
just hearing i swear
that simple surreal
song "in the jungle
the mighty jungle
the lion sleeps
tonight..."


version #6

She was healing me
      while i was slowly dying
            i suppose another term
                  for watching our life pass us by
  or the physiological/psychological
              sensation
                  of 'to forgive & forget'
                        pleasantly to no longer exist
              whispering sweet-nothings
     light as a feather


version #7

Please do not tell me there's no smell
for hurt and pain and guilt and loss for
words that got spoken spewed and shot
for broken hearts and shattered glass for
primal mythological howls in the wee hours
cuz just get sick of the petty power struggles
while one does not ever quite recover from
deep down loneliness and a life which just
seems to break you down around every
corner the plaintive pensive ticking of
a grandfather clock no different than
a time bomb or toaster oven roaming
the home like a ghost with incessant
recurring nightmares no matter how
much you redeem yourself and move

on in this laborious existence which
still seeps through the pores of your
consciousness they sure love their texas
down in football i'll take any day humphrey
bogart and *the last picture show* the tv will
tell us when the sun will rise the tides and
when she will show up and sleep by your
side one knows the sign of a great film when
the critics finally shut the fuck up and go silent
with tears in their eyes young lovers and old
timers refusing to leave their seats and teenage
concessionists and old ticket takers looking like
ushers at a funeral parlor cannot stop shedding
these abundant tears of sorrow at the bewitching
hour into my cup of joe mothers give birth to their
first love and mourn the one who came before...


version #8

Seeing myself as one of those disappearing acts
not sure which way i am coming or going and
am neither here nor there looking deep down
the top hat and the only thing that comes up
are the echoes of the deep blue sea not sure
who i am as there have been so many mailmen
and lived in so many homes of that eternal smashed
window from a number of different balls letting in
the different brilliant mercurial seasons the garbage
men who out of rage and a certain amount of humor
turn the tables and end up chasing the dogs round
and round the dead end the insecure ghost who just
decides to pack it all in and become a traveling sales
man in his token black suit with his token white hankie
looking like one of those ole time skyscrapers piercing
through the smog in the evening a night train with no
real destination rattling to the horizon a whole line of
chorus girls passed-out on stage like dominoes from vertigo
while the spoiled wealthy daughters give a round of applause
nodding-out not sure whether to be seductresses or scholars
critics as always like faceless toy soldiers heading towards
the doors *the national union of elevator constructors* on strike

while that humble stud gigolo stripper no longer able to entertain
the very aggressive slobbering suburban women and put food
on the table of those he loves knowing that those keystone
cops are all just really jealous and corrupt cause couldn't
get a job in the mob and end up taking on a whole other life
of crime while in fact ironically become the real petty criminals


version #9

At the group home they teach the boys
to count backwards from 10 to try and
reframe defuse and control their anger
(wonder if get into the negative
numbers will help to heal and get
to the source of all our problems)
wondering if you can do this too
with time and figure out where it
all started going wrong in life?


version #10

If jesus died for
me i died too for
bukowski dostoevsky
jean-paul sartre camus
i promise you on
an everyday basis
for james dean in
"rebel without a cause"
even "east of eden"
kathryn hepburn
in *long day's journey*
having turned into
a morphine addict
in that tragic tumble
down mansion ghost
of her former self in
denial completely
unaware of it
when all you

hear in the
distance is
the melancholy
chorus of ghostly
foghorns like some
haunted beacon
nihilistic real-life
self-fulfilling
prophecy
that day
when you
just feel like
you've lost
it all when
in fact got
so much
more to
live for


version #11

When no one ends up believing you
does that make you something
like the opposite of god?

no problem as never much believed
in myself and thus in a strange sort of
psychotic way inspires me to move on


version #12

Rimbaud weeps into clawfoot tub
where his saintly naked sister
an angel to die for who works

a swingshift at the off-season tavern
has given birth to a wild seraphim who
just hangs out on the corner and smokes
opium between the cobblestone and ocean

a lemon tree blooming right over
the prison where they keep all
the smugglers and swindlers.

through the sea-stained shutters
one sees a choir of school children
and lonesome widow rinsing her rags

a lake where they keep the lunatics and aristocrats
ferry of kings & queens coming in for the season


version #13


Techniques on how to hose down
the elephant cage on a late tuesday
afternoon on the outskirts of providence
to help to heal a bit and reduce the base-
line of temporary loneliness, melancholia
self-loathing, and situational depression


80

I seem to make a connection with all those who clinically
could not make a connection; the true-blue alienated starving
artist and poverty-stricken desperate for escape and experience
and promise you not on purpose but real down home suffering
like genet and dostoevsky; kafka and kerouac, rimbaud and
baudelaire who bared their souls cause deep down they really
had no one else out there (on a literal and existential level) and
cared and gave a damn and had no other choice in the matter
and nowhere else to go so those times when i can just scrounge
up a couple bucks and get a cheap plane ticket always find myself
(like some pleasant ritual without all the predictable rituals of ritual)
returning to the south of france like some poor transient aristocrat
whose soul and imagination always goes naturally instinctively flying
(fluttering, levitating) when suddenly comes into contact with the
image of the palm trees of the mediterannean and taking in all the

natural liberating scents of the ocean and olives and lemons; all
knowledge in the expression of a wild, wide-eyed, vagabond kid
(the american always seems to obsess and brag and harp on the
concept of what it means to be 'a free man' until it almost gets
nauseating from an ethnocentric point of view and want them
just to shut the fuck up as always appears like they're talking
way too loud for their own good around the tourist bed & breakfast
table and just don't have the experience of other countries and
cultures around them and simply ends up sounding silly and shallow
competitive  and recycled following those exact same behavioral
patterns and non-verbals of never listening which becomes the
sickening irony as if everything from a privileged and entitled
point of view should cater around them) getting back to lonesome
traveling and the senses and anonymity this is what always
does it for me instantly instinctively which really has all to
do with (being 'anonymous' and the real 'true-blue stranger')
the core concept of identity but maybe just perhaps perversely
ironically feel it the most keenly (experience fleeting sensation)
and thus not having to think about it i mean feeling it most fiercely
while simultaneously just forgetting it all (and thus getting away
from such psychological dynamics and defense-mechanisms of
so-called 'intellectualization' or 'internalization' and 'externalization')
which has everything sincerely to do with freedom without having
to always absurdly advertise or talk about it so cerebrally


proof:

An ode to the tremulous trunk, the skin & sky-blue bark
of the pouting & pockmarked, insanely stunning plane
tree, sprouting sporadically along the mediterannean
always seeming to be barely blooming in off-season
whose distorted figure goes weeping, wailing somewhere
between coincidence & fate in the spirit & exact same
moment of the brilliant, transcendent ages, weather-worn
by the wind & waves of history, profound, keen, especially
along bourgeois boulevards of forgotten cemeteries & sea-
side cities like nice, whose bulging, ancient pods have been
throbbing since ancient times & dwarf muscular ribbed anatomies
knock-kneed, twisted, sculpted by the wind & sun & sea-stained
seasons, bleakly rise up from the slums to the stars where skeleton
shadows get tossed against the lattices of the opera house & orphanages

& petty thieves & pompous bureaucrats got their start, such as perhaps
travelers like young runaway vagabond rimbaud who embarked,
bronzed, camouflaged in the palms, wild & intoxicated, hysterical,
hiding-out, on-the-run with that decadent bum verlaines deep in
some wasted porthole in the jailyards & schoolyards & vineyards
of rainy glistening cobblestone, knowing every single shortcut, stray
cat, slapping, creaking windswept shutter & haunted, pungent, damp
kerosene alley whose selfsame antiquated planes like a blissful wicked
dream instinctively led from murky mystery to the deep hollow core
of the hoarfrost of the raw keen senses, winding up to the opulent
cathedrals & castles of aristocratic villages where incest & nepotism
ruled the day nestled way up on top of the hill, looking out to the
magnificent blinking bay of half-crazed slave ships & pirate ships
of blackmarket opium & spices whose blessed cursed life caught
up with him eventually contracting syphilis & dying in the lamp-
lit lap of his saintly sister; this juvenile-delinquent, world-renowned
poet who became famous at 15 & gave it all up in his twenties
as the rains came pelting down on the provencal streets of plane
trees piping & steaming somewhere between the promenade
of freaks & the pristine cactus & carnival sea


81

1, Why do the pseudo-intellects always find the need and
compulsion to be the first ones to laugh in the movie theater
as if always trying to prove they get it first while ironically always
got to get 'the last laugh' in as well with their very formal highly-
competitive highly-intelligent higher-education really got nothing

2, How they consistently exhibit behavioral patterns
of always having to act cryptic like some passive-
aggressive way of pathetically seeking attention

3, Constantly acting coy really a 'fear of intimacy'
fragmented personality, and form of 'avoidance'

4, Almost every intellect i have ever met
seemed to betray and contradict their
exact supposed selfsame morals

and ethics (so far from anything
consistent, kind, or compassionate)
almost as if playing some 'hard to get'
futile game of opposites and thriving
off semantics, and could use a good dose
of practice what you preach (if you knew
the paradoxes!) and self-actualization or
for that matter some sort of father figure

5, How much will they keep stealing from you?
the intellects with their attitudes and how they
make you feel and doubt and question yourself
sort of feel very much like the opposite of god

6, Question? why are they always the biggest
aloof & arrogant assholes trying to make one
feel so small while ironically got no idea?


proof:

The only membership i want
    is that ol' faded chlorine-stained card
                              from the y
    & the first time i got laid
thinking i was in love…



82

They talk about all those parades they should have thrown
(or at least not spit or thrown eggs) for those veterans in vietnam

well how about chaplin after mccarthey
deported him back to england?

a long funeral procession for lenny bruce from
the bronx, ny all the way to the shores of los angeles

83

The ones considered real smart even the geniuses of society
are the ones who simply know how to work the system
and keep the secret and lie more convincingly…


84

Corrupt corporations in america after they consciously
deliberately lie and steal and swindle you, for their curtain
call in so-called commercials and advertisements try once more
to take advantage, and declare such see-through mistruths like–
"we're re-committed to you" which only blatantly and obviously
(*patently*) absurdly reconfirms the (emotional and spiritual) abuse


proof:

We learn our rights or our right to have rights (the hard way)
after having been abused and taken advantage of way too
many times by faceless, dehumanizing, bureaucratic, might-

over-right institutions, who thick with irony and hypocrisies try
to disempower (because they can through disinformation) the little
man who so desperately seeks their necessary support and guidance

and communication only works one way to their advantage
and there's no way to get in touch with them
and then ask you to take a survey…


85

The real issue and problem with politics
is that people (and the masses) are
desperate and naively looking to be
saved trying to find that 'one savior'
to show them the way and to believe

in and when they eventually find out
their leader is a phony and fake who
breaks practically every one of their
promises (which helped get them
elected purely out of self-interest)
internalize and feel betrayed when
most likely was a bit crazy to think
that this figurehead (in any way)
would  play the role of some father
figure to figure out their problems
and lead them to the promised land


proof:

Politics is worse than any dirty business like all that meanness
experienced in middle school by someone you thought
a best friend at best an acquaintance and didn't know
what you did to deserve it and turned out devastated
as always had the best of intentions with kindness
and compassion and generosity and innocence

the media, "the experts" are there to break down
and deconstruct all the whispers, gossip, and rumors
but just never ever really come close (due to the compulsive
need to always objectify and hyper-intellectualize) while simply
don't get it's all just the basic vulgar and disgusting contradictions
and hypocrisies of the psychodynamics of animalistic human nature

government is the panacea when you've run out of ideas…



86

If only grownups were more personal
in their professional lives and more
professional in their personal

87

In the long-run, often 'the good' will give up on themselves.
it is hard to tell exactly when this happens and why and where
as usually it comes from the smallest of things (literal or a trigger
or symbolic representative) some ridiculous, overwhelming, aggressive,
obvious and blatant behavioral pattern of man, which can only make
him feel existentially 'a/ban/done' (perhaps not even care or give
a damn…) to relate or engage anymore with his psychosocial
environment and either becomes abundantly clear or some symptom
it is not going to get any better and that form of melancholia or
existential revelation of feeling eternally cursed forever, which
gradually just gets the better of him or just spiritually feel like
there's no more fight left, and therefore thus, somewhere in the
long-run the good (not sure necessarily the precipitant event or trigger)
will just naturally give up on themselves losing a sense of 'perspective'


88

The rich always seem
to be celebrating each other

(weddings and funerals
even become political)

with a very convenient
and collective amnesia

which almost
seems criminal


proof:

The affluent like to make a claim to 'culture'
because they are exposed to it and can afford
it but the very distorted and ironic paradox
usually more times than not, it is the poor
the down and out and impoverished, who

through whole different mediums and creative
styles and forms (different ways of 'getting
on') of art and language actually create it


non-proof:

It is a perverse dynamic how in the rich family
with all the politics and bullshit and family dysfunction
they often have the potential to make one feel poor and
unwanted, while in the poor find certain creative ways of
making one feel like they belong and a sense of importance


89

All those really rich people i've ever known lived the life of ghosts
(always 'at a loss' on a spiritual and psychological level, haunted
hollow almost as if trying to recapture a piece of their missing soul)
never ever seeming to have family around, but still thick with tension
closets full of skeletons and never anyone out on their lawns (all except
of course for the help to help keep the illusion going) yet ironically still
with the need to keep up with the jones', their reputations and people
they so desperately (a whole other illusory way of maintaining) had
the compulsion to make some sort of shallow superficial impression


90

Some of the biggest secrets lie in those upper-middle class
families with all those subtle superstitions, routines and rituals
(which they remain so passionately and pathetically committed to)
and all those personality disorders which kept politically so well
hidden to desperately and absurdly keep up their
mystique and leverage and illusion and reputation

## 91

Rebellion's not really rebellion
when standing up for one's
identity and fighting injustice

that's the way in fact the coward-devils
will want to try to have you believe it
and confuse you who live by the lie
and do all their shit from a distance


proof a

The reason why things frequently get so awkward
because one party clearly not acting in good faith
while ironically the exact same party who shows
little to no remorse or doesn't give a damn; all
the lovely little things we learn about man…


proof b

Being placated is just as offensive
as all the reasons they don't get you


proof c

One has to make it through all the doubters and haters
like the tributaries to the river to the miraculous ocean


## 92

Anyone can be a thief and a liar
for some it just comes natural
been way too romanticized

have you ever met someone
of the opposite dynamic?



93

Guys never ask questions…
they always seem to be giving
answers when weren't even asking



94

I don't know…why do i find hardworking women
in their gardens so much more original & creative
doing something positive & productive than all
those wannabe gangsters riding through town
all loud & hostile in their pre-packaged posse
attention-seeking with their pre-manufactured
anger supposedly supposed to represent
something all rebellious and cultural?
they almost seem as tough as those guys
in their pickups driving real slow always
leaning back at the perfect cookie-cutter
angle trying way too hard to intimidate
like bullies who never quite graduated
(always seem to get real frustrated
when you imitate them, even get
a bit flustered and don't appear to
quite know what to do, confused)



95

Everyone's always offering a piece of advice
but pretty self-serving and rarely addressing
the conflict or crisis as strangely perversely
always seems to come back being about

them; their life experiences and losses
failures and shortcoming weaknesses
so when it really truly comes down to it
not really genuine support or guidance
when it more accurately has something
to do with their own self-interest and
more likely their own way to get closure

one ends up feeling more
lonesome and abandoned



96

In truth the clinical narcissist sees himself
as both a martyr and savior and does not have
the cognitive potential (nor does he really care,
mildly sociopathic) of how his ignorant/arrogant
behavior is really affecting and damaging others



97

For the convenient scapegoat
if only not so convenient

what a play of words!
oxymoron to be more specific



98

There are those who somehow try to make their point
through constant indifference but never could quite figure it
'cause wasn't sure what they were getting at and why they were
trying so hard in their conviction in an opposite dynamic without spirit

99

The way people choose to make a statement
to me never seemed like much of a statement

proof 1:

Why is it the biggest squares always
the ones talking about being centered?

proof 2:

That lazy cliché expression
"i was just doing my job"
as you think to yourself
in the back of your mind
i wish you *were* just
doing your job...

proof 3:

People hold onto grudges yet should make
little more of an effort to try and hold onto
the opposite which is the spirit of love
and passion and all things romantic

proof 4:

To die with honor
but how many
truly live with it?

proof 5:

That perplexing paradoxical play
of words once again of an oxymoron
like quality–'over my dead body...'

## 100

I remember working with this dude on this alcoholic
painting crew who would make these idiot outlandish
claims like the reason he was depressed or like never
made it was due to the music they were exposed to
or forced to listen to back in his generation and used
to think man is this guy kidding making such excuses
but you know now that i turn on my radio every morning
in the kitchen to keep me from hanging myself i think
you know he might be onto something and hear myself
saying to myself out loud–'what the hell is this? is this
even music? what the heck happened to rock n' roll?'
and suppose i guess may be just a little bit more
sympathetic but you know ain't gonna go
so far as to blame a whole generation


proof:

I can't stand these days even when you turn on
the classical radio station in the middle of the day
to try and calm your hurt and damaged soul they got
hospitals actually doing commercials bragging about
how good they are (and are # 1) in that specific field
i mean has it really all come down to that? what's
next? funeral homes *billions and billions served*?


## 101

I want to show up to my funeral
and spit on my grave not in a bad
way but in the good "brother" way
maybe like good ol' clint eastwood
in that movie where with mad moxie
he felt the compulsive need to spit on
practically everything to christen things
even his poor mangy dog who always
stood loyally nobly by his side whining

## 102

When they finally finished wrapping up filming
of "guys & dolls" they asked some director think
it may have even been kazan maybe not how brando
had fared in his role with his song & dance skills
& he curiously quixotically responded was able
to hold his own while just a little later on at one
of those infamous hollywood screen tests jimmy
dean the first & only time beat him out for some
part forgot which one it was right around when
the guild gave an x-rating to "midnight cowboy"
& jon voight took home the academy award
for joe buck (of course the projectionists
as always on strike, while the old timer
ticket takers & young kind psycho ushers
just wanting to make a little pocket change
for cheap bottles of wine) manifest destiny
making it through mafia philadelphia coal
mining pennyslvania those strange winding
tributaries in the eerie evening of glistening
ghetto of toledo crossing over that unknown
border just west of the mississippi with your
$7^{th}$ bride $7^{th}$ daughter with her rosy cheeks
red hair flowing over shoulder & quilted
sky-blue dress draped over whale bones
belting rogers & hammerstein to the bliss
ful blue heavens with all that mad spirit
sense of humor & the whole wide world
ahead of her while men in ten-gallons & top
hats duking it out for a piece of the american
dream & rest of the posse of mad scientists
& magicians always had some quick money
making scheme to invent some panacea
secret potion cure-all to cure degenerative
arthritis & alcoholism taking nips of moon
shine beneath the stars while the rest of the
cast of castaway civil war soldiers without a home
& ex-cons got their first taste of freedom ecstatically
square dancing like doing some insane break dance
from the bronx by the campfire somewhere between
denver, colorado & reno, nevada where the balloonists

& bone collectors set up shop maurice chevalier on
one unicorn & lewis & clark on the other shuffling
from the snowcapped grand tetons through dense pine
forests of swollen over melting rivers & indian territory
only to finally at last miraculously glean the wild
crashing ocean through the towering redwoods
of oregon where they kept the leftover dewy
donut shops with dope addicts nodding-out
& bubbling hot springs by the railroad tracks
& boxcar diners & little lego towns of lumber
mills & $2 movie theaters over overcast majestic
rivers & industrial bridges all the way at the end
of the universe traipsing in their gold dust rags
to the holy & sacred shores of the folklore of
san francisco where the tenderloin district
stood proud & sure like some keen brilliant
mystical sacre-coeur where supposedly they
stored a quarter of jesus' broken heart way a
top monmartre for their last supper ceremony
of *mad dog 20/20* & a great big gigantic
burrito which could last them the whole
day & right around dusk feeling totally
turned-out down on their luck homesick
for home about 3,500 miles from home
all alone somewhere between the trolley
cars & ferries still having the ability
with holes in the soles of their high
top sneakers to stand nobly up on
top of russian hill right by some neat
& clean chinese laundry & have visions
& dreams gazing over the sparkling pacific
somewhere between alcatraz & san-simeon
with one single solitary pawnshop transistor
hearing through all that static to just a simple
literal ethereal crack of the bat as the giants
took on chicago over at candlestick stadium
& had to learn how to gauge & figure
out which way the wind was blowing

proof/kronology:

        1

Rimbaud! imagine doing a wild
vigorous fugitive mythological
impossible backstroke down
& out down out-of-control
half-crazed raging river
disappearing to flaming
horizon pot of gold at
the end of the rainbow
where the dwarfs & elves
runaway genius criminal
kids & streetcar sisters
of the mountains live
past all the kerosene-lit
prisons & institutions
dance halls & missions
where the only language
they're fluent in the fluttering
fermenting change of seasons

comedian really a long-lost romantic…

        2

A charlie horse cowboy clown still on silts
and in ten-gallon pumps gas at the desert
gas station while in town the empty barber
waits for his customers and becomes
something of a tradition and custom

both have drinking and girl problems
and looking to make their killing...

3

He calls up the oldies station
and thanks them for playing
inspiring music from his
childhood; the allman
brothers, elton john's
"i'm still standing"
then all you hear
is a gunshot and thud–
"we're gonna have to break
for commercial" and in a strange
obscure way it all comes around full circle

103

What to say about that band of mad traveling actors
still trying to make it get their big break on broadway
living in rent-controlled apartments for $325 a month
in the upper west side right around riverside park
that brilliant plot that thank god most of the
tourists don't know about hugging the hudson
with wild puerto rican picnics drifting loners
and poets just like yourself and can still feel
the spirit of all those brave courageous explorers
steering their huck finn rafts through old man rockefeller
young teddy roosevelt mansions making their living
cutting hair at *bendall's* madison avenue beauty salon
waiters in the shady romantic cobblestone of soho and
cozy taverns in chelsea even belting burlesque in amsterdam
avenue barrooms those strange cousins always estranged in
childhood who couldn't quite see their way through college
on polluted stagnant connecticut rivers and so much more
preferred the art scene of warhol and jean-michel basquiat
in the lofts of lower manhattan shacking up with stud sculptors
from switzerland who prove to be the real soulful forgotten actors
of america not what you got now a team of typecast action heroes
fitting into the cookie-cutter formula making the world safe
for democracy and can't and will never be able to relate to

proof:

Would have loved way back in the day
being one of those radio personalities
who doesn't so much crave the fame
but more so the anonymity being
heard and not seen waking up every
morning and heading out in my wrinkled
linen suit in my chevy convertible down
sunset boulevard for my regular of
a western omelette hashbrowns &
a cup of joe while the pharmacy stools
start filling up with cigarette girls looking
to be stars and you do fall in love with a
poster girl and marry her and move into
one of those fine humble mid-century
frank lloyd wright mansions up in the
hollywood hills where you'll never be
bothered again and live happily ever
after...get visits every so often from
abbot & costello superman & chaplin


non-proof:

Going to the movies these days (all your idiot
commercials & reality shows on tv) in america
like some automatic gigantic freak game of flinch tag
with a fist which comes crashing through the screen
(of course your token killings & quota of explosions)
and the first one who actually gets rattled & screams

104

The Amerikan Scream:

take 1

All these strange half-crazed fucked-up
hypocrisies of these united states where
we historically have started wars around
the globe all for the sake of freedom and
democracy and dominance and control
killing millions of innocent people yet
*dominoes* has come out with a brand
new gimmick and policy called some
thing like 'insurance' just in case
should happen to come across any
dangerous conditions on your way
to your destination and may drop
your pizza on your way to suburbia
get a brand new one; claim instead
of an apple a day which used to keep
the doctor away take a *bayer* aspirin
to fend off any serious heart palpitations
all these brand-new pharmaceuticals for
all these brand-new disorders we've never
even heard before with side effects even
more lethal that can kill you or make you
suicidal or delusional and fast food chains
which will conveniently deliver your burger
and tater skins straight to your car door and
don't even have to get out pressing your
garage door opener on your way home

black man straight from the ghetto holding out
from training camp and even willing to go the whole
season to get what he believes he deserves at least 20 million

take 2

All these wannabe asshole aristocrats in amerika
(most likely newly-retired or their whole life having
had things handed to them, or just got their inherent
dance) in their retro convertibles desperate for people
to stare at them and get attention, and then if one should
look anywhere in their general direction act all aloof and
arrogant and offended like how dare you even consider
being a part of their grand delusion of grandeur and their
body language and expressions just seem to indicate completely
empty and vacant (you wonder why they're never considered
for drive-by shootings or assassinations) while in the other
direction pass moronic motorcycle men with their pre-man-
u-fact-erred anger who have whole other absurd reasons
(seeing themselves as 'rebels' really grownup bullies
or selfish and silly little wannabe heroes supposedly
so independent and individualistic in their conformist
posses) for why they don't want you to stare at them
rumbling down the fashion runway making their
choreographed commotion still living with their
mommies in the mean mountains of new england
bicyclists with the compulsion to always be wearing
their very competitive spandex racing uniforms and
wonder what happened to the days where you would
just throw on a t and pair of cut-off blue jeans taking
off through the bleak brilliant trees of the suburbs to
hang out with your friend at the end of the dead end
while these days white trash gangsta bitches all scowling
in their fold-out chairs they got for a steal at *the dollar
general* wanting to get their spot staring down at their
smartphones as they're setting up for the floats on the
parade route; later on at sundown all the pasty-faced
dr. jekyl & mr. hyde alchies will stagger through town
while they blow up the dumpsters with blasts from m-80's
literally triggering your ptsd and think america just raises
and brings up a bunch of brainwashed zombies with their
need and compulsion to worship flags and monuments
and believe we would just be so much better off if had
like some sort of real-life self-help manual to teach these
schmucks just basic politeness and manners (something
apparently never taught to them) or just a little subtlety

and tact, while in fact seems like never quite had any
sort of maternal or father figure influence, or even
perhaps one of those pocket pamphlets we had
when growing up and were in the boy scouts
of how to tie the perfect knot or how to rescue
a kitten from the treetop or walk an old lady
across the block as believe it or not straight
up in my opinion and estimation would have
such a more unique and creative make america
great again' nation so much closer to the original
vision what all those great courageous forefathers
and statesmen had so sincerely earnestly intended


take 3


I hear the cops can now issue tickets to you for driving intoxicated
on your lawnmower; picture that! showing up to some poor miserable
father's postage stamp lawn working this awful interminable 9-5 job
barely hanging on wanting to hang himself one step from putting a
bullet in his brain; his wife and kids having lost all love and respect
for him with last vestige of independence and freedom and pig just
standing there in his wrinkle-free nazi uniform with his ten-gallon
scribbling him some ticket and ripping it off at sundown and wonder
what we can attribute this to? american know-howmaking his quota?
american exceptionalism? our brilliant punitive democratic justice
system? making america great again? while those all-american
heroes peel through town on their motorcycles with their straight
pipes (to amplify and make the sound as loud as possible) draining
every last piece of you on the parade route triggering and kicking
in once again your ptsd not sure whether to fight or flee cry or scream
so wasted and wired don't even know who you are anymore breaking
you down wearing you down to your wits end while there's some
ridiculous madman in his benevolent association uniform
just planted out there issuing a summons to a broken
man with head down in the sand…

take 4

In amerika they just love to  throw their token parades
(while wish little less pomp & little more circumstance
everyone always marching off to war) & would just
love if they had a parade for when the parade finally
leaves town (the carnival & rowdy repulsive tourists)
returning the land back to the natives, humble
& softspoken, drizzle falls on the dandelions


take 5

So the white man has stolen practically
everything from the american indian
and his culture and way of being
while in their 'life of leisure' they
have their token fiberglass kayaks
strapped to the tops of suv's with
miserable unhappy wives silent
and resentful in the passenger
seat and 2-3 zombie brat kids
looking out the window on their
way to the sea and after all the
parades and beer drinking and
making the scene with the onset
of evening never a time i feel
less a part of things and empty
and alienated with no real sense
of identity or meaning as instant-
gratification idiots of self-interest
and conformity just look to satisfy
their strip mall fast food wants and
needs (with the compulsive need to
be seen and show off their things
soulless and greedy) you find you
have developed something of a case
of dysthymia in a dystopian society

all seems like porn without the intimacy
as the ambulances return with
the clowns and freaks…

take 6

In amerika all the real martyrs all the real matters
have been forgotten and we have been taken over
by cartoon characters and a cartoon commander who
spews propaganda while followed by his ridiculous
republican coward sycophants and what they refer
to as his percentages his base and approval ratings
who are the eternally spiritually brainwashed and
rape convenient scapegoats with fear and hate as
live in a land of billionaires and those working 3
jobs who can barely afford to put food on the table
as must be brought to the attention once again for
the sake of culture & civilization real music or rock
& roll does not even exist anymore; they're cartoon
characters as well with reality show health club heart
throbs of mock attitude and drama and exact same
synchronized cookie-cutter dance moves safe and
secure soulless sluts taking selfies with their cell
phones while the exact same silly custom occurs
in the 7$^{th}$ inning stretch of "take me out to the ballgame"
can you freaken imagine which used to just be about
the collective whole now close-ups of some posing
schmuck as one cannot help but to feel so damn
lost, while are now in 3 separate wars, what
they're for really not sure anymore (all over the
globe making the world a safer place for democracy)
that does not clearly exist because it is policy not
to show any tv clips or real-life carnage over your
local news station as that tragic quota is reserved
for your school system and synagogue and shrine
(by some suburban child whose soul has gone
psychologically numb and senses turned off
only turned on by that real hot cool blood
and gore he gets right off his play station
and social media and satanic commercials
and formulaic special effects movie super
size me! and get me an all-day all-inclusive
ticket for obnoxious and privileged and entitled
caucasian family down in disney *down in disney*...
and put me up in one of those little pretty theme
mickey mouse club hotels with your psychotic

waving mickey and cinderella but now gotta watch
your back in orlando in the stripmall in the sunshine
state in the movie theater cause considered the stand
your ground state and doesn't matter what state they're
in or you're in have every right if find them in any way
shape or form to be mildly threatening to protect yourself
with your weapon so says the late-great charlton heston
moses man of the people and your cartoon president
who refuses to reveal his taxes and pay his workers
and has over 16 cases of sexual harassment against him
yet "will make america great again" this grand wizard
wheeler & dealer in the hospitality business keeping
out all those dangerous poor poverty-stricken migrants
fleeing gangs and hunger those monster under your bed
rapists and drug dealers looking for just a safe simple
place to rest their bones and raise their kids (so the tv
will show close-ups of exotic dog food with fresh slabs
of beef & chicken & fish but a whole mess of immigrants
locked up in cages fleeing danger just to get to freedom)
off to the marble mcmansion mission where never see
out there any one of them that great big empty museum
in the stars where it's just the gardeners keeping up
with the jones keeping up appearances keeping up
the lawn to make it look like some perfectly neat
& tidy glossy paint-by-number mural so off to
the grand illusory mall and food emporium to
be saved by air-condition and tater skins to
get yourself and parking ticket validated
and rush back up the highway to get
home safe and securely to beat rush
hour and the bewitching hour and
the falling nightfall and carjackers
and all those lonesome elements
in the sudden change of seasons


take 7


Sorry please forgive me
but democracy in amerika
these days just seems like
way too many options and

way too little opportunity
the customers never happy
(loading up their plates at
the grand buffet with things
they don't even necessarily
want) taking it all for granted


take 8

In the land of amerika all these very tough
little white trash posers pretending to look
all scary & suspicious (all part of the exact
same cookie-cutter attention-seeking act
with their pacts of manufactured anger)
still living with their mommies & daddies
as try just once one day living in the projects
and then can see how rough you really got it


take 9

Satire 1:

1, a close-up of the killers in the crowd
2, sexless soulless sisters behind sunglasses
3, couples never happy but always too proud
4, apparently with all their down
   time they turn neurotic and numb
5, they are here to root on the blondes
   and the question becomes to shun or be shunned
6, dusk does become more than the bewitching hour
7, all sponsored by pharmaceuticals and techno
   national bank and cashmere cleaning products

take 10

Satire 2:

the before & after the before & after
came way before all that marketing
for the symbolic & subliminal ad
vertising of virtue & innocence
helps the whiskey & wine go
down easier; there was a reason
in those ole time movies why those
cowboys & soldiers suddenly broke
out in song (while in the madness &
horror of it all) at least provided some
sense of hope; 'of being' meaning &
purpose in this desperate fucked-up
cursed blessed existence & to may
be even return home in one piece
to that 'happily ever after' home
in suburbia to their girl & son &
daughter & pay off their car &
mortgage; a stack of pancakes
with *aunt jemima* syrup & nice
little job at *alfred j. tickle co.*


the origins/derivation of marketing strategy:

'survival of the fittest' translated to man
is the one who can stand and put up with
the bullshit the best…can be most single-
minded with the ability and potential to forget
a sense of perseverance, perhaps even, having
the least conscious (having no problem instantly
rationalizing & compartmentalizing) when being
a cut-throat & competitive & making his quota
what it means to be 'a success' in this ridiculous
& monotonous slow-death type of absurd illusory
life of constant repetitive ritualized free-enterprise

take 11

Satire 3: the not so secret secret of advertising

1. these are my breasts
2. this is my smile
2a. these are my breasts & my smile
3. this is my beer bottle
3a. these are my breasts & my smile & my beer bottle
4. this is my slight seductive shift of shoulders
4a. these are my breasts & my smile & my beer bottle & slight seductive shift of shoulders
5. this is my product
5a. these are my breasts & my smile & my beer bottle & slight seductive shift of shoulders & product
6. this is my message
6a. these are my breasts & my smile & my beer bottle & slight seductive shift of shoulders & product & message
7. this is my freedom on the ocean
7a. these are my breasts & my smile & my beer bottle & slight seductive shift of shoulders & product & message & freedom on the ocean
8. this is how your life will turn out
8a. these are my breasts & my smile & my beer bottle & slight seductive shift of shoulders & product & message & freedom on the ocean & how your life will turn out
9. this is what will happen
9a. these are my breasts & my smile & my beer bottle & slight seductive shift of shoulders & product & message & freedom on the ocean & this is how your life will turn out & what will happen
10. this is your figure from every angle
10a. these are my breasts & my smile & my beer bottle & slight seductive shift of shoulders & product & message & freedom on the ocean & how your life will turn out & what will happen & your figure from every angle
11. this is your scenario of living happily ever after if you purchase product
11a. these are my breasts & my smile & my beer bottle & slight seductive shift of shoulders & product & message & freedom on the ocean & how your life will turn out

& what will happen & your figure from every angle &
scenario of living happily ever after if you purchase product


take 12

Satire 4: age of communication

how about a statistic or demographic
(or one of those commercials for some
psycho/tropic one of those all-inclusive
cruises to the tropics) for all the times
in amerika a man heated just calls
the *home depot* because his wife
is just driving him up the wall
and being impossible to deal with
and moody and erratic and hollers
out loud over the phone–"fuck you!
i just want a fucken human being!"
and that placating mechanical
stepford wife repeats over and
over again in that patronizing
tone of voice–"i'm sorry i didn't
quite get that? did you say heating
and refrigerating?" again–"fuck
you! i want a fucken human
being!" and get–"did you say
heating and refrigerating?"
until all you hear is them
going back and forth like
some silly little futile ole
time vaudeville act with
out the comedy which all
"might just be recorded"
and the simple sweet
sound of some gunshot
and the thud of him hitting
the floor while the recording
just repeats over and over–
"i'm sorry i didn't quite get
that" do they have a statistic
or demographic or population

for that? you know the madness
of the hypothetical (the mundane
and the mechanical) and all those
little things in life which just push
you over the edge? a statistic and
demographic for the newly dead?
some store policy or money back
guarantee if not fully satisfied and
content and decide to just give up
on this ridiculous existence because
have tried so damn hard with the best
of intentions and just not worth it and
just can't seem to get over to that grand
department of kindness & compassion
so they just keep on pushing you and
you keep on pushing this button and
pushing that as you finally see these
foreboding shadows all standing over
you offering all these different night
marish mechanical options but never
once ever the chance of getting through
to that district manager in receiving
(as still trying to locate him) for every
thing that they had originally promised


take 13

Satire 5

mermaid rules

1. do not touch
2. do not feel
3. do not yell
out like some
hysterical tourist
without sex appeal–
"i saw a mermaid!
i saw mermaid!"
4. do not whip out
your smartphone

for whatever fucked
up reason pod people
whip out smartphones
5. do not send
postcards to those
you feel the necessity
to send postcards to
6. do not let your
obnoxious spoiled
brat throw stones at her
7. do not try to shoot or harpoon
tuna or dolphin of mistaken identity
8. do not do the breaststroke or insane version
of the crawl because think she will save
your soul or restore a loveless marriage
9. do not even tell an ole best friend
from childhood partner or neighbor
from the dead end but keep it all
on the downlow on the terrace of
your off-season motel and simply
bow your head in reverance and
keep your no-tell tail to yourself


take 14

Satire 6: a found poem: work experience

"*Superthin Saws* is looking for a full-time Production
Team Member to work Monday through Friday
hours typically 8:00 a.m. to 4:30 p.m.

Ability to carry out repetitive work requiring good
hand-eye coordination, rapidly, to achieve quality
standards while performing both the loading & un-
loading of components & tooling setting up machinery
as well as maintaining neat & various types of tooling"

you see why man turns to repetitive things like drinking
to repetitive things like trying to find ways of forgetting
to repetitive things like mowing the lawn
to repetitive things like mowing & drinking

to repetitive things like mowing & drinking & sun sinking
to repetitive things like cheating with other women
to repetitive things like other women & turning to religion
to repetitive things like proselytizing whole other form of pimping
to repetitive things like trying different ways of killing himself
to repetitive things like watching nonstop tv just watching
sports & weather turning to heroes & mythological gods
to repetitive things like hollering at the one he truly loves
to repetitive things like trying to find a second job
to take her to places like vegas & cape cod
to show her how much she means to him
to repetitive things like feeling no pain
feeling no pain feeling no pain & finally
at last that sensation of may he rest in peace


take 15

Satire 7: amerikan manifesto


1. my theory the american dream
comes at way too high of a price
too many burdens & bureaucracy
(too many obligations & broken
promises small print that always
seems to work against you) to
ever straight-up realistically
realize 'the dream' & truth

2. ironically has all these *blue*prints
& boundaries rules & regulations
boards & committees & faceless
institutions (absentee landlords
full of hypocrisies) where you
constantly have to get their
consent & approval even
pay taxes & pay your
dues to the abuse
of power sexless
shrew to keep
the absurd

illusion
going

3. "follow directions"
to keep garden growing
to keep wife & *hoa* happy
electricity turned on & to
be forgiven not forgotten

4. a stickie on front door reads–
"for the love of god mow your lawn"

5. clean-cut neighbors on local cable voice displeasure
(with their drinking problems & fine reputations) having
started major battles over all things territorial having
absolutely no idea towards basic communication
always taught to hold things in or go in for the kill
case will be determined not so much on merit
but a strange sort of country club nepotism

6. there's a reason bury treasure
at the bottom of a box of cereal.
for children, that hope & desire
(& imagination) means the world.
at the end of the night you devour
a bowl with the sports & weather

7. beware of suburbia
of the waving people
of that pot of gold
at the end of
the rainbow

of child developing a drug problem
because parents never home & no natural
consequences & family lawyer always providing bail

8. guns & flags & the pledge of allegiance
will keep them all safe & secure holy & sacred–
"your call is being monitored for quality assurance
thank you for your patience...thank you for your patience"

9. housewives obsessive worshiping of appliances
substitutions for husbands no longer
showing any interest in them...

(they tell their fare-weathered friends
on the dead end they are convinced
he's gay or through some half-crazed
fucked-up form of munchausen find ways
of blaming the kids who decide to either hold
in their feces or present with suicide ideations)

10. one gets awfully lonesome...

11. miserable 'life of leisure' citizens
always kvetching & complaining
who can never get happy even
with everything handed to them

12. constant bullshit & bickering
to try and prove they're 'living'
(like the opposite of descarte's
"i think therefore i am" theory)

13. having a difficult time trusting
the most trusted man on tv...


take 16

Satire 8:


-12

thunderstorm watch underway
i wonder how the royals are doing?
the seine? the thames? state of tibet?

what's that river again
of forgetting and no regret?

-11

what happened to those good ole chain letters
from back in the day actually made you feel
a part of something and crazily in a fantasy
like way might actually make a change


-10

war in lilliputia still underway
with a gigantic empty catapult
and whole heck of a lot of eggs


-9

geriatrics gathered around global warming pool
revealing card tricks to their grand kids
about the best they can do...


-8

planning family get-togethers
you turn to drinking while exactly
a week later you stop completely


-7

the best advice one can give is none at all
like brilliantly figuring out the solution
of some long math problem while in
fact its answer really doesn't matter


-6

marriage with the moodiness of it all
the best we can hope for some sort of
obnoxious overboard cruise ship stranded

with an open bar *lake champlain* chocolates
murdered conductor harp used by fallen angels


-5

that high-rise condominium
for the out-of-work actors


-4

different dentists' sons strangely
enough go back to their parents'
old vinyl record collections and
come up with ahmad jahmal


-3

the best hash neatly rapped up in tinfoil
when their parents take off to their
second home in the berkshires


-2

the jazz organist plays a mean solo
to a ballroom full of embezzlers
giving away their daughters
while their wives get down
with their gynecologists


-1

they ironically give long laborious
speeches with the words in it–'don't
feel like i'm losing...but i'm gaining...'

0

oi vey! all those old time movies
with hot-air balloons escaping...


take 17

Satire 9: large buxom lesbians in stewardess
dresses with sawed-off shotguns involved in
drive-by shootings paying back girls from high
school who used to cruelly mock & ridicule
shattering the windows of little safe & secure
suburban dead end homes & sills all filled up
with those larger-than-life come-to-life collection
of dolls. husbands always gone missing-in-action
on those infamous business trips & conventions
dressed up as slick sleazy salesmen selling their
soul/pharmaceuticals along with those suitcases
they came in while all these women ever really
wanted were immaculate lawns with hedges
high enough where they can finally be left
alone. homes which look like wax museums
without the figures & just the leftover sterile
perfect plastic furniture. tchotchkes which
look like they came straight out the pawn-
shop window with bowls of wax fruit & vases
of plastic flowers. busts of bruce lee, buddha
& batman & robin. those ominous domineering
foreboding haunted murals of fathers with their
chest plunged out in pomp & circumstance posing
proud like a pair of bookends or candlesticks
who will always protect them eternally love
them & can do no wrong who come from a long
line of old money...corrupt judges born & raised
on the compound & country club & just enough
extra room for swinger acquaintances who look
like those attractive relatives you see at weddings
& funerals but never know where they come from.
twin sisters who mix it up & throw fists at each
other but still look out for each other & got mad
love for each other down-to-earth salt-of-the-earth

radiant & as good looking as you can get & even
sleep in the same bed like bridesmaids with broken
limbs who have paid their dues & just as deserving
of love & spoon each other when life when night
mares get the better of them usually due to some
past boyfriend who abused or took advantage
of them. victims survivors & now strange sacred
daughters of dysfunctional dollhouses. a rear set
of stairs & dumbwaiter for runaway abandoned
brothers & finally at last that long-lasting very
convenient fantasy to have just enough downtime
to have enough downtime to contemplate suicide
long sighs or never ever to have to worry again
about hardwired hallucinations & such absurd
unrealistic expectations of living happily ever after


take 18


Satire 10: think all i need one of those real pretty operators
you'd see from like one of those doris day *bye bye birdie
movies* who will simply just sit by my side all day and all
night with her board of bright lights inputting and replacing
wires with grace and style, but think because i've become
something of a loner and social pariah she'll have absolutely
nothing to do with her time and ask her if she might be able
to make me like a tea with honey and ham sandwich and can
she help with my awful arthritis when i creep in and out of
the shower and she'll still just be sitting there cute as a button
interested attentive with a smile no matter how fake or not just
to provide support due to all those coward devils who try to
damage your soul and break your heart and at the end of the
week of course pay her her just due under the table and it all
really be worth it and when she takes off wonder why you
never saw in front of your window one of those ol' time
streakers from the seventies who would just suddenly
show up out of nowhere in the middle of some ballgame
and for no apparent reason just streak across the field
in their high-top sneakers while the out-of-shape
bloated security used to try to track them down
and round them up like some madman at the asylum
as you'd literally hear the color commentators start

to get into it and go something like–"and there he
goes rounding first second third coming home"


take 19

Satire 11: i have decided even though we really don't have a penny
to our name to literally test out the old cliché 'fake it till you make it'
and bring over a whole different list of contractors to give us an
estimate for clay tennis courts as i've noticed all those affluent
homes i drive past with no one ever out there, or no one on their
lawns, have clay courts but the way i'm gonna differentiate ours,
is i'm going to ask them to include some miserable, middle-aged,
aristocratic white woman who's never happy in her all-white tennis
uniform sipping from her token bottle of vitamin water stuck to a
white tennis bench. also i'm going to request a beekeeper dressed
to the "t" in his beekeeper armory jumpsuit and helmet for when
those holes suddenly open up and materialize out of nowhere
chock-full of bees and hornets (as of course learned a long time
ago about the illusion of beauty and that nothing's ever perfect
in the universe) a random golf cart which serves absolutely no
purpose and to get completely carried away to convince myself
of my being, might even be one of the few who puts one of those
huge judge's high chairs in the middle with some expressionless,
semi-retired old timer from the suburbs in his sunglasses with a
whistle and you know if this doesn't help to at all change my attitude
or baseline of moods or for that matter standing in the community
at least i'll know every morning when i peek through the blinds
will have that fine clay tennis court, a miserable middle-aged
aristocratic white woman sitting down on that white bench
sipping from her water, some strange beekeeper skulking
around in his armor, a random golf cart, and old timer
sitting way up there in his sunglasses with a whistle,
indifferent, keeping an eye out and judging it all…

take 20

Satire 12: something of a non-linear version
of human stages of growth & development


1

i had
sub
stance
when
i used
to stroll
the sills
of the sky
scrapers
taking in
the winter
& summer
scenes
dreaming
out the garment
district windows
of lunch break
buildings to the
side of ancient
red brick alley
lofts (the shapes
& forms of young
girls doing yoga
& the life & times
routines & rituals
of methodical
pigeons just
minding
their own
way up above
somewhere a
round herald
square greek
orthodox cathedral

thievery holiday season
how each single street
had its own particular
spirit & sensibility
feeling & personality
& bleak ephemeral
familiar identity)
all the way from
the pea soup green
1950's façade midtown steam
of *harcourt brace* to hell's kitchen
to holy & sacred forgotten junkie hotels
of the upper west side i swear on my life
wandered every one of the midnight bridges
bleary-eyed between manhattan & brooklyn


2

a whole treasure chest mess of
leather-bound books by pushkin
discovered dumped & discarded
deserted by the trash can fires in
the beautiful mire of twilight gutters
of the autumn of new orleans in many
ways defines the history of the world


3

how is casanova
always with a
dozen roses
& immaculate
powder-blue
tuxedo constantly
found sneaking
out at sunset
found on his
deathbed?

4

honestly i never really cared much about other's
perception of me 'cause deep down inside knew
it was all political & have always been apolitical

(& if it's all about perception really
means nothing at all rumors passed
down from generation to generation)

spending that whole summer reading
spinoza wittgenstein sherwood
anderson hemingway freud

& dostoevsky so honestly deep
down inside why the hell i care
about what they think about me?

caddied whole summer for obnoxious wallstreeters
& their slut daughter-in-laws was all brainwash
& what else could i do but go on bronx runs

to pick up my bag of ganja
& make all these burdens
& illusions more bearable

bronzed, handsome, rebellious, on-the-run
turning all situations & scenarios
into satire & sarcasm...


5

pain & pleasure
in the derby hat
in the top hat
in the mad hat
of shakespeare
watching his back
over the hedgerow

of the mean mal
icious & mono
tone his masses


6

it's only when i began
using poor judgment
my instincts kicked in


7

existence a series
of broken romances
with spirit at its nucleus


8

to know the truth of the universe lies
somewhere between the eternal echoing
of the musical seas deep in a conch shell
& that liberating cascade of water flowing out
a city hydrant during sweltering summer evening


9

the reality of a poet-philosopher trying to figure out
all of life's problems (for that exact reason whether
does or not an eternal type of struggle and survival
like beautiful dead flowers in a vase) eventually in
the long-run for the most part always ends up alone
while still grossly misinterpreted and judged by those
who couldn't even begin to know so all's left to really
do but to appreciate the natural wild beauty around him

take 21

Satire 13: image of buddha with fingers in his ears
to drown out car horns in bumpdabumpa rush hour
not exactly looking so calm but more so with a howl

amerika used to have classic actors you
could really believe in like steve mcqueen
brando jack lemmon and deniro in *taxi driver*


take 22

Satire 14: finally the father
just hollers–"can we all
just eat supper together!"
and see them creeping
into the television
one by one
looking out
the screen
blank-faced
at the light
at the end
of the drive
way
like
some
holy
beacon
illuminated
as that evening
the pharmacist
decides to just
turn the tables
and randomly
strangely
serendipitously
pull a gun
on a customer
having had it

pulling
a clown
mask over
his head as just
gotten so sick
of the public
and the side
effects of the
walking dead


take 23

Satire 15: we live in a time and age where the new
scandal of the day a cell phone is caught cheating
on another cell phone and on its day in court will
literally be found throwing itself on the mercy of
the court and for support is shut off and slipped
into the pocketbook of some pop star and since
it is its first offense will simply be given a
couple months community service. after
that token grace period of paying its dues
and spending several years out of the lime
light the cell phone will have its comeback
tour and because amerika is known to be
such a forgiving country (or convenient
amnesia brainwashed by the media) all
will be forgotten and take home several
awards while all the teenyboppers (also
in the form of cell phones) will carry it
around as if nothing had ever happened
and will climb that infamous well-known
ladder of success and now be given the status
of "legend," as it's persisted and beaten all those
so-called odds and obstacles while this contraption
full of icons is now considered an american icon…

take 24

Satire 16: did you know in fact that nixon
actually was not the first one to make those
secret illegal tapes while being in the oval
office and goes as far back as roosevelt, eisenhower,
kennedy, and johnson as the scholars inform us the
background noise represents 'other people in room
or putting feet up on desk…' who knows maybe
we should go through the whole impeachment
process again or have like one of those brilliant
directors like michael moore or oliver stone do
a movie on them and just sort of make it some
mash-up non-linear film and we have to guess
who is who with a broken fragmented feedback
loop and the stooges hitting each other over
the head while doing a closeup of spiderman
getting a makeover mohammed ali's refusal
to enter the draft clips of frank capra's first
film interviewing scientists as far back
about the devastating effects of climate
change and global warming and kurt
cobaine wriggling on stage screaming–
"what is wrong with me?!!" as that to me
would be the perfect socio-cultural insightful
documentary on the rise & fall of american hx

take 25

Satire 16: the candidates all lined up in a neat little row
behind their podiums like game show contestants going
in for the kill; you name them, i dare you 18,19,20,21
getting ready for the great debate; the personification
of always the right thing to say who we put our blind
faith and will decide our fate and supposed to decide
who seems the most sincere in their conviction (who
will keep their word and not break promises) who
is the most convincing actor-substitute-savior
who'll pick us up from the hole we're in

make that microwave movie popcorn with real butter
and wash it all down with a six pack of *budweiser*...


take 26

The clanking of dishes
proves that i exist & i am
not alive that i have a wife
& a marriage & just trying
to get by just trying to get
through the days & survive
my nightmares & haven't felt
in so damn long & they're all
just a bunch of wannabes having
no idea what they want just know
they want something from you
that they perceive out of envy
& jealousy they ain't got &
find yourself nodding-out
in your easy chair to the
breaking news & buffoon
make-believe president
who's never cared about
anyone but himself with
a whole swath of brain-
washed working class
washed-up & wasted
in the heartland & rustbelt
who like madman mothers
under some maternal spell
claim he can do no wrong
as you fall back into your coma
dreaming of *dr. pepper* & leftovers

A Hx of Amerkin Existentialism (Suburbanization,
Gentrifikation, Anarkey, Angstidy & Melankolia)


1

Today i applied
for a government job
i won't tell you what it was
but literally had to take a number
while of course there was always
that asshole security guard
pretending to be something
he's not stuffed in his box
staring you down paranoid
& way too bold for his own
good with his insular little
absurd napoleonic complex.
i took my seat in the front row
of the pews & something
told me to suddenly look
up & there staring down
at me like a bunch of
freak gods with these
glossy glued-on
televangelist smiles
each in their own man
dated personal gold frames
was the president & vice
president of the united states
like anti-christ batman & robins
& right at that exact moment real
lies how absurd my life had become



2

I think with this idiot clown
prince i would prefer one
like the late-great eccentric

recluse howard hughes who
at the end of his existence
due to severe cognitive
damage refused to
come out of his room
(my dream come true
would be for that to
happen to the senate
& congress too…)
& then would get my
full approval rating
breaking news
would be how
there'd continue
to be no breaking news


3

I think with this pathetic pussy
pence if he was in fact really
one of those so-called good
christians he'd just type up
his letter of resignation &
in keeping with his muted demeanor
take off on some steamy sweltering
summer evening in washington dc
to some dive where he would not
be recognized & wash it all
down with *michelob light*

there comes a time in every man's life
when gotta just sit down for his rights

4

I know it sounds crazy
but i just want to start
a news station with a
dummy & ventriloquist
who'll just be sitting there
on a stool right in the middle
of the screen lip syncing all
the present day stories & events
of our present day government
& swear trust me will be
just as rational & relevant
(& pretty damned cathartic)
& in a sort of half-crazed way
make a hell of a lot of sense just
as much when cable first came
on the scene in new york city
in the late-seventies & some
time right around midnight
be this variety show narrated by
this real down to earth bleached
blonde with her saggy bosoms
just hanging out who for some
strange reason the guys were
crazy about when they all struck
out stoned off their step mom's stash


5

So when you got a country whose main industry
for profit-making & to make a killing are prisons
& pharmaceuticals (some of them even use the
latter to put to sleep the former) & a president
& commander-in-chief captain-of-industry really
a spoiled little rich kid who got everything handed
to him & as offensive & insulting & corrupt as you
can get (who manages to offend practically every
last single one of our allies around the world &

takes full credit for the stock market; who mocks
'the retarded' & women who have been molested &
at his little pep rallies through the dynamic of bullying
puts all his idiot constituents into hysterics) you can
see why maybe just might feel a little depressed?
you know that old proverb or expression where
you feel far more lost & lonesome in a room
all full of friends & acquaintances?


6

While our commander-in-chief was busy tweeting
all of rome burned around him, which of course
he took absolutely no blame or responsibility

pipe bombs sent to all his perceived enemies
by some madman down in the sunshine
state not terribly far from his estate

while just a couple days later came the mass
shooting in the synagogue in one of those real
true-blue all-american towns mr. rogers is from.

one who has the clinical dx of narcissism
matter of fact meets almost every element
& criteria trait & characteristic in the dsm

(with psychological disconnects) along with
being a spoiled little rich kid who has never
had to face any sort of natural consequence

(perfect storm close to being sociopathic)
in fact proves to be dangerous & can
never ever be the leader of men.

in fact he looked like he was in over his head
even from day one without the substance and
just the fluff; some higher-than-holy hotelier

pretending to be that man of the people, really
some old beaten broken barker at a burnt-down
carnival trying to construct & create his own house

of mirror kingdom from his delusions of grandeur but
what a clown fears the most is when they actually
turn to him for guidance & answers & wisdom



7

If only our government & politicians
put in at least half the effort america
does in making the perfect vacuum
cleaner to get out every last stain
& crumb off the floor. sometimes
i wish there was just one more
god (for the snobs & slobs) on
an administrative level let's say
a god for human resources who
would just take care of all the
hypocrisies & contradictions
of human nature. you look
into your morning mirror
& see why perhaps always
the need & compulsion to
have to hit the road & travel
you wish at the end of all this shit
the late-great johnny rotten would
just show up from the ruins & with
that infamous snarling snicker simply
burst–"ever feel like you been cheated?"



8

Sometimes democracy works. sometimes it just doesn't.
sometimes it just makes you nauseous. sometimes they're
just a bunch of mass idiots when put all your faith & trust

& belief in politicians, as implicitly, they are a direct reflection
& microcosm of human nature, which historically & philosophically
all the great historians & philosophers have proven is so full of
hypocrisies, self-interest & contradictions, more accurately, has
to do with a whole hell of a lot of impulsivity, projecting, acting-
out, displaced hostility, passive-aggressive reactive-attachment
(fragile identities) playing the blame game & as the pattern of
history & culture of mankind has consistently & painstakenly
taught us, looking for an instant scapegoat & savior or vice-versa;
why in this case honestly (& not trying to sound short or glib) are
you in any way, shape or form shocked & why think it would be
any different, as in my opinion what i find most shocking is people's
collective-amnesia whether recent i.e. george w bush & dick cheney,
or remote; go back to any war or dictator, while concretely some of
the most profound & devastating tragedies have sparked from simple
complacency; how man can be so easily brainwashed & manipulated
when they are down on their luck & desperate. so america i guess
you might call this my apology letter but not really & am sorry &
please forgive me, yet simply numb & indifferent at how you so
blatantly, consistently make the exact same mistake & can be so
easily persuaded. there is a psychological phenomenon where
when one is being physically, emotionally, spiritually, or psycho
logically violated or experiencing some form of brutal trauma, they
'disassociate' & have reported the 'bizarre' sensation & phenomena
(through their coping & survival mechanisms of being there but not
really, entering "the surreal") while simultaneously also feeling separate
or a part from it & observing the incident from a distance; this may
seem like something of a stretch (& know it is) but might ask you,
upon reflection & a bit of soul-searching, to possibly consider,
at least briefly, the damage it inflicts on the human psyche


9


The weather girl looks like the weather girl
looks like the weather girl looks like the weather girl
with her weather girl blouse & her weather girl hairstyle
& her weather girl smile & her weather girl riddles & her
weather girl dialogue & the weather girl will help us to get
by & weather life & the lottery numbers of 8 4 6 0 all look

about right & the stocks all look fine for *ibm* & *world
international paper* & there is your token recall & your
man hunt is still on & satisfaction guaranteed & today
will be cool & chilly right around tichonderoga valley


10

Awwh! this arthritis is killing me
getting the better of me so decide
to fondle myself by the microwave
while the local weatherman looking
like a pedophile of sorts like some sort
of frankenstein madman who my fellow
damaged social worker who grew up
in the slums of south boston said if one
of those preachers ever touched his kid
would literally kill him and believed him
and supported him as knew he had been
through it the raw rainy winds coming in
from quebec canada right down the spine
of i-35 desolate flatlands into the swathe
of silhouetted mountains of north country
blowing here to the literal red brick factories
hugging the blue swollen rivers of the capitol
city where see literal rabid fox trot past your
window who honestly once tried to scare them
off and held their ground and wasn't scared of
nothing at all some cub at dusk turned loose
by his mom casually on all fours swaggering
past for the neatly stashed trash at the end
of the driveway while believe or somehow
convince myself that caressing my ass
by the microwave feels damn fine and
settling while always beside bach violins
always tuned to the local staticky classical
radio station way up here in the mountains
when the winter comes down rolling in out
of nowhere against your own will and volition

11

Sometimes you just have this wish
that your visiting angel quips i think
all you need is a kiss & you instantly
respond to her as long as it's desperate
& endless (never been one of those cats
who trusted those with strict boundaries
as a matter of fact trusted & respected
them so much more when they didn't)
& just bent over & went ahead with it
& ironically the opposite happens
& instantly heals all her loss
& trauma & open wounds
& just seeing her reaction
chemically & spiritually
provides a panacea
& heals yours too


12

Good buddy of mine
from the lebanese
section of detroit
& i used to laugh
when looking back
at our life whenever
might happen to get
into a street fight
would abide by that
age old tradition of
removing watches
so as not to damage
(as though everything
wasn't already fucked
up & damaged) as if
this was one of the few
things which held value
& now ironically think
about how fast time has

passed & really cherish
those past broken times



13

"Man-o-man-o-shewitz wine!" some of those deemed to
be the real freaks of society by the frightened & the phony
who have always had things conveniently handed to them
on that infamous silver platter those mechanical-robot-pods
who always seem so comfortable in their skin in their home
away from home in the mall on their cellphones always with
that ridiculous omniscient sense of belonging who look down
on those with real-life freak rigidity in their freak reality while
always having the comforts of living anyway getting back to
my point i swear always ironically the ones who seem to be
those deemed as freaks the poor borderline fragile suicide girl
my client from the group home who loves to somersault down
the escalator in the mall the kid who's been bullied his whole
life with asperger's & taken advantage of the homeless black
man in the park who used to be a well-known artist
& gave exhibitions at *the whitney* & *the guggenheim*
while interestingly poignantly the ones who come up
with some of the most keen & perceptive comments
of all time as these 9-5 idiot-conformist-pods who
act like false gods & some honor to be around them
(with clinical delusions of grandeur) still staring scared
shocked from the side of their sockets strangely enough
with the obvious desperate need & compulsion to have
to turn them into freaks & scapegoats & when you look
at them closely from the perspective of the park bench
or camped-out all day in the window of some modest slavic
diner can absurdly cookie-cutter style see who the real freaks are

14

Film noir is the reverse art of war...
it's a skyline looking through a venetian blind
it's the shadow of a man that's taken over his life
& a wife who stands nobly by his side through thick
& thin the innocent victim guilty until proven innocent
being brought in for questioning leading to less answers
& the undercover detectives just as defensive & damaged
while the only witnesses are those who sit in the audience
who do not have the street smarts or experience to come
up with the right conclusions as proven most of existence
is just a rush to judgment by the insular & ignorant which
is the whole pathetic tragedy of it while the smoking gun
planted more times than not by the haves who have not
those who have been eternally petty & jealous their whole
life & had absolutely no qualm guilt or remorse in setting
the whole thing up a matter of fact even saw themselves as
martyrs justified in starting the whole denouement & drama


15

We fall in love with noir because we are just barely hanging on
& all those things in life which have done us wrong which always
just seem to elude us while it appears as well to touch on our everyday
existence of brooding, perseverating & even situational depression &
in reality we all suffer & are all so alone, isolated, distant, engaged
in that lone journey of 'quiet desperation' not too dissimilar to
the nature of gangster films which always seems to contain an
element of poetic justice, as deep down inside (can never accomplish
in real life because of societal norms or what freud alludes to in his
"civilization and its discontents" as primal, animalistic urges that get
repressed) & those who sincerely deserve it, as well as asking for it
& symbolic & representative even cathartic of people in our reality
& past experiences who should have just been 'ended.' the same
holds true with westerns & that instant medium & connection
with escapism, while in essence (when we break through all our "role
playing") are so impulsive & primitive, searching for that deep down
rare justice which for the most part contains an element of violence

16

A well-made western helps one to get to bed
cause simply deals with the living & the dead
devoid of all those little things in between
which has a tendency to confuse & bring
about a certain amount of deep dread



17

Hard to say can't say
why i've always had
a hankering for the
gangsters in the ole
time movies falling
asleep on mid-century
freudian sofa clutching
onto his cocktail glass
with a gun by his side
bruce wayne with his
morphine habit pleasantly
passed out like the joker
unable to get to batphone
& the rest of the hitchcock
crew hiding out in the china
town darkness & edward hopper
cobblestone shadows the virginal
daughter with her madonna-whore
complex shimmying in front of
jukebox while her older brother
with a heart of gold & not a mean
bone in his body can't stay out
of trouble always taking the rap
waiting for a call from the ring
leader at his country club as
his lovely wife in black velvet
& pearls getting on his nerves
& driving him up the wall
not caring or giving a damn
& taking mad chances while

every last single one of them
for similar reasons not willing to
go out without going down swinging


18

I liken mankind to king
kong as that afternoon
found calmly browsing
in the souvenir shop
of air-conditioned lobby
for a pack of *wrigley's*
& one of those neat
little black combs
having an interview
on the 63rd floor for
an advertising gig
set up by his pal
in a gray flannel
suit just trying
to get his foot
in the door
while if he
only knew
what would
befall him
later on that
warm summer
night as simply
a real-life gentle giant
& die-hard romantic
minding his own &
probably should have
just stayed home to
watch the midgets

19

I had been scrounging around
for my used brown suit i had
purchased at this thrift shop
on broadway in the east
village (guess historically
which had been boosted
straight off the rack) then
suddenly woke up in a sweat
on a warm sweltering night
& saw humphrey bogart was
wearing it along with a hanky
he had stuffed in his breast
pocket that one that jackie
gleason had lent naughton
& told him it was for showing
& not blowing while this was
a humphrey bogart movie
i had never seen where he
was playing the role of a
slapstick comedian & not
particularly good as never
a huge fan of over acting


20

The american dream
was that old jew
hyman roth...
eating his lunch
on his dinner tray
watching college
football down
in the sun
shine state
semi-retired
in technicolor
pastel life
of leisure

& al pacino
paying him
a friendly
visit to try
& figure
out if it
was him
who tried
to do him in
this nice
old cut
throat
jew
who
knew
how to
work the
system
offering
him some
thing to eat
with his fine
nice silent
wife by
his side
& that in
famous line
which went
something
like–'this is
the business
we chose...'
pretty much
normalizing
placating
ration
lizing
it all

21

American cinema does not exist anymore
as now kills off its protagonists & heroes
by absurd glamorization, commercialization
& prostitution of simplistic & shallow archetypal
symbols of one-dimension (everything i swear
has turned cartoonish & computer-generated
or some form of brutal violence & horror) in which
we could not possibly connect to or for that matter
feel any sort of compassion or really care about
(absolutely no sense of character development
or nuance) while the whole absurd tragedy of
it all, this is the primary core reason of why we
even chose to go to the movies in the first place


22

I remember hustling a taxi way out to forest hills, queens
from new york city during a graveyard shift & apparently
the fare really liked me & wanted to train me as a manager
at one of his movie theaters. this one happened to be *the arts*
on 57$^{th}$ st. in manhattan but the lady who was training me was
the meanest bitch of all time & even admitted it (me thinking
in the back of my mind, damn why do you have to be like this
& so damn plain & phony & obvious in how you're glamorizing
it) & just another one of those people in life who turned me off
to mankind; how she taught me like some sort of robot always to
remain completely focused & never to be talking when counting
all the drawers & the safe, how not to treat the employees working
under her very nice & with any kind of respect & how they should
never become friends, like the candy concessionist, the very old
man & kid with a cognitive delay who collected the tickets both
with very quick & innocent sense of humors i supposedly was
not supposed to get started, the projectionist, the teenage girl
in the ticket booth always with an obnoxious attitude & aloof
or the actual writers & directors of the films we would meet
& give a viewing to make sure everything was to their liking
& aesthetic & sensibilities & even once scolded me (right in
front of them) for giving them praise explaining i was being

trained & could see by the awkward look on his face not sure
what to make of it & was thankful & not too appreciative
of this automaton who made it all that much more hard
& finally i got to that infamous profound point of my
so-called tutorial where i just didn't give a shit anymore
nor give a flying whether i lost my job or not & started
treating the employees with mad heart & took great interest
in them & all of their eccentricities; their family problems
& personality disorders & supportive of all those little things
which helped them get through their life struggles & finally
at last when she was not around & was allowed to take my
allotted half hour break would just go up to the dark balcony
of the movie theater (usually during one of the holiday matinees)
with one of these really sensuous sex scenes between the lead
actor (& his lead lady) who was severely traumatized from
concentration camp & now living out in brooklyn & trying
to survive having flashbacks looking to re-acculturate back
into society & live a normal life & taking this beautiful
sophisticated lady from behind & the scene was really
gorgeous & intimate & think i was very much able
to be sympathetic & make a real connection & finally
fed up & turning pleasantly indifferent would just
jerk-off to the beauty of it all take great pleasure in it all
then sneak off to the bathroom & wipe myself off as what
was i going to do throw myself out? eventually though, just
like everything else, i was only able to last at that job for so long
as of course i never saw that very nice man who originally gave
me the job & way too much of that snake woman which she
actually called herself & in the long-run just got sick of it all
playing this subservient role in a system & bitch i had absolutely
no respect for, while strangely enough, upon reflection, took great
pleasure in the relationship i was able to develop during the bleak
holiday season way up in the very dark balcony of the arts on $57^{th}$

23

I don't know…when i first got married & moved to the suburbs
seemed like everything inextricably proportionally got more shallow
& absurd like those annoying, nauseating proverbs passed down
from generation to generation of 'build back your credit, build back

your credit, build back your credit, build back your credit…' like
some amorphous anonymous asshole automaton was going to judge
your integrity & good intents heart & soul & morals & ethics even
instincts & good judgment based on some random arbitrary number
of building back your credit, but how come no extra credit for being
there on all occasions in all periods & phases & crises & life-transitions
for friends & acquaintances & would never ever waver no matter the
weather going all out for damaged girlfriends from impossible over-
bearing fathers who left them feeling eternally guilty & vacant running
these consistent compassionate clinical groups & always being there
for them for all those boys abandoned in the group homes & shelters
of providence rhode island able to relate to them cause i had been there
& made sure to get them out of there whatever need be done to a safe
& secure home so you move to the suburbs & tell you you have to
build back your credit & wonder why you end up feeling more aimless
& depressed empty & vacant & what based on this ridiculous logic
& mathematical equation like who runs things that idiot napoleonic
life insurance salesman who obsessively mows his lawn known for
his explosions & episodes & real-life scowl always on the prowl
& starts up with almost everyone & doesn't have an honest bone

24

I remember where we used to live i had this neighbor
who once told me he wished there weren't so many
of these gorgeous towering pines & wanted to cut
them down while our homes which were in the woods
not too far from shore wish they were much closer to
the stripmall (i think to have better access to *dunkin
donuts & home depot*) & back then really didn't
know what to make of it & think blocked it all out
almost like everything else back then while his wife
used to bend over almost every time she saw me
as supposedly the story was that he had turned off
to her & hadn't touched her in ages and wasn't sure
who i felt more sorry for as felt like the grand metaphor
& long-lost illusion of what it meant to live in suburbia

25

I know this may sound strange but i find i trust people
far more who are m.i.a. & leave their garbage cans out
a couple days (with damp colorful leaves scattered all
around) similar to the girl next door who i like to imagine
checking me out with a pair of binoculars through the blinds
of my nighttime window & perversely find i can really
relate to & always try to look as natural as possible

What to make out of this hole existence
where you have been made to feel like
some sort of secondhand paper-mache
pawn or possession in some other's clinical
narcissistic (some turn to narcotics) reality
which has always left you feeling cheated
or taken advantage of (with an eternal case
of the down-in-the-dump doldrums) in regards
to identity awwh! what is that i hear? the beat
& the rhythm of the beaten & battered 'march
of the tin soldiers...' on your son's drum pad
through the paper-thin walls which somehow
heals your tragic fragile soul (you think your
wife is in town seeing for like the third time
in a row "a star is born") ahhh...who is that
angel stranger weather girl where you'll be
happy to be controlled (go all out for & be
sacrificed & slaughtered) looking like that
cute girl i grew up with next door on that
dead end of child/hood why you always
seem to turn happily ever after towards
the deep blue dusk of the rain & snow

Weather just becomes a moot point & thankfully
a lower rate of tourists due to suicide & divorce
both having something to do believe it or not
with the romantic principle & concept of the
difference between faith & fate (or function
& form) on one of those point-plot graphs

## 26

We appear to make our greatest mistakes in judgment
during very trying desperate times but who are they to
pass judgment as could not even begin to comprehend
the nature of such overwhelming circumstances while
in retrospect might very well have been our best way
of functioning & coping (as long as not hurting any
body) experiencing the most change & wisdom


## 27

Whenever i feel like i'm most down & out
& just can't make it no more deep down in
the middle of the night i try to think of such
things like that fine mean domineering lifeguard
not really so much in a sexual manner but more
so like a portrait of some queen-princess way
atop her throne soulless a heart of stone pasted
up against the silhouette of those undulating
rolling bushy mountains brilliant juxtaposition
of pale white skin against black swimsuit
long legs crossed like some country club
suburban slut not really caring at all about
anyone down below while spacing out in her
own little world aloof arrogant alone looking
out to the mute madness of humanity cooling
off letting it all go in the slow natural haze of
a half-crazed melancholy summer while every
once in awhile she'll use her whistle like some
warning from a sadistic warden with an attitude
pretending like she might actually give a damn
but that's only really when she does not want
to be disturbed & they're getting on her nerves
& you dream of her maybe like one of those real
obnoxious untouchable girls back in high school
whenever you're desperately trying to get to bed

28

You waking up in the morning to something
called something like *jltv* which is like jewish
tv out of israel that helps you to escape your reality
& shows this good looking young israeli teaching
some cute zionist how to fend off a terrorist going
on the attack with a knife from the back (of course
she's got that classic coquettish grin when she
mimics him somewhere between taking him
serious & not too serious) while love the fact
that i bought my pretty wife a beautiful blue
& white striped dress for the summer &
always wears that beautiful blue & white
striped dress which i guess pays me some
respect & allows me to connect & really
love her my favorite part of the season
where it's always coming down in
torrents with lightning & thunder in
the mountains & through the translucent
white flouncy curtains can see the deep
verdant hills filling in with the sunlit strip
of wildflowers beginning to bud in the pasture
& the fragile delicate white blossom of the snow
drift crabapple & natural wild apples exploding right
on the border between the lush backyard & forest
reigniting your senses starting to thaw once again
after a very long miserable interminable winter

birds take to the wire whose seesaw
synchronized rhythm all a part of the
same strange solitary exotic life cycle


29

I have bought her summer dresses
driven through lakes & mountains
to purchase exotic chocolate
& stolen roses & orchids
& helped her out through

impossible drama with her
abusive & absentee father
rescued her from her histrionic
hoarding mother in the bronx
but still somehow manages
to wallow & blame me for
all her problems when we've
reached the top of the mountain
while summery drizzle just starts
to come down in the high grass
of the holy fragrant meadow at dusk
the sacred gurgle of overflowing rivers
surrounding the village & threatening
the stray cats madwomen & cathedrals
eventually bearing aimless roosters &
rainbows roaming up the side of the hill


30

When you & your wife are not getting along
when she's just going back to her old ways
of going on the all-out attack & never once
admitting she's wrong just for the fun of it
might check out the 'research' engine
to look up past girls from high school
their shapes & forms who literally just
as horny came onto you at 'house' parties
during note taking in 'ap history' rubbing
their contours up against your anatomy
as honestly don't know what's wrong
with her these days while going back
to her old ways of fits of jealousy & rage
& in many ways don't even care if she's
going to hold me hostage with this type
of brutal & barbaric bickering & see nothing
wrong to try & shake it all off going back to
that real nice down to earth girl i used to walk home
with & gorgeous to die for daughter of a korean diplomat

31

There should be a play
or indie or poem or hymn
written about this wise ass
badboy kid in school can't
keep himself out of trouble
& this good deed doing
straight-a girl who sees
so much good in him
& tries to save him
& long longing stares
across the classroom
& sometimes even
sneaks secret glances
at him while strolling
down the hall when
he makes it a ritual
to stay everyday
after school leaning
back holy & hand
some in detention
hall & there's
a hell of a lot
of pleading
& begging
& weeping
& eventual
dramatic
smooching
& it's all so tragic
& beautiful this kid
who gets crucified
& condemned
on a daily basis
with his head
crooked to
the side
with tears
in his eyes
holding it
all in from

some ridiculous
authority figure
& that absurd
proverb of before
you die seeing
your whole
life pass
in front
of you
sees this
on a daily
basis not
even aware
of it while
just doesn't
give a shit
& this little
angel trying
to save this
poor damaged
soul who's far
better than all
of them put
together


32

Witch nun came up with the sadistic shtick
of whacking a kid on the buttock in front
of the class having him sit embarrassed
with a dunce cap on in a chair turned
to the corner pulling him out by earlobe
like getting yanked by a hook off stage
as it was almost as if they ran out of
parts of the anatomy & wonder what
stage of growth & development they
thought that this might improve
their character & personality?

33

I would have wanted
to see a *twilight zone*
episode where some
older character was
addicted to clocks
perhaps hunched
over in his basement
fidgeting & fixing them
a whole home full of them
just sitting in a room full
of ticking clocks & then
the last scene having
the camera pan in
not sure if he's
dead or alive
if it's him or not
& all you hear is
the assuaging
tone of some
metronome
& the cadence
of a tick-tock


34

Have you ever seen one of those automatons
standing behind trump at a trump rally?
looks something like a psychotic peanut
gallery of bullies & brainwashed white trash
& soulless tourists & by the way does absolutely
every middle-aged woman in america have to
be a bleached blonde with those cliched signs
which read–"finish the wall" "drain the swamp"
like some really poor distorted form of feng-shui

i.e.

Pride for your country…
there's nothing i can think
of more obvious & boring

people should work on
being more complete
& less controlling


35

I want to toss an afghan
over my head & slowly
stroke a cello. when i
come out i will put a
conch shell up against
my ear & hear the echoes
of evolution & the history
of the world & finally
at last know after all my
pain & suffering am cured

"cubs/reds
rain pouring"


36

Women who keep on speaking about
their boyfriends over and over again
have real issues problems with men

in brooklyn we used to literally stick
our heads in the freezer to cool down

i had an uncle from oceanside
used to tumble in the dryer
to try and impress his pals


37

The image of some spare solitary priest bent
over giving final rights to a football player
spread-eagle on the gridiron while some
gorgeous voluptuous cheerleader with
a pasted-on smile stands on the shoulders
of some ken doll mythological god rooting
on the roaring crowd of white boy wannabes
from the fraternity & sluts from the sorority.
inside the drawn curtain of the concussion
tent silhouettes slow-dance cheek to cheek
while some stand-in sneaks with a sandwich
from the catered deli platter. after the body
has been removed follows the traditional
funeral procession of mascots & alumni
& time for the halftime ceremony where a very
attractive asian girl peddles in with her unicycle
balancing spinning plates on her straight upright
profile & then the marching band in matching uniform
comes melodramatically strolling in in their regimented
choreographed line dotting the "i" with the final dramatic
ritual of some fine decked-out warrior royally swaggering
in lifting a sword above his pugilistic helmet & planting
it in midfield sealed with your token quota of sponsors
from both rival colleges of quasi-higher education
trying to prove their merit showing very diligent
students the movers & shakers of the future
in their goggles in the science lab with all
the new state of the art equipment guess
leaving out the part with the beer funnel
& beer goggles desperately trying to prove
their worth & loyalty & attempting to fit in
in what they like to refer to the college experience

38

The keen thing about the college cheerleader
is they always got that nonstop unconditional
smile while shuffling moving those pompoms
in single file; it could be a slaughter a mass-
acre the apocalypse & still through the act
& art of seduction will be rooting on the
roaring crowd knowing they got full control
over the male student body with every eyeball
focused & fixated & fantasizing about them
eventually will marry someone like a dentist
a prelaw or premed premeditated murder
giving birth to 3 kids 2 cars & 1 lovely
home in the heart of suburbia sedated
stunned & safe & secure the substitute
& panacea for the punchline of living the
life & living the lie of happily ever after


39

The best thing about past girlfriends
was just taking showers with them
watching them go through their
grooming rituals as if you weren't
even there honored to be a real-life
voyeur while they put bottles & bottles
of shampoo & conditioner into their hair
as if they've been going through this tradition
as far back as can remember being impossible
seductive teenagers seeing their eyes tightly
closed with all those suds running down their
hair over their face eyes neck & body some-
times even a loofah might be involved making
all these strange distorted contorted expressions
as if re-experiencing all their phases of trauma
& loss & pain & crisis when going through these
routines & rituals & you just standing at a quiet
distance from this ceremony a silent observer a

naked stranger honored to somehow be involved
& included in this very rich feminine institution


40

Videos on how to have more satisfying sex
or where to take shelter during a hurricane
ironically taking on similar & overlapping
symptoms & traits huckleberry finn
just leaning back on the raft reading
"the adventures of huckleberry finn"
remember spending that whole
summer on the lake just making
love to her remembering that lake
& simply making love to her in no
particular order, the constant formation
of new disorders, popping up out of no
where & new & improved pharmaceuticals
(from the farm of pseudo-calls) to make
your life proportionately better, more
comfortable, that middle-aged eternal
safe & secure smile & phenomena
of the real-life 'happily ever after'
all the propane tanks & port-o-sans
getting delivered to the suburbs for
the start of the season along with
those convenient rebels on motorcycles
living in their mommy & daddy's base
ment making absolutely no statement
like nuclear bombs being dropped &
never going off for purposes of attention-
seeking & pathetic pre-manufactured
patriotic worshiping of america (want
to put a bat to them like shattering a
yule log on television & piecing it all
back together again like some pretty
little postmodern picasso & make
it just a far better world to live in)

best one can hope for is to get high
& a buzz & to be left the hell alone
always hated those loud angry drunks



41

The best thing i learned was
from my poetry workshop teacher
at *the new school for social research*
who casually mentioned to me–
"the yuppies always seem just
one step behind" while i started
laughing there right on the spot
as thought that's one of the best
lines i heard of all time like that
haiku from that chinese hermit
who was hanging on for dear life
off the side of a cliff & took a bite
from a wild strawberry & said that
was the best thing he ever tasted
right before he fell to his death

that summer i wrote all my poetry
from my sweltering rooftop in brooklyn
looking down on the whole universe with
the tugs coming in around lower manhattan

my final dream to be hanging backwards
like one of those glazed ducks in the
alcove of *wing wong's* in chinatown



42

Blow-up buffalo discovered
eating mock apple pie
off the windowsill

of
women's
penitentiaries

the creatures
have overtaken
tongue-tied terrariums

cashiers on strike
at the creamery sick
of poor working conditions

& being treated poorly by
old timers who gather up in their
charcoal suits on the lawns of funeral

homes to escape
their long-lost widows
in the institution of marriage

perverts & playboys
playing the roles disguised
as hardworking good family men

mistaken identities
all well & good
those thought

stoned to death
were in fact
resurrected

in the imagination
& hated once more
for their ability to grow

in all-weather conditions
to also persist & survive
the doubters of the world

like kindling & cords
of wood sitting outside
*cumberland farm* at dawn

the last-ditch hitch hikers
from wealthy old money families
get in the cars of fugitives on-the-run

heading to similar-like destinations
of closed-down tourist towns
of brokedown boxcar diners

& liquor stores
& all those motels
& factories on the shore

to all those old sea captain homes
with views of gleaming hospitals
& methadone clinics with lit up

florescent beacons like signs
which tell us the lottery numbers
& sales on cigarettes & paper towels

& usher in all the brilliant
madness & mercurial elements
of the magical bleary-eyed season

all the all-night delinquents
& dope addicts come in from
the slums right around where

paul revere made his infamous run
& shuffle down the magazine aisle
to get their prescriptions filled for

the holidays & their take-home
dosages of methadone heading
zombie-like past the alcoholic

choir of firemen & police benevolent
associations & that old immigrant
mechanical woman playing piano

at all hours of the night
in the blinking midnight
wild wax museum window


43

X-mas coming around the corner with massive
consumerism & commercialism & the compulsion
& codependence for every necessary electronic gadget
known to man ('mama must really love me…') as the
collective unconscious if there really is one (all's gone
numb) or any real will or volition or independent thinking
is for the cookie-cutter pod people to actually believe all
the bullshit brainwash & that betrayal just was some sort
of arbitrary coincidental situational aberration (even common-
place and become complacent) of the century rather than
a constant and consistent/erratic behavioral pattern of
mankind and human nature of where's waldo? jesus?


44

Staggering drunken
through the snowstorm
after karaoking through
lone midnight of sleepy
hollow stumbling downhill
towards that brilliant blue
gray fog on the hudson
with that sudden throng
of foghorns like a prayer
for lost souls gods and
goddesses barely hanging
on having died so long ago

45

Behind the postcard resort is a lot where they dump
the toxic waste & p.c.b.'s & old mayan indian bones
& this is what they like to refer to as the ancient ruins
while white women from the suburbs in their bikinis
& perfect health club bodies get tipsy off their all-inclusive
pina-coladas & mix with the natives to prove their diversity
(i guess that recent voting demographic which just turned
from republican to democratic) whereas just after the disco
& dinner buffets, serenaded by rastas & their tin drums the
horny sons & daughters having worked all day on their glowing
golden tans test their potential for primal attraction (& action
& adventure) try to feel each other out feel each other up
in the effort to bring fable & folklore back home for
winter vacation to make names for themselves


46

I remember i used to hang out at those friends' houses
who usually were like the cutups or burnouts in school
& their parents used to always have like these very well-
groomed perfectly formal living rooms or dining rooms
& never could imagine (even somehow seemed more
abandoned) as would never come close to that idealized
fantasy or vision while never saw anyone in them 'cause
the parents were never around & nowhere to be found
& siblings missing-in-action having taken off a long
time ago & always just felt just a little too sad & silent
solemn, melancholic, even a bit haunted, like ghosts &
phantoms with way too many stories to tell (could almost
feel the spirit of their absentee non-spirits & souls) while
always just seemed too quiet for its own good, like those
scenarios set up for those prepackaged manufactured token
happily-ever-after regimented real-life representative rooms
in museums you never saw anyone in but always tried to make
them look all pristine & immaculate, overcompensating for you
knew was some pretty deep damaged fucked-up dysfunctional shit

the pictures in picture frames with all their
taboo secrets always just a little too distant

47

Looking back at my existence i can't believe how many
of my intimate & very close friends turned to coke
(& back then showed absolutely no sense of guilt
or remorse trading you in for drug friends) & turned
so unoriginal & uncreative spending all their time
measuring each line & making sure each one was
right & which one they wanted & turned so obvious
& just like that right in the moment sniffed it all right up
& just like that felt like they traded all this for our friendship
& felt like what did i do to deserve this & just like that that
was it what it was like like i never even existed & looking
back at my existence without even being aware of it think
i went into an instant situational depression feeling an
overwhelming sense of grief loss desertion & abandonment
& back then not being very in touch with my feelings probably
used coping & surviving skills & defense mechanisms as it is
strange only until many years later end up realizing these keen
& profound emotions & kind of ironic not quite sure if ever recovered

48

You used to roam during your
lunch break like a sleepwalker
through the parks of the northern
bronx through what looked like
unfinished sci-fi buildings so
stark looked like giant cinder
blocks almost as if the architects
just didn't give a damn or had
run out of funds feeding into
your sense of fragmentation
alienation & situational de-
pression & could see why

if people lived there would
just give up hope & turn to
dope with the distant clatter
of the el going nowhere
somewhere right around
your internship as a social
worker at the rehabilitation
center on the reservoir so
drained & wasted literally
had to fake it till you made
it & almost couldn't take in
the seasons really not sure
if any of this would end


49

There's a certain point in your life where loneliness
just smacks you & takes a hold of you & you're not
exactly sure where it came from whether it's always
been deeply embedded in your subconscious or some-
thing symptomatic & 'prodromal' & can either spend
the rest of your existence trying to avoid or run away
from it or embracing the insane emptiness & facing
it like some ridiculous puppet searching for its long-
lost ventriloquist without even being aware of it...


50

They say they do not use the term melancholia anymore
because it is outdated & that it's just more clinically
apropos to refer to it as depression but i don't know
always felt melancholia to be so much more personal
& intimate (even leaving some room open for recovery
& the imagination) matter of fact even felt myself getting
more down in the dumps (in these ridiculous exchanges)
when one of those all-knowing, out-of-touch schmucks
threw around & made instant diagnoses based on like
a half hour visit & ironically even felt myself getting

more hostile & pissed (with a deep sense of resentment
& counter-transference over those who in fact looked
intimidated with napoleonic complexes) thus so much more
prefer melancholia over something they know nothing at all


51

Some weird shit we used to accept as kids
like that 1970's commercial of mr. whipple–
"please don't squeeze the charmin!" while
there was this middle-aged asexual man just
hidden-out & planted somewhere in the aisle
when some housewife (one of those suburban
caucasian kleptomaniac women) suddenly has
the compulsion & desire out of nowhere to just
squeeze a pack of toilet paper, most likely 'cause
her husband isn't paying her anymore attention
(sick of being taken for granted or feels taken
advantage, even feels something of 'a stranger'
forced to act-out to prove it) & passive-aggressively
needs something palpable of instant-gratification &
her expression & body language & reaction is completely
orgasmic while all of a sudden that sleazy merchant mad
man shows up again with that psychotic smile & giggle
& a close-up of him, declaring–"please don't squeeze the
charmin!" (as it's so fluffy or like some transitional-object
safe & secure item, which will instantly heal all problems)
& for the sake of advertising this is his daily job & function
having to deal with all those obsessive-compulsive mothers
who cannot (keep their hands off, or) control their impulses
while this just became a part of our everyday natural lexicon
& cultural collective unconscious as children & adolescents
& just accepted it while was a perfect distraction
for being able to avoid any type of thinking
or fixating about our near to remote future

52

Followed by peter pan sailing around
the kitchen in leotards for *peter pan*
peanut butter; fred flintstone with his
sidekick buddy barney always standing
faithfully by his side with an advertisement
for *winston* taking a drag in the backyard
living a life of leisure; a commercial for
*mcdonalds* & that mechanical mantra
ingrained in our brain you constantly
hear repeating itself over & over again
like some pavlov's pledge of allegiance
"two all beef patties special sauce lettuce
cheese pickles onions on a sesame seed bun"


53

Your very first memory & recollection as a kid seeing
the constant image of richard millhouse nixon's thick
5 o'clock shadow, pale pasty demeanor persistently
plastered on the television for something couldn't make
sense of but seemed very serious; that great big *i dream
of jeannie* capsule not sure could have been apollo landing
from way up in outer space safely with those heroic *tang*
astronauts in the deep blue sea being scooped up by navy
seals seeing all this while in elementary over the tv resting
on a set of wheels either in home economics or science lab


54

Then one showing your token american indian
who just happens to be conveniently standing
there along the side of the highway while the
white man during rush hour who doesn't give
a damn just callously tosses his trash out the
window bringing a tear to his eye having of

course to do with the dueling archetypes of
self-interest & excess & kindness & compassion
& the theme of the effects of pollution on america

man…how fact truly is stranger than fiction
& how it all in real life came back to haunt him



55

I saw it all as a thoughtful boy
in my canvas pants with that
great big bandana patch & light
blue worn flannel floating deep
within those bottomless massive
leafpiles the sicilian gardeners
used to leave out on each
& every corner like sacred
pyramids wondering (or not
wondering at all) how they
got there becoming a part
of the lay of the land when
the chilly brooding dusk
was turning to mercurial
nightfall falling deep
into the spell of the
naturally warm lone
some leafy shelter
once again letting
my imagination run wild
& innocently worrying
about the future already
nihilistically contemplating
without being aware of it
about man's inhumanity
to man like some solitary
secret prayer with no
beginning & no end

56

On your deathbed will be a final request
to get one of those non-stick egg pans
made out of titanium (think might be on
the infamous periodic table of elements)
will at last have satisfaction guaranteed
& be complete before i meet my maker

i.e. they mentioned
when they opened up
secretariat they said
he had a heart practically
twice the size of a regular
horse (i guess the true-
blue heart of a champion)

i think when they open
me up they'll find a mess
of seltzer & chicken bones


57

I remember as a kid me & my best friend neighbor
would have these great sleepovers where we would
draw up these intricate elaborate maps to raid the
kitchen which would involve a whole heck of alot
of ducking & crawling & maneuvering our way
through certain pieces of furniture & parts of
the house but we never ever seemed to quite
make it as our lids would get heavy & sleep
take over & always wondered that exact time
when we fell into slumber in closets in sleeping
bags in different positions in different parts of
the room in the deep shag rug but i guess it was
all about those elaborate maps & our secret plans
& strategy of attack which i suppose in retrospect
was the only thing that ever really seemed to matter

58

And so yes i guess back then there was this
all-out primitive competitive race of who
would get there first & take first place
& how much of that was really true
how much of that was really fake &
yeah i guess were the first to land a man
on the moon even became something of
a cognitive-behavioral metaphor for when
we had something else to try & prove but
what else can we really say about it all &
what really happened thereafter? vietnam?
the nixon era? watergate? inflation? endless
gas lines? disco? coke? crack? reaganism?
self-interest? big business? the trickle-down
theory? the blues? real-life global warming?
politics which just keeps on getting sleazier
& sleazier by the minute? so yeah i guess
it's true we landed a man on the moon…


59

I really don't have particularly high expectations
for myself & just hope one day they erect a statue
of me right by the lincoln memorial & i'm just sitting
there on the dock of bay just giving him something of
a sideways glance like yeah you the man. i can't stand
that they never put one up of kurt cobaine in seattle…

how about chaplin in los angeles who got blacklisted
by mccarthey & deported back to the shores of england?
when i used to work as a social worker with troubled youth
in massachussets most of them never even heard of jack kerouac

how about joe buck when he just ripped up that postcard
& tossed it out his window like confetti from that seedy
hotel way above the hustle-bustle of it all in times square?

## 60

When coming into shore one of those cold bundled-up
immigrants from the old country first thing i saw was
the brooklyn public library while wasn't able to afford
one of those posh lovely brownstones right off the park
but was able to afford hanging out all day focused
& loitering trying to make something of myself seeing
through those lone solitary shadowy windows of brilliant
blessed gloom & doom change of seasons my favorite
greta garbo's were silent & not the ones where she
infamously wallowed—"i want to be alone" which i
never could really quite understand feeling so much
at home with the subway getting stuck & delayed
in the sweltering summer on flatbush avenue getting
turned on & falling in love with black girls with
my heart & soul on the bed & of course mandated
one foot on the floor with that wild orchid in a vase
in the caged window to keep out strangers or neighbors
or younger brothers without father figures & protective
sisters having become dope addicts trying to case apartment
& the holy hollow blast of foghorns creeping up from the
east river straight up the alley to keep me company allowing
my imagination to run wild with that wild orchid i kept in
a vase i got from the heather gardens uptown in manhattan
in cloisters where i saw all the explorers come up the hudson
& literally swear had visions reading freud's "civilization
and its discontents" on park benches with my own private
manifest destiny crossing that majestic george washington
in a greyhound from port authority deep into the palisades
of william carlos williams patterson new jersey zooming
straight out towards the mississippi with that accordian
bus ticket to denver des moines cheyenne wyoming rogue
reno midnight being & finally like some mythological
distant pristine sparkling spire & steeple of good ol'
holy & humble tumbling saintly sister san francisco
suddenly miraculously rising bleary-eyed in five o'clock
shadow from the new day dawn of the reborn pacific ocean

## 61

Allman brothers *fillmore east* those long blues
jams what i used to write to when i was blue
& had no one to turn to & returned home a
former ghost of myself dead to the world dead
tired to the bone so tired actually experiencing
phenomenon too tired to sleep from those bleak
neverending insane graveyards hustling a yellow
taxi in new york city & had to pass the mafia
dispatchers pure bribery a 20 with trip sheet
just to get out in the streets best pick-up were
the ones with the cop engines in them returning
home to 12th st. lower east side lucky lou sy ano
flat where he got his start finishing off a blunt &
quart of *ballantine* in merchant marine sweltering
summer dawn looking down empty vacant & alone
the best that you could hope for while wasted wired
in rastafarian garden my god how they could jam
almost made you feel like a new man "cause there's
a man down there might be your man i don't know"

## 62

One of the best scenes i ever saw
was when they showed a close-up
of mama cass in her supersized
sunglasses at monterey & how
this sudden look of complete awe
just raw wild wonder washed across
her face & actually saw her mouth
in slow-motion go wow when she
witnessed for the first time janis
joplin's booming voice & her
boogying on stage almost like
witnessing a miracle unfolding
& a shame & just wondering
why things like that don't
happen more these days?

63

The greatest albums of all time
that actually get better & more
interesting every time you play
them which is a rarity as opposed
to boring & more repetitive the clash
"london calling" the doors "l.a. woman"
the beatle's white album velvet under
ground the one with a banana on
the cover rolling stones "exile on
main street" carol king "tapestry"
miles davis "kind of blue" & that
whole album of duets between
ella fitzgerald & ole satchmo

all of them during one time or another
having helped me to make it through


64

'Goodbye pork pie hat' nyc 1959
around 57$^{th}$ st. on the upper ease
sigh when staggering off martinis
& long mingus blues so low all
raw & rainy up from blow staticy
smoggy skyscraper where swear
you saw the spirit of fantoms
behind the tragic sacred battle
ments of ole money aristokratic
windows looking down on it all
when you ponder got everything
to look forward to nothing to look
back on not always just necessarily
hell's kitchen latin quarter times square
blues bee-bop also went down around these
parts if in fact this is what you were about

## 65

That whole summer some
where around 1977 was
drinking a whole heck
of a lot of *schlitz* beer
with a handsome tan
bronx runs to pick up
hawaiian gold rolling
them into thick stupid
blunts hanging out at
friends' countryclubs
having wonderful
delusional dreams of
a decent future reading
sherwood anderson's
"winesburg, ohio"
dostoevsky's–
'the idiot, notes
from underground'
& freud's early case
studies on hysteria
listening to a whole
heck of a lot of neil
young that spiritual
native american
twang lead
guitar solo
the a-side
everything
you knew
& b-side
you never
listened to
unknown future
with the early rise
& fall of the clash
falling in love with
a whole mess
of girls & think
a couple may have
even loved me back

never quite making
that move making
it all that more
romantic...


66

What happened to mayor mcfish
or was that mayor mccheese
& the hamburglar & all
those other *mcdonald's*
characters you always
wondered what they
did in their down
time like those relatives
you never knew what
they did for a living
& only seemed to
show up for family
gatherings & used
to try & guess
most likely
were like
bookies
or drove
trucks for
*the ny times*
but all pretty
nice guys or
might just every so
often make those
tasteless jokes
more likely just
like everyone else
with nowhere else
to go hanging out
on the weekends
with their old timer
pals at their local

mcdonald's checking
out all the young girls


67

Was thinking should do a photo shoot
of like melania in front of floods
in front of western wildfires
in front of whole towns
leveled by tornadoes
in front of long food lines
in her chic casual leather line
with that great big elastic smile
& the wind blowing back her hair
& the back of her leather coat with
that cryptic motto "i don't give a damn"

her man (with the master plan) in his own private
psychotic pep rally signing bibles in the wasteland
of alabama meeting every criteria for narcissistic
personality disorder having already tossed paper
towels to the ravaged victims out in puerto rico


68

I want to be just like one of those all
loving nonstop action adventure
families in a *disney* commercial
where they always seem to be
running towards some sort of
miracle happy hysterical
pointing up at some god
maybe like some flying
dumbo/cinderella coming
sweeping down the staircase
of i guess that mock enchanted castle
for the little spoiled suburban daughter
mickey serenading the privileged punk

know-it-all bratty son & when the parents
get back to *the magical kingdom condos*
mom whips out the whips & humiliates
the idiot salesman & then gets on all fours
where he sticks his tongue up her bunghole
to tease & tickle & titillate & make her howl
to the stars both acts proving how much they
still love & are committed to each other, of
course the do not disturb sign put up on the
doorknob of this already very disturbed perfect
all-american couple who not by coincidence quite frugal
leave a cheap tip of loose change tossed on the night table



69

Who invented the first dance steps?
that very square square dance?
the exotic cha-cha-cha?
the fancy-schmanzy waltz?
the schmaltzy tragic melodramatic tango?
the grandiose mood swing of the bunnyhop
when you're the very last soul on line &
the rest leave you for reasons you're still
trying to figure out left all by your lonesome
after you sober-up all the way to the apocalypse
when you just ain't got enough dough anymore
(as if you ever did) to fill up the pool anymore
but just enough sun in the back to get burned
by the american dream of global warming?



70

I think i view a lot of our existence & reality
like the opening to stanley kubrick's *space odyssey*
where all those primates are jumping all around wildly
with old dead bones & aware or not (that's irrelevant)
end up killing one off then just tosses it up in the middle

of the air turning instantly into a spaceship sailing in the midst
of the constellations, thus it appears it's all a cross between
something primitive & very advanced yet not too terribly
different to a certain extent constantly in existential crisis
& eventually becoming self-fulfilling & destructive
or self-destructive; in my dreams with a whole heck
of a lot of self-loathing i'm always trying to figure
things out & desperately somehow trying to make it
nihilistically concerned that some foreboding figure
or spirit is going to get me, while i suppose it all comes
down in our cognitive reality that our existence is just a whole
hell of a lot of drama & how often just bring on our own trauma

ironically, i first saw this film smoking a bone
with a buddy of mine from the upper west side
while we were both working at one of those
video stores in the middle of the sweltering
summer & just passed-out on sofa during
that horror/bull period of the crack era...


71

I remember reading one of nietzsche's
recently discovered unknown writings
going over of course that theme about
living in a world without the support
of a god or the loss of a moral guide
on some park bench outside one
of those high rise projects in harlem
& it was for the most part on a fine
chilly autumn morning with dappled
colored leaves gathered on the asphalt
& it was my job to check on & deliver
a monthly social security check to this fine
kind older black woman in her simple & spare
apartment with only a couple pictures on the wall
& was so softspoken & grateful & looking back
at those few moments i used to spend with her when
i used to do home visits maybe perhaps that's just what
this existence is all about as without a doubt meant the world

72

I guess in the end if you put up
one good last final battle against
the devil bureaucrats & soulless
system like mohammed ali doing
his infamous rope-a-dope the whole
fight against foreman in "the rumble
in the jungle" backed up in the corner
taking every single punch, secretly
wearing him out, then suddenly
coming out fighting & knocking
him out, gracefully, poetically
to the insane roar of the poor sub-
jugated oppressed natives in africa
al pacino, al capone, clyde barrow
jimmy cagney's concept of freedom
claiming–'i'm never gonna go back
to prison! they won't take me alive!'
& puts up one last final desperate gun
fight as pride's got absolutely nothing
absolutely everything to do with it...


73

Those couple times those coward
brave men in blue harassed you
& just decided to pay your dues
& do jailtime but how much keener
everything felt & looked more lucid
& appreciated it so much more when
got out into the early morning clean
fresh air & sun beating down  hitting
your head; everything so much more
strange & surreal; your soul opened up
that much more still stunned trying to shake
it off aimlessly wandering home damaged
from the devils trying to process why
& what happened but more soulful
cuz survived it all when they were

putting the fish out on hester
hosing down all of chinatown



74

Called up *gentle dragon taekwando* on river road
because no other dojos are getting back to us
for lessons for our son and some schmuck
with that little whiny yuppie voice suddenly snapped–
"why would you call someone at 6 in the morning?"
(honestly just wanted to leave a simple message
if they're a business to see if they were offering
lessons) i returned his lovely rhetorical question
with "because i got your phone number off
the internet mofo" and hung up the phone
while wife never returns calls after mine had
spoken to her several times; finally figured
out they were the joint which just shut down
right next to that chinese where it was found
out not particularly savory things going down
in their kitchen, while this gentle dragon didn't
really seem exactly so gentle; matter of fact seemed
like one of those punitive napoleonic vice principles
you grew up with or maybe they're just going through
some sort of divorce and in a sort of weird way almost forced
me to love and to appreciate my wife and kid that much more



75

You wonder if tarzan ever woke up
in the morning & just didn't feel
like getting up or letting out that
token hi-holy howl as just got sick
of the white devil having to constantly
prove himself to jane & boy & just
remained coiled in the fetal position
while felt far more safe in his dream

world maybe suffering from a bout
of melancholia, as the gorillas &
crocodiles & cut-throat hollywood
producers could just wait as sure as hell
had sacrificed & kept up his half of the bargain


76

Curly always with an available
pair of wrenches & pliers a part
of his defensive arsenal just in case
awful humorless straight men two
faced backstabbing betraying liars
tried to get the better of him while
things really ain't that funny when
the producers & directors can't
even return a simple phone call
babe ruth spending the rest
of his waking adult life alone
by the phone for a call that
just would never come
to think how he devoted
& sacrificed practically
his whole life to them
made more than the president cuz
of course that year had a better one
grew up in the baltimore orphanages
& had the experience & skills
to just be so good with the kids


77

So please forgive me but so much more prefer
the good ole days when someone with the stature
of let's say a yogi berra in his puffy plume of fresh
clean cotton yankee pinstripes would whack the ball
a mile long right over the wall which might read some
thing along the lines of *pabst blue ribbon* or some sort

of frankfurter or hot apple pie & all of the mad blissful
poverty-stricken boys from the neighborhood would go
hustling after it like insane spiders running for their lives
as if this was some kind of final holy grail rare gem diamond
scuttling under the body of a *buick* in some used car lot in the
bronx & show yogi heroically slowly still taking his time (literally
taking it in stride) trotting around the bases while taking it all in
in his zen-buddhist moment cuz in that moment that was all that
mattered whereas with all our day to day pain & suffering we
all might as well collectively appreciate it & wouldn't worry
about being hit the next time up out of some idiot male code
of retaliatory respect cuz in fact he was actually being quite
respectful to the game in a sentimental & passionate way

78

They say similarly mickey mantle once hit a home
run so far just missed by like a foot or so going over
the high balustrade in the outfield of the old yankee
stadium clearing the whole park. wow! they don't
make 'em like that anymore & must have sailed
somewhere in the range of about 525 ft (now
even with the baseball specially wound tight
lucky to get it maybe 435) & heard he used
to literally spend nights before getting drunk
& into fights in bars; said sometimes he'd
even go up to the plate the next day with a
hangover or sometimes a bit tipsy & when
they asked him how was he able to hit the ball
he simply recalled how he saw three coming at
him & just go after the one right in the middle
shoot...now i can't even get air-conditioning in
my car while the used car salesman where i literally
just laid-out about twenty grand said how do i know
it didn't break down on my way from his garage
to my house (i still regret that i never followed
through with a private firebombing) while on my
weather channel ironically still can't get the local
weather & just show me all the towns & cities east

& west of the mississippi you pick 'em; yeah so i guess
my point being, just don't make 'em like that anymore

the cruise ship coming into port
with another case of food poisoning…


79

Spotted early this morning
those 2 missing roosters
that 1 siamese cat
that blue crow
that purple pimp hat
that red-haired angel
in her tattered rucksack
missing-in-action
who got damaged
& life got the better
of her by the riverbed
behind the traintracks
that ghostwoman
who was last seen
screaming hysterically
in the overflowing
river last season
during solstice
not sure if she
slipped or some
thing far deeper
hollering holy
& haunted
behind the dairy
cream & movie
theater & if
you should
happen to
see them
please
don't

scare them
as trust me
are very
sensitive
& just
seen
enough
of what
this life has
brought
them


80

To know eventually how
one long passionate kiss
can actually save your
sad solitary starving
soul right there in
the nitty-gritty
anonymity of
it all on some
steamy sweltering
summer evening
everything falling
down all around
you & the acute
senses & sensation
of what it means to
persist while simul-
taneously everything
ceases to exist right
there in the swirling
mist of bleeker street

81

In stead of a map
of the united states
of america i'd prefer
a pillow of all the
states past girl
friends put me
in (those wildly
gorgeous lost
goddesses who
made the past
more perfect
present little
less tense
& finally
at last
future
unknown
no worries
or concerns)
blowing those
wildflower weeds
running blissfully
through graveyards
keeping the secret
to yourself you
can tell the future
& is exactly where
the blues came from


82

First of winter's snow
coming down on the last
bras of ballerina in brooklyn
still not taken off forgotten
clothesline in autumn trying
to have seduced upstairs neighbor
to know we're all just lonely & suffer

the silhouette of steeples & derricks
going down at dusk along the river
where hand-me-down widows
sweep up the leaves & stars
of husbands who will never
return home as got cheated
on a long time ago by fate
& phantoms & alcohol

the foghorns & church bells
are too familiar a reminder


83

How did the stooges end? did they just fade
away like everyone else a gang of jewish
cousins from brooklyn & just sort of got
sick of it all sick of life & how everything
just had befallen them or maybe outlived
& outdated their audience & didn't want
to go the way of game shows when every
thing turned from classic black & white
to color or perhaps it was just like how
we lost touch with all our best friends
from child/hood for no particular reason
still trying to make sense of larry moe curly
& later on shemp or did he come before missing-
in-action on the side of a milk carton when still
a little buzzed & wasted in a midnight delicatessen
in bayridge brooklyn trying to make it with a girl
you're really not even that interested in deriving
great pleasure out of seeing how they mislabeled
all those cartons of chocolate pretzels as chocolate
'pretels' & cracking-up & she doesn't seem to get it
or perhaps just not want to make the effort (not sure
which one is worse) like that section of queens which is
devoted solely to funerals to know it's all just one big industry
or perhaps riddle which you appear to be the only one privy to

84

Wandering always wondering what
was going down spent days doing
this could literally feel one season
shift to the next with that first warm
day of spring melting all the maddening
mounds of snow in the red brick factory
gutters along the kosciusko canal in down
town brooklyn & like some miraculous
revelation, literally right in front of
your eyes changing properties beaming
burgeoning gushing streaming downhill
in fine sparkling rivulets of blue; almost
a spiritual rebirth or sense of redemption
coming out of hibernation turning alive
again past funeral homes & mafia social
clubs to the long-lost conduit of avenues
taking off to the great golden unknown


85

Out here we know the change of seasons
when the signs go up & signs go down
at the *tasty cream* just out of town
when the distant stars start to beam
just a little bit brighter over the barn
when the colorful strung-up lights
blink that much more in a pool of
blazing lights in the in-town homes
when the crimson & scarlet mountainous foothills
start rolling in orange & white & wolf pumpkins
when through midnight windows can smell
the smoky stray scent of succulent forests
like the smell of grilled cheese & bacon in a boxcar diner
when you're forced with just a little resistance to knock
down the hornets & birds nest as you tried your
best yet seem to take advantage of your kindness
when the rivers start overflowing & flooding the town

as there's one on each side by the railroad & graveyard
when you go over once more with a schoolboy's passion
that sign for sleigh rules outside the elementary school
which reads true like the declaration of independence
when that poor schizophrenic dazed & disoriented never quite there
is no longer there or stands all day outside his home without a care
when the stud soldier just sweet talks the high school cheerleader
in an alley with crabapples in the gutters & sweet aroma of chinese
when those trucks all loaded up with sticky logs & split wood ramble
down the road & literally disappear into thin air as the cold winds
out of nowhere just naturally come in & gotta prepare yourself like
some weary wizened old man for the sneaky thief chill of the season
when the fogs & mists turn just a little bit thicker
& whether aware of it or not think a bit more about
your existence your mood & mortality & final destination


86

I remember cities by the desolate
breezes blowing down bleak beat
down early morning streets from
the not too distant & secret sea
& each one i swear depending
on its location & region having
its own concrete olfactory scent
becoming a part of your spiritual
being & transcendent consciousness
blending its natural configurations of
sweeping swathes of mysterious rolling
hills & rivers & blooming barrooms
& breweries season after season; the
pawnshops & pharmacies & funeral
homes smelling of formaldehyde &
rose; the slight faded light from the opaque
sun holy snowfalls & glistening iridescent
rain beaming down alleys & cobblestone
while those sad solemn sacred shadows
swallowed you up somehow strangely
making you feel more at home where
in the late lonesome hours of the evening

everyone emptied out & everything at last
turned vacant & missing quiet & blinking
when you really got to know them intimately
like a girl who suddenly shows up out
of nowhere & fall in love with &
wondering where she's been your
whole life & now just naturally
sleeps gracefully by your side


87

Opening warm winter window in brooklyn
crying out for more kielbasa in chicago
san francisco always starving
partners like real-life ghosts
of former selves nodding-out
on the chinese laundry corner
in the mission at sundown
lunatic lament in louisiana
not so much different
in midnight biloxi
than mobile & memphis
bible belt mad dog 20/20 orange
cool breeze sharing with ex-con
woebegone & free in the deep woods
of the carolinas waiting for the next
*greyhound* to arrive in dusty evening
bums breaking bottles beneath your
*southern pacific* motel window in reno
literally seeing steam shooting out deep
dark oregon barrooms with silhouetted all
night ole timers leaned over their highballs
disappearing in the foggy valleys & gorges
misty matchstick hills of portland & seattle
winding back home through homeless
idaho & low-hanging clouds of montana
dead tired falling fast asleep in the pews
in the blues in the hues of the train station
in the dusty doldrums of denver; that great
big grand bathroom mirror like some brilliant

redemptive dressing room for a self-destructive
actor shaving your five o'clock shadow
& putting on a fresh new pair of blue
jeans & flannel with fellow madmen
slapstick characters shufflng in & out
desperately trying to make names for
themselves along with petty thieves
& drug dealers & hustlers & grifters
looking to hook up with past girlfriends
crawling back through lonesome chi-town
waking up in the trainyards of patterson
somehow making it back to the foghorns
of sleepy hollow which blows like some
holy hosanna on the mythological hudson


88

Was a reason why the great sculptor
had to go out each & every morning
with his hammer & chisel & go
at it (sublimation of his struggling
& suffering & society's injustices)
& whittle & break down & bring out
(with a keen active amount of passion
& perseverating) all the brilliant traits
& characteristics of culture & civilization


89

I remember when i called up my old pediatrician
having to get my records from when i was a kid
& hadn't spoken to him for like ages & asked
him how retirement was treating him & said it
was killing him & found the first time i was really
able to relate & connect with him suppose having
something to do with coming around full circle &
that infamous life cycle & used to live in this perfect
little suburban home with a postage stamp lawn

& this great big golf net in the sideyard i imagine
used to hit golf balls into his own true-blue version
of paradise & i guess life just got the better of him
& eventually faded with time & he asked me where
he wanted my records sent & told him my lower
east side apartment & wished him the best & told
him to hang in there & nice chatting with him…

90

They still used the saxophone & horn & xylophone
in the seventies & still some of the hippest & hottest
music ever created still able to afford a rent-controlled
apartment in the upper west side looking out & feeling
the warm wild breezes of riverside knowing every
single shadow sprung out from the trees to the lobby
while still able to dream & let the imagination run wild

*ventura highway in the sunshine…where the days
are longer…the nights are stronger than moonshine*

91

Finally those secret x-ray glasses
ordered from the back of the captain
america comic books arrived while
after 50 years showed up to my door
& apparently they tracked me
down over the years but i don't
know i kind of lost my mojo &
really no desire anymore to look
through the clothes of the cute
jewish sisters next door or my
french teacher me & my per-
vert pals would always call over
for oral help & would bend over
in her low-cut button down blouse

feeling her warm breath right on
our necks while hearing my friends
howl hysterically in the background–
"hey joooey!" & of course instantly
blurt back–"hey jean-paaul!" as those
pair of marvel x-ray glasses just sit there
now on my nighttable like some pair of
binoculars or good ole bible strangely
enough seeming just as meaningful
as i thought they'd be 50 years ago


92

I remember when i used to work at these
boys shelters & group homes & would do
some crazy shit & acting-out & attention-
seeking usually due to some form of deep
damage & abuse & neglect then suddenly
i would see them every so often after these
sudden explosions so thoughtfully reflect
with such a sincere sad & solemn sense of guilt
& remorse & an inward intense almost sacred
expression of like what did i do to deserve this
as if making some spiritual connection with their
disassociation or source to their problems & why
they were where they were (tragically not by any
fault of their own) while these kids did more living
than most grownups i had known as feel this phe-
nomenon & psychological dynamic is not so much
different than how we feel when we get much older


93

That kid who everyone saw & stigmatized
as a bad boy in providence, rhode island who
had run away multiple times due to a negligible
mom who married a new husband & didn't
get it & treat him very well & spent far more

time with him as ended up at one of the group
homes on the edge of town & found him a job
ironically working at the police barracks grooming
the horses & there was no one more hard working
& caring & compassionate & supportive & even
developed a good & decent relationship with
the exact cops who had once arrested him (& fought
the stereotype & changed the narrative) & now with
this new chance & opportunity developed a reputation
as a really nice kid when you had to take him back home
to the group home on the weekend where the mother would
always promise to visit & never once show up while all you
saw was the image of him just hanging out in the window at dusk


94

When you get older thanksgiving seems to just creep up
on you so much quicker. perhaps it's the warm weather
but feel more at a distance & colder. when we were boys
it almost became tradition to play tackle football in the school
yard killing each other & getting all full of mud with our shirts
off however cold it was; maybe it was just the necessary ritual
& primal instinct to subconsciously try to relieve our anxiety
or get our ya-ya's out & adrenaline & blood running knowing soon
we'd be stuck in very formally decorated living rooms at very formal
family get-togethers having to listen to relatives tell tasteless riddles
which would go on forever & being the nimble & natural athlete
you were would just sneak into your room in the faded overcast
brilliant blue dusk with a little frost on your window & perhaps
put like bob dylan's "nashville skyline" on your record player
& dream & brood & have visions with your leftover plate of
turkey & gravy stuffing & ambrosia the leftover scores on
the television of the detroit lions who always had losing seasons
getting slaughtered by lopsided scores & finally when the family
was all gone & everyone in their bedrooms late at night to retain
your buzz would finish off mugs of wine from the refrigerator
hopefully catching such classic films like "it's a wonderful life"
dozing-off on the sofa faintly subliminally hearing the dialogue
as if you had somehow become a part of the plotline feeling a
sense of belonging with jimmy stewart & donna reed. this year with

my own nuclear family i'm going to try to get close to something of
a similar sentiment & intimacy & head over the bridges out of town
following the burgeoning rivers through the mountains over to the
*price chopper* & pick up a couple rock cornish hens & *saucy susan*
& a 16 pack of maybe *pabst blue ribbon* to almost try to trigger &
initiate these memories like tossing loose change to the drunken
choir outside our door which used to be my alchie painting boss
who i loved to death & one of the few people i can think back
to in this existence with fondness who i actually was able to trust


95

I have memories of my aunts at past family get-togethers
by the very subtle, schmaltzy perfume they used to wear
like blackmarket bottles they picked up for sale in herald
square trying to persevere & desperately cover up & keep
down all those real-life nightmares of what existence &
marriage & fate dealt them; all those taboo secrets from
the schtetl & synagogue & split-levels in the shadows
of the lush suburbs & how that exotic scent might just
provide an instant panacea & somehow save them (whose
sudden sweeping aroma in the moment might allow them
to forgive & forget) or transcendently help them to survive
& cope & last just a little bit longer & isn't that a lot of
what life is all about when we naturally, instinctively
look back at it; back to those strange phases which
seemed like a whole other lifetime ago, containing
something of a nostalgic, magical sentimental quality

we try to find different creative ways to substitute & sublimate
our suffering which pervades & permeates all the quixotic
conflicts (all that perseverating & neuroses) of our being


96

Be very careful & wary you may have in fact
already realized your dream(s) while the greatest
absurdity or tragedy is not in realizing it or perhaps

forgetting or maybe not having the insight & wisdom
to consider looking back to those simple things like memories


97

O! one of those nightmares again
being stranded in some beatdown
dusty empty town right around dusk
where paul revere got his start trying
to find my way back home & this time
happen to follow some elvis impersonator
in his green chrome muscle car with a
drinking problem just as down in the
dumps & in the doldrums & lost
but a real nice down to earth guy
willing to try & get me there yet
the real problem deep down in
my heart & soul in everywhere
i've roamed not exactly sure where
or what i exactly from an existential
point of view can call my home &
if in fact i even want to be there

wife suddenly shows up
& rescues me as always


98

Petsitting: a communication log

"i tapped on his bowl
and mostly he just
wants to be left alone
he sort of wagged his tail
sort of dead sort of alive
and i gave him encouraging
words saying–"how are you?

you're gonna be ok!
you're gonna be alright!"


99

In the morning you just wake up
to your muted tv with henry fonda
spinning bette davis round & round
in circles in the opulent ballroom &
that is how i'd like to just imagine death
to be swinging & swirling happily ever
after through the pillars of the pearly gates
no need for it to say the end or even for that
matter the beginning just waltzing eternally
the girl & the one you love up into heaven


100

The firetrucks arrive on the pastel watercolor scene
helping c. brown get his tangled kite out of the tree
after he gets blindsided literally seeing stars when

lucy out of the clear blue sky obnoxiously yanks that football
from him just one more time & him laid-out on the mound
after getting knocked-out with his clothes tossed all around

gingerly lifting him on the stretcher & sympathetically asking
if he's alright & having gotten used to it becoming something
of a tradition routine & ritual inquiring how are the wife & kids

back then with never an adult around in the comic strip
returning home from the hospital all bandaged up bit
disoriented & seen hitching on the side of the road

no opiates painkiller
just a long horizon
& a whole future
to look forward to




101

Man will fight quarrel cut throat & kill
for his own little plot of land whether it's
his postage stamp lawn in queens or king's
castle on the english countryside walt whitman
asking the operational question what is grass?
which is some pretty deep shit if you stop
to think about it as one day eventually
we'll all be six feet under say queens
more people buried below than over




102

In my mausoleum i'm gonna have a beautiful
miserable red-haired girl with no expression
at all simply sitting behind the counter like

one of those aloof moody candy concessionists
with an attitude as if she doesn't want to be there
the opposite of buddha asking what do you want

which will include either milk duds seltzer blunts
booze brews blues or a room with a panoramic
park view to do some real downhome brooding

a postcard carousel of either the bright blue
brilliant ocean or majestic mountains which
will measure the path you have taken & all

those half-crazed stages of growth & development
with all those women you have met & known along
the way realizing all really was just a mood you were in

## 103

I get all my news about
the destruction of the world
from one of those old russian
men with his shirt off letting
it all hang out on the warm
wild summer boardwalk of brighton
beach, brooklyn with a little black
transistor planted on his shoulder
eternally stuck to his earlobe trying
his best to make out the message
through all the static & shriek
of seagulls literally lost in translation
while measuring his very measured
stoic & sentimental expressions
as often so hard to tell while
such a fine line between every
day survival & the end of the world

## 104

Where i swear i felt the true-blue spirit of phantoms
was paris at the end of that park in le tour d'eiffel
& the pillars & tenebrous ballroom windows of
that antiquated royal holy & haunted palace taking
the tgv speeding from le gare de lyon through the
industrial slums when the miraculous palms of
the mediterannean suddenly show up out your
window & see the signs for cannes nice monte
carlo like some tearful revelation taking the ferry
from naples through the tick-tock evening to the
misty shores of sicily the acropolis rising out of
the smog of the slums from athens to the long-lost
island of atlantis being those white cliffs that sud-
denly spring from the aegean being that of santorini
all those ancient streets of the holy land the secret
clandestine alleys of the arab market in downtown
jerusalem the climbing vines of the wailing wall jaffa

haifa herziliah tel aviv like lower east side delancey .
orchard pitt st. where all your blissful poverty-stricken
ancestors in those faded black & white photos hail from
& you returned roaming contemplating along the promenade
of the east river all hours of the night from season to season
when all those lit tugs & barges slowly silently slipped in
under the rippling brooklyn & manhattan bridge with meaning
& purpose harlem & hell's kitchen no matter the hour all areas
i've settled cloisters & the heather gardens along with
the sweet seductive delicious scent of aromatic orchids
whose pungent olfactory scents felt like you could never
ever once again be lonesome overlooking the romantic
nomadic hudson that delivered newfound explorers
out & ancient explorers in & coney island the last
stop on the trains feeling like the final empty vacant
existential end with that eternal smell of beer & pralines
living in some ragged ramshackle shingled home always
with the hypnotic echo of the seashore like living inside
a conch shell lo & behold the last lonesome window in the
world feeling like the last shipwrecked soul in the universe
later on the spirit of all those restless kid civil war soldiers
when escaping with a girlfriend from sleepy hollow over the
mason-dixon keenly feeling their sweeping swirling spirits right
around gettysburg through kitty-hawk & kill devil hills where
wilbur & orville through pure will & volition tested their
courage & conviction sputtering in that rickety rice paper
bi-plane all the way out to the outer banks of north carolina


105

Shouldn't have let kerouac
become a drunk & alcoholic
& should have been more
of an effort to save & rescue
him from that cottage down
in the cotswalds of florida
as he sure as heck gave
enough of himself
sacrificed himself
for his fellow man

mankind & america
moses started out
on a raft on the nile
jesus ended up on the cross
kerouac stated i'm a good catholic
so i won't kill myself but i plan on
drinking myself to death still don't
get why no one tried to get him out
of there back to the hilltop & fogs
& stars of denver & san francisco

logs rolling downriver from lumbermills
to those unknown misty destinations
of dostoevskian dandelions & thrills


106

The tugboats the same in new york
as they are in paris as they are in
istanbul the foghorns in london

no different than sleepy hollow
man still tries to get away from
it all up on top the mountain with

his flock of sheep & lighthouse
along the shore so please tell me
exactly what's all the fighting for?


107

The tulip clouds sprouting
from the morning mountains
jesus suffering all night from
insomnia from visions & nightmares

& will one day rock-a-bye-baby sleep  
again gently & those candles lit behind  
translucent curtains will lead him through  
midnights back to the moonlight kingdom



108

Left moses cleats in synagogue
                all that dried-up mud
                            turned to sand
       a trail to the beaten
                & battered land
                    of mistaken identity
                                  skinned knees
                                  aching bones
   a sign of boyhood
              & moan!
                    forgot to suture
   up ripped jeans
            heart & soul
blanket of fog
        slipping in & out
                the pine of mountains
      heal up all
            that pain
                & damage
 waiting for it
   to turn a smoky
              violet
& it all just vanish
all just be forgotten
              saint dusk
                    what'ya say
                          we grab
                  couple...

## 105

Those with a keen perceptive intuition
and even a sixth sense are left to feel
awfully lonesome and isolated as see
through all the bullshit and betrayal
and hypocrisies and contradictions
of human nature sometimes so much
so just want to fold or cry out loud
cuz however hard they try just seems
like they don't care or give a damn or
know who and what to turn to anymore
i mean how much more are they gonna
try to rip at and tear at our heart and soul
why the sensitive artist often turns to drugs

anti-proof:

I tell you at times at times it takes a man
of great courage to feel a lack of courage

proof:

May all those betrayers & backstabbers
live happily ever after in the bad karma
and character of the plots they created
and hope they eventually find each other
and forced to live with each other in their
misery loves company drama like a reunion
of shakesperian villains who will inevitably
turn to victims from all their wicked efforts
and intentions to do harm and damage the
reputations of all those innocent romantics
simply minding their business to find there's
such a fine line between fate and coincidence

106

Depression's self-incrimination
from the petty crime of living
and a pattern which repeats
itself over and over again
usually from something pretty
'situational or circumstantial'
and people who make you
feel like nothing at all 'cause
so full of shit and irresponsible
and rarely following through
on their words or promises


proof 1:

Please tell me what is the opposite of fate
and if it's just everyday frustration and
tedium can see why they came up with
(based on empirical patterns) which often
feels cursed such symbolic terms like fate


proof 2:

The subtle colorful language of best friends
growing up…everything thereafter really did
not exist at all and be lucky to get a return call


proof 3:

Still can't get
  that image
out of my head
  that kid
waiting every
  weekend
in the window
  of that

group home
   & his
mom never
  showing
    up
don't really
  know
how the sun
  comes up
how the sun
  goes
down until
  you
seen some
  thing
like that
  going
     down


proof 4:

The first man to land
on the gloom & doom


proof 5:

Eiffel tower with a view of room
its arms wrapped around my blues
when the rain starts pouring down
in the pawnshop dusk of my solitude
what the heck? is chicago supposed
to be venice with that long-lost canal?
lost love is a postcard with a ridiculous
glossy smile taking the elevator up with
the drag queens that plays country-western
at the forgotten welfare hotel in the whee hours

when i die i want them to put me out with my recliner…

proof 6:

She once told me she didn't want to leave me
that evening cause i had the same look on my face
when she tried to commit suicide (while that never
ever really crossed my mind) and thought a very fine
and romantic sympathetic gesture and why not could
really use the company as it's moments like that where
you peculiarly perversely remember the most while in a
sort of really mad dramatic way feel like they really care
and give a damn more than most people i can say i ever met


proof #7:

What drains you is not so much the work
you're doing matter of fact never the work
you're doing but the people you're working
with and the constant excuses and incessant
bullshit that goes on forever and don't know
how the fuck to stop them and when you
return home actually feel a bit violated
and taken advantage and are so drained
take that long hot shower and drink
a couple cold ones as that's the stuff
in the long-run that just does you in


proof 8:

Brawls in the jai-alai parking lot
in the thunder; at least they're still man
enough to do it with fist-a-cuffs and feel
all your senses come back with the first stray
breeze of the hurricane through the purple palms


proof 9:

Coyote finally shows up with my food
i leave a leftover bowl of sangria for his tip

see him staggering blissfully back to the wilderness
right at the bewitching hour minding his own business


proof -1:

When man gets older he appears to try
and get more sincere at being insincere


proof -0:

Nothing can be symbolic without the tragic and cursed
(or coincidental) course of events which often seems
to plague the consciousness of the innocent hero


proof +0:

The visionary poet always a little haunted
running from his past towards
the unknown future


proof 1:

Why is it that man gets so excited
when he discovers a new and ancient civilization
but seems to forget about his fellow man on a daily basis?


107

After all our adventures all our defenses
all our challenges all our obstacles
all our coping all our survival all
we are left with is just the silence
(the sadness, the normality) of our
mortality but please don't ever forget
the barely burning wild and flaming

stars beaming outside our window
over the barn during the seasons

108

We are all these lost & lonely absurd futile prizefighters
just trying to stay up but why not try lying down
everyone once in awhile and dream a little?

109

Our dreams are made up of archetypal symbols and surreal images
of our present day moods and feelings (all those doubts and fears
actual people from our past symbolic of guilt and anger and con-
flict) which may have been hiding and lingering for some time
and suddenly springs up for no apparent reason and desperately
try to make sense of deep within our subconscious and psyche

counterproof:

Likewise (similarly), it's not necessarily in essence
that something quote on quote is superstitious or symbolic
it's that its origins for the most part came from something
so severe and profound and traumatic there is that natural
fear of it repeating itself and happening again, and thus
when faced with similar-like nihilistic images and psych-
ological triggers the mind through its own signals of intuitive
coping and survival skills and defense-mechanisms sets up
cognitive forms and objects and even rituals as preventative
measures through objectified and externalized machinations
while it being the brain turning cognitive and cerebral and
becomes hyper-internalized and transferred to the surreal
language of symbols and superstitions out of a natural
protection and fear of it happening again

110

He just lost trust and gave up
on people somewhere along the way

(most likely due to those who had given
up on him a long long long time ago)

111

In the long-run you just kind of become real hollow and lonely
not necessarily out of anything major but all those little petty
people you knew would never follow through on their word

(they always have the right
thing to say and naturally
forgiving of themselves)

112

Why is it always that one little thing which pushes us over the edge?
perhaps maybe it's all the thousands of ones that just led us there!

113

There's no more scarier feeling than becoming a slave to the system

114

Paranoia is simply all those truths your nightmares told you

115

We have a tendency to demonize or glamorize our past
depending on our mood, cognitive-behavioral state
of mind, anxiety, 'fear of failure or success' being on
the precipice, or present day conflicts and circumstances


proof:

Quite often we will fixate on triggers deeply embedded
in our past when often it has absolutely nothing to do
with that or even relevant to anything in our present
and just the fear and anxiety of it happening again.
there are reasons why we so desperately cling onto
and hunger for romantic and sentimental memories



116

That arrested stage of development
you remember exactly what and where
it all began with overwhelming circumstances
way beyond your control; what if never gave
up and was persistent and never sold your soul?
any chance at all in getting out on good behavior?



117

Life should be as mysterious exotic
as one of those glossy postcards
of that gigantic jesus with arms
stretched out over the whole
length of loco lego city rio

shuffling bleary-eyed to the buffet table
from the night before with a hangover
those tin drums like ancient artifacts

leftover and you just feening for black
sausage real strong cocoa bean coffee

so humid and sweltering in the plantain
morning not caring or knowing what you're
doing the rest of the day just heading towards
sheltering shadows of any anonymous palm tree

making sure you don't get robbed
even kidnapped and held hostage

and getting wasted...


dream #1

My recurring nightmare always seems
to take place somewhere in south america
on one of those very decadent beaches of
freedom, claustrophobic and overcrowded
in the smog of humanity where i'm always
somehow left alone and solitary, and the
young thieves have stolen everything; my
wallet, my clothing, my friends, and my being
even my third cousin, isabella rosellini where
something tragic's always absurdly happening
lonely and wailing, histrionic and holy, and
simply scavenging for her in the tumultuous
waves, voluptuous and naked, as deep down
inside we sincerely love each other, but some-
thing always existentially appears missing
obviously impossible to explain through any
comprehensible language of mutual understanding
and have a history of making love to each other
out of a hollow empty sort of overcompensating.
i am forced to accept awfully quickly that she is
gone forever as i pick myself up naked with nothing
to call my own and wipe the sand off my bones and say
goodbye to all the fine young couples who speak foreign
languages worried about their finances and the future
and the old perverted giggling and grotesque husbands
and wives who are still madly in love with each other.

i head back to the chic and cosmopolitan graveyard in the
high-rise posh hotel on the postcard in the smog of my being


dream #2

The third world dictator expressionless with a flat and dull
affect in his cheap over sized polyester suit is led into the
interrogation room accused of your basic and fundamental
everyday routine and ritual human rights abuse of power
those central american countries which customarily get
overthrown have gotten so used to in crimes against man

and genocide with invisible alarms strapped up and down
his anatomy surrounded by a simple row of tables forming
a square with just laptops on them which will be the tribunal
probing and peppering him with a whole battery of questions

while right above is the bulletproof plateglass mezzanine
of automaton human beings deeply damaged and traumatized
more so the victims of family atrocities observing the ceremony
and a giant tv screen which will be receiving and spitting out these
questions in their muffled tones as when he responds it will naturally
show a whole subterranean boneyard of the lay of the land of where

he is from in this banana republic jungle of gigantic plantain leaves
and banana trees, and a long dusty road which is the main conduit
which leads its citizens into town that houses bamboo resemblances
of a cathedral and disco and schoolhouse and fruit market and corner
barroom and the only ones willing to be interviewed are the very old

ancestors and ancient shaman who have done their share of living
and no longer give a damn what happens to them or care about
the consequences; some may call them martyrs, some may
call them madmen and in the end the laptops make the final
judgment of whether guilty or innocent, and transported in a
sudden bolt of electricity straight to the screen that will swiftly
mutely in muffled tone commute him to his ultimate destiny…

on the other station they play advertisements for ska and reggae
at nightclub lounges and hometown island liquor and detergent
and motels with cable and air-conditioning and one of those

electric vibrating belts to strap around the waist
for angelic housewives looking to lose weight
call this the nature of contemporary society
or just a reenactment of the origins of reality


dream #3

Jesus
    just weeped
             on the cross
like kafka
    guilty of a crime
        he didn't know of
then all
    the jigsaw pieces
             just fell off
a strange jumping-off
        place for civ. 101
                & culture
how long's your guitar
      gonna be in the pawn
                shop window?


118

Most peoples' judgments are based on resemblances
and preconceived notions which is so far from the
actual core of the element of the truth and ironically
leaves "them" completely open to interpretation


119

Those who make those ridiculous and cliched
sweeping generalizations (with proclaimed traits
and characteristics) of some form of bias or prejudice
rarely ever truly have the exposure or experience and not

too ironic or by coincidence always fall just short of it; of
those things desired and wished (and delusionally imagined)


120

The instinctive origins and configuration of language
form like the natural musicality of waves crashing
against shore while their stirring and echoes and
repetitive patterns are the deconstruction into
concrete colorful words and their intonations


proof of parallelism:

We in fact and without facts do in fact learn language
from beat and rhythm and intonations, feeling and emotion
ask and observe any toddler or child, all you hear babbling
and echoing in the half-crazed, anonymous hustle outside
your window in the city or even suburbs strangely coming
together like some mad symphony in the late noon and
early evening (the subtle steady stir of dogs and birds
dying down at sundown) the natural and lucid sharing
of thoughts and ideas and their articulation in a close
and intimate relationship with a woman (the brilliance
of pillow talk, keen deep emptiness of sweet-nothings)
the same holds true in the moods and murmurs of those
you trust and believe in, the sound of the wind and ocean
which leads to natural contemplation and revelation (consider
when you put your ear up against a conch shell and hear the
consistent eternal pattern of the stimulating soothing sea)
one might even present a hypothesis that those olfactory
senses which provide an instinctive, intuitive trigger to
previous memories provokes a certain concrete, active
and internal spirit without even being aware of it, later
on in life humming all those precise melodies and
masterpieces like sentimental mantras from the
heart which bring about nostalgic images and
moments that got you through the hard stuff
even the cadence of one's palpitations
breathing patterns on their deathbed

121

Language and the natural creation of words
is directly connected and related to images
and memory and even thought pattern like
the factors of a mathematical equation and
its instinctive logical resolution or the dynamics
of a scientific theorem and its functioning; when
we make such natural claims like–"i am at a loss
for words" we sincerely empirically are and cannot
find one (as there is nothing in the moment fully
accurate or describable, or even for that matter
relevant or necessary) for the traits and characteristics
of this unfamiliar experience or high-expressed emotion


proof 1:

Often words that we forget are connected to those things
and events we feel guilty of or a deep sense of guilt, and
thus experience the phenomenon of a profound form of
psychological blocking or the keen sensation of becoming
'numb' and the ones which are very clear and lucid in our
memory (and are able to express and articulate) either
have a 'positive' or palpable experience, or without being
aware of it, go through the psychodynamic machination of
actually making the attempt to project from our subconscious
into the consciousness of our being, while often representative
(in one form or another) of our intrinsic character or behavior
in our day to day experience, and thus, these things, elements,
and dynamics happen far less or infrequent from what we believe
and are convinced for reasons being quixotic and of coincidence


proof 2:

Language at best becomes a representation or extension
of feelings and emotions but interestingly as much a natural
deflecting mechanism when within the fluidity of conversation
(while not even being aware of it during a moment of discomfort
or awkwardness triggers a whole new thought pattern and formation

of language) also trying to escape
those selfsame feelings and emotions


proof 3:

There are those linguistic proclamations which start
with a sort of negative connotation of false neutrality
and hold very little meaning like–"i'm afraid to say
we are not going to be..." but interestingly in
a fragmented way when you deconstruct and
separate (the sentence) and individually repeat
it over and over again does appear to hold precise
meaning like–"i'm afraid...i'm afraid...i'm afraid...
i'm afraid" or conversely–"i'm happy to say there
were no lives lost" yet when follow the same
linguistic law get the same results of–"i'm
happy...i'm happy...i'm happy...i'm happy."
this pattern and dynamic appears as well
to apply (to function and thrive) with instant
clarity and a sense of comprehension and
understanding through simple childlike terms
(and phraseology) of action and musicality
like "whoop-si-daisy" where its definition
(and meaning) becomes implicit and self-
evident right away or likewise consider such
spiritual terms like "hallelujah" (whose definition
appears to take on the exact meaning of its
multi-dimensional structure and configuration
cadence and mellifluous beauty almost deriving
from a self-soothing stimulating sort of trigger)
so in conclusion we see these linguistic patterns
of clarity in repeated words of emotion and feeling
and sole (surreal) words of pure action and musicality
but if follow this same grammatical ritual and routine
with just our everyday random words they tend to elicit
the opposite effect and lose their meaning (or not so much
proverbially 'speak for themselves'); take for example such
words like 'dog' or 'boy' or 'man' or 'lake' so it appears words
didactically, empirically, keenly, acutely, and even accurately
adopt and maintain their 'true' meaning when attached for the
most part to a concrete foundation of emotionality as well as

state of flux or pure and primitive musicality but not so much
so arbitrarily or 'absolutely' without these most necessary
colorful contexts (of active 'life and spirit' and being...)


proof 4:

The term 'wetlands' suddenly somehow came up in conversation
and told my kid it referred to certain stagnant bodies of water
like marshes or bogs or swamps or lagoons and he said
i thought it meant when you walk on wet grass and it
goes squoosh (which i laughed a little and thought
was so cute) and wondered why not while within
(or without) context felt just as valid and accurate


proof 5:

I always found myself confused and conflicted with the proclamations
and expressions and supposed analogies and allegories and metaphors
of language, such as–"don't scream fire in a crowded movie house"
ironically not even knowing didactically what that meant in the first
place and what it was even referring to, and would even argue a sort
of strange and surreal proverb which does not help to really elucidate
or make things any clearer, for example, if we were just to simply
rearrange the words of this phrase and declarative statement and
swap and change it perhaps to–'don't scream movie house in a
crowded fire' or 'don't fire movie house in a crowded scream'
or 'don't scream crowd in a movie house fire' would  that really
sound or feel any more profound, or, just the actual repetition of
these words over and over again of–'don't scream fire in a crowded
movie house...don't scream fire in a crowded movie house...don't
scream fire in a crowded movie house' as this supposedly self-
explanatory statement instantly becomes diluted and all of this
loses its true meaning and significance if were to happen to take
out the context or consequences or not attached to a real-life high-
expressed emotion, and thus language at best is just tangential or
slightly helps to describe the true desired empirical nature of the
circumstance, the concrete range of feelings and emotions, the effort
to flesh-out a scenario or conflict, and true core to the course of events

122

I never understood those expressions
with mixed messages which appeared
more in my opinion to be manipulative
and to take advantage like stealing cookies
from the cookie jar i mean if it was left out
there on the counter like shaking one of those
snow globes, or this is going to hurt me more
than it hurts you those starving children in Africa


proof #1

I could never stand those sweeping clichés
like 'if the young or old' as in my opinion
they both sold their souls down the river


proof #2

"I beg your pardon" whose configuration and paradox
and twist of phrase(s) and subtle sarcasm and intonation
when deconstructed is the exact opposite of the nuance
and bizarre declaration of the original statement intended


proof #3

All those 'sincerest apologies' never seem
particularly sincere or for that matter
very much like apologies...


proof #4

"Where is that gonna get you?" is a linguistic cognitive
statement opposite to the hypothetical question both
just as useless and unhelpful, usually, mostly just in
desperate need of some sort of necessary validation

proof #5

"I didn't think you had it in you"
what an underestimating sort of
statement (reaction-formation of
mistruth) of projection, ironically
coming from the aloof and arrogant


proof #6

Those statements like 'brutally honest'
present as something of an oxymoron
considering how conversely the former
appears far more honest and the latter
perversely brutal, whose proclamation
seems to stem from something of a
passive-aggressive reality to manipulate
and take advantage and eventually confuse

consider too the quixotic configuration
casual play of words like–'pure chaos'


proof #7

"Seriously" adopts something
of an opposite meaning…


proof #8

"I don't have any reason not to believe you"
which pretty much means got every one to

proof #9

Whenever they used those cliché expressions
like–"you never get a second chance to make
a first impression" ironically it was always in
situations where i never really cared or gave
a damn turned off to the sleazy art of persuasion

proof #10

That expression 'the proof is in the pudding'
another one of those strange vague (lazy
inaccurate) sayings and proverbs i never
quite understood (by an idiot raconteur)
as what pudding were they referring to
and was this a special pudding as would
always dig deep and find absolutely nothing
but maybe that there was the whole ridiculous
existential fucked-up futile point of it all (the
paradoxical lack of purpose and meaning)
finding nothing and the emptiness of it all


proof #11

I can't stand those who say such shit
like "could of, should of" like some
kiss ass translating irregular verbs


proof #12

The man who lives his life
in anecdotes tries to convince
himself and really sees nothing at all

proof #13

Such futile and generalized specific statements
like 'where did it all go wrong?' would imply
there was a time when it actually went right
so thus would it not prove more accurate and
concise to precisely inquire when it *did* go right?


proof #14

I have heard certain expressions like
people 'fighting for their marriage' but
doesn't seem very much like that yet
something that was given up on a long
time ago and that brutal sadistic crowd
at a boxing match getting it all out looking
for a little bloodshed, cruelty, and carnage


proof #15

Patience is a virtue but if hold onto
too long comes back to haunt you


proof #16

I hate those placating statements, as just ironically
makes me more hostile and angry like–"let's just agree
to disagree" as feels so damn simplistic and sweeping
and obvious and lazy, and really honestly when it came
down to the nitty-gritty was most likely not even taking
it that seriously nor even looking for any sort of resolution
or effort to convince that individual to agree with me, or in
any way shape or form to prove i was right as just looking
to engage in a little intellectual banter and repartee and
just wanted them at best to get my point of view or validate
or possibly consider opening their mind (to another reality)
or make a mild point of clarification for purposes of commun-
ication, so all that boring bullshit like let's agree to disagree

when originally it stemmed (and if deconstructed and broken
down) from the origins of the empirical phraseology of 'let's
disagree to agree' why honestly in the long-run in any
way shape or form would i care to agree to disagree?


proof #17

All those pompous people who love to make
those pithy and predictable claims like–"everything
is open to interpretation" what seems more germane
to the traits and characteristics of these rather obvious
and mundane people by the old mathematical proof
of the law of opposites and even more accurate is
–"everything is closed to misinterpretation"


proof #18

I hate when people give me advice
like 'take your own advice' as the
first thing that comes to mind is
mind your own business as wasn't
even asking so stop questioning...


proof #19

All i ever really try to do is self-improve
but just can't seem to get in the groove.
i wonder when i get in the groove
if i'll just simply forget to improve
which will only prove how truly
overrated is self-improvement


proof #20

They always talk about the elephant in the room
well wouldn't it be more apropos
the room in the elephant?

i'm a big believer
in nothing…


proof #21

In fact fable was really built out of fable
for the selfsame need for there to be fable


proof #22

Self-loathing and low self-esteem
in fact has its own language (to
itself) we're not even aware of
like that painting "the scream"


proof #23

Sometimes in listening to music i just find
myself breaking down crying and don't know
exactly why; could be the simplest rock song
or swear a single note from a symphony with
no need to define or understand such things


proof #24

Those who make that impulsive, defensive statement
of rationalization and overcompensation "i have absolutely
no regrets" when you break it down and look at it closely
really in fact have regrets for having absolutely no regrets


proof #25

I have always found that expression "marked for success"
more than ironic for its selfsame description and definition

while those who are a real and genuine success do not need
such a desperate random arbitrary and objectified reference


proof #26

Think about the absurdity of that expression—"the higher-ups"
and only wish there was someone a little higher up when all
those higher-ups don't return your call all a part of that je
ne sais quois meant to make you feel lower than them all


proof #27

Man (out of a fragile insecure identity)
makes claims about all these great deals
or tiny little successes, but just can't quite
ever seem in his real life to really get honest


proof #28

I have learned picked up so much more
from those i met on the road and similarly
turned away from their home, from the thief,
the runaway, the convict, the trucker, the hustler,
the streetwalker (i guess you'd call them life lessons)
and all seemed initially to come from these really down
to earth, compassionate places i could always relate to
and spiritually stayed with me forever so much more than
i ever learned from any scholar or one of those who earned
their doctorate as honestly just didn't have the street knowledge


proof #29

"I never stopped loving you" is just about one of the best
things one human can say to another considering the complex
complicated and conflicted nature of our everyday being and reality

proof #30

O what beauty and brilliance picking
up those mathematical proofs so easily
and came so naturally as had always
been streetwise and intuitive and able
to break things down and figure things
out at the drop of a hat and now i had
this whole list of laws to prove it like
an actual law of opposites through its
logical contrary variables and sequences
proving and providing evidence to
eventually get at the original truth


proof #31

"If you only knew" should be the true-blue adage
of the misunderstood poet-philosopher who's
been around the block more than once


proof #32

In essence don't most punchlines
really come before the riddle?


proof #33

That lame befuddling expression
like "losing one's confidence" as
if it ever existed in the first place?


proof #34

'To tempt fate,' what an odd & strange play of words
considering the nature of the eternal & empirical state
has already been determined by the stars & the gods &
elements & factors on a whole other metaphysical plane

proof #35

The expression "the rise and fall" of certain societies
and cultures is such a ridiculous and naive proclamation
as implicitly by nature and history is already self-fulfilling
when you consider what illusory, fragile, one-dimensional
dynamics or principles, and a lack of moral and ethics
and thus, inevitably, inextricably, through (in)human
machinations will eventually clash or implode or
turn self-destructive, while having always stood
on such unstable, shaky ground and foundation


proof #36

That expression "the coast is clear"
what exactly did they mean by that
as for the most part is it not clear while
within context and periods of crisis usually
pretty far from anything having to do with
a horizon or endline of some sea or ocean?


proof #37

Certain such strange like statements like–
"vouching for one's character" as when you
think about it or repeat that what an absurd
and bizarre configuration and statement, as
well as the actual process and dynamic, while
always found myself a bit hostile and resentful
(maybe possibly passive-aggressive) like how
could you possibly know one thing about my
character from those who supported and ad-
vocated it to those who were the judges who
were to make the determination, as deep down
always kind of found them (full of it) to be lacking
in it and knew from experience (with them) rarely
a man of their word, and when the time really
came (through thick and thin) and the nitty-gritty
would more than likely be nowhere to be found

proof #38

Those always talking shit like they got eyes
behind their head always seem to belong
to that species of human and population
of former ghosts of themselves half-dead
slurring their words in something of a
drunken stupor reminiscing about things
you can never really relate to and if in fact
got eyes behind their head would have been
killed several times by those out to get them
man lives in a house of shattered mirrors
trying desperately to maintain the vision
really delusional in the effort to hold on
to the illusion fooling himself for purposes
of vanity and reputation and so full of lies
and contradictions in this absurd house
of mirrors when it really comes down
to it does not even know his reflection


proof #39

I don't trust people with "reputations"...
just think what a fucked-up and shallow statement
having spent a whole existence 'establishing a reputation,
developing a reputation, has a reputation, good reputation
bad reputation,' and when i met them there already was
a linguistic pre-conceived notion towards this sweeping
generalization and characterization and thus the image,
sentiment and core essence of behavior and character
came nothing close to the advertised (advocated)
description and definition or anything i had imagined
instantly finding contradictions in these claims and the
efforts towards everything which had been established


proof #40

I am offended by almost every group
and culture who finds the need to declare
(advertise and promote) their definition(s)

as to a certain extent are just as exclusive
(insular) self-righteous and unwelcoming
as those they're so vociferously railing against

also too ironically try to come off
as individualistic and independent
but not quite exactly when live and
thrive and function within the exact
same acronym and performances
of suffering with exact same rhythms


proof #41

I can't stand people who say shit like–
"if i didn't like you i wouldn't be..." having
no idea ironically how much i don't like them
and don't want them to spend a minute with me
like it's some honor to be around them (as only
confirms their obsessive and insecure need to try
and exert control over me) while just don't get it
aesthetically or intuitively, and so predictable
and boring with their anecdotes and soliloquies
and all-knowing knowing very little personalities


proof #42

I could never stand those sweeping cliches
like –"he's just reaching out for help" as it was
exact shit like that that made me not reach out for help


proof #43

I think in real life that useless expression
would be far more apropos due to the nature
of mankind and human nature as–'there are
a lot of people not rooting for you' all coming
from that infamous group of misery loves company

proof #44

Any time somebody asks for something in the rhetorical
more times than not trying to get something over on you


proof #45

Statements like 'i urge you to' usually lacks the sincerity
of its conviction more so pontificating and usually having
to do with one or both parties having already given up


proof #46

That old expression 2 steps back and 1 step ahead
just remember in that first one not to drop dead


proof #47

What makes us tick? do they also ever ask
this existential question when we are broken?


proof #48

Those who quote such things like–'it's my ethical duty' or 'i'm
under sworn obligation' usually, ironically, not by coincidence
fall just short in spirit, principle, practice, and integrity of this
actual reality and if you only really knew what perversely went
on behind closed doors with all their convenient abuses of power,
breaking of confidences, betrayals, and very casual inside jokes


proof #49

People who don't get your jokes and are not quick or clever
and turn hostile are clueless and to a certain extent sadistic

proof #50

Adults used to use that old used expression
when playing golf (which is supposed to be
a sport based on the honor system) "i was just
improving my lie" which really meant they got
caught casually kicking their ball a little out of the
rough and always thought wasn't that just the perfect
metaphor for the nature of human nature and mankind–
"improving my lie, improving my lie, improving my lie…"

proof #51

'People skills' just listen to that one and always
got a real kick out of and found laugh out loud
if you repeat that over and over again–"people
skills…people skills" like people who actually
put this down on their resume (and are proud
of and wonder if they were born with or acquired
through some sort of 'life experience') like what
does it really mean to have people skills? seems
like those aliens who just got off their spaceships
in those old time sci-fi movies–"people skills…
people skills…people skills…people skills…"
and what the manager at the movie theater
and clothing store are looking for (along
with of course becoming some sort of
responsible team member *of course*
until they decide to let you go) finding
yourself getting instantly turned off
and not even applying for the job

proof #52

I can't stand those who think they're being all cute
and original, while casually use cliched expressions
like "don't shoot the messenger" and in fact wasn't
even thinking of them, as they're all just a bunch
of freaking incompetent grownup little kids (with

poor judgment and awful communication) and
honestly just for making such boring idiotic
statements want to fucken shoot them
and the assholes who sent them

rob them and steal the god
damn horse they rode in on


123

Then you just start to think and can't stop thinking
and don't want to think have you ever once really
found one honest man how you've become that
one honest man who could not find one honest
man or down in the dump philosopher forgot
what his name was who spent his whole life
searching for one honest man and still could
never find one and honestly you never ever
were really looking for one and only came
upon it upon *trial* & error and the principle
and concept and flesh & bones of its high-
expressed emotion because ironically innocently
interestingly (originally) was never ever looking
for it and became a 'common' theme but when
can't even find it in a best friend or a boss or a
brother because of the most base & vulgar traits
& characteristics of envy and jealousy and inevitable
betrayal i mean come on they gave a nobel peace prize
to yassar arafat and then just a year later went back on
his word back to his old violent ways with all those terrorist
attacks see maybe why bob dylan got one because had to
keep on creating to just get him through it all through the
madness of it all and 'keep on keeping on' as what else can
you do when everything crumbles all around you and got no
one to turn to and can't believe in one living breathing soul
and then honestly what the fuck does honesty even mean
anymore i mean isn't it just a term and a word and when
you simply repeat it over and over and over again loses
all its meaning and means nothing at all (and becomes
absurd) and maybe all you can really try to find and turn

to is love or some form of reflection or solitude or maybe
even having to fool yourself a little to stop yourself from
driving yourself mad and what start playing the role of fool
like the wise man playing the fool but hell no will never go
down that path again and then realize the only thing can really
turn to is the true-blue thunder and that sudden blast of wild
downpour coming down in the mountain like a revelation
(with the sensation and liberation of the senses) and then
silence and then comes the brilliant beaming prisms of some
miraculous rainbow and then comes another and you forget it all


124

Real time does not exist anymore!
i'm telling you comrade as we spend
all of our time, the brave and courageous
souls that we are obsessively trying to capture
real time with all of our gizmos & contraptions
all of our cell phones perched over our skulls
gathered in herds & hoards all aimed exactly
in cookie-cutter fashion right at that desired
targeted goal, the conformist brainwashed
souls that we are absurdly believing we
are doing something unique and creative
creating our piece of art for some obvious
reason when we show up to a sporting event
pick up/take down police brutality, some
pathetic pompous politician at his podium
and then the operational question becomes
when do we gather up that posse, the people
person that we are of friends and acquaintances
family members and witnesses with our chips
and dip and white wine spritzers to watch that
home movie screening when you felt the need
(didn't think at all) very mechanically callously
passionately in the past tense here & now
to capture the future perfect of real time

proof:

I don't know...in my opinion the sign of a real true-blue
democratic society will actually be allowing us to make
our own free decisions like i honestly don't need some
quasi good deed doer to tell me they can't deliver me
a rare cheeseburger due to some ridiculous litigious
directive or card everyone on my line to make sure
they're all 35 on some fine higher than holy sunday
honestly know i've finally found the land of freedom
when i can simply stroll into a *sunoco* gas station
and pick up a 6 pack of beer go a little further up
the road and into the mountains and pick up my
fireworks and maple syrup and pumpkins and
if i'm in the mood which i usually am pick up
a hitch hiker to find out what's really happening

sound of lumbertrucks motorcycles
sputtering into the distant mountains
not sure why but so nice and cathartic

                         sunrise & awaken


125

I think i'm starting to become
a lot like my grandfather
who was a very quiet
man & wife used
to dominate him
only difference
his hair turned
all white by
the age of 20
& owned with
his brother
a pharmacy
on the corner

in bed sty, brooklyn
when they used to
sell heroin as a
stimulant over
the counter
& mix ice cream
sodas along with
*the brooklyn eagle*
neighbor/hood
newspaper
when it used to be
a nice all italian
neighborhood
& had very few
jewish people
& whenever
my dad went
over to a friend's
place the mom
would scream aloud
"it's vinnie's jewish friend!"
& literally would walk
every evening after work
over the brooklyn bridge
just to learn the language
& only took off every
other sunday
yet ironically
think i live a far
more lonely solitary
life in this day & age
& o yeah maybe that
part about being dominated


In middle age
sinking back
into easy chair
sticky sweltering

you dream of all
those girls in high
school you used
to fantasize to
who used to
wet dream to
pretty sure
they did too
one you used to
dirty dance with
drunk at keg parties
one who you'd
mutually get close
to in the shadows
of cubbyholes and
lockers and think
if maybe with all
their divorces and
miserable marriages
somehow found them
and got familiar might
actually make your life
a bit more bearable
perhaps maybe even
a little more complete
swimming all the way
to the bottom
of the deep end


127

I have always had something of a strange and lucid keen
6$^{th}$ sense but when it came to all the other senses no sense
& nonsense & no sense of common sense which pretty
much left me a rather ridiculous lonesome old man

x,

You see them much later on and supposedly this is what
they are when they grow up and become mature and think
you liked them so much more before they became what they
were way back when when you didn't know what they were


y,

It's all that little shit which gets you in the end
all that pathetic petty trivial bullshit bickering
i mean have you ever heard anyone say it was
all those words and power struggles and sem-
antics which helped me to rise above as people
become self-destructive with things they once loved
the shattered glass of the crystal ball of the fortune
teller who tells you your future the shattered snow
globe of *rosebud* the ridiculous systematic 'big brother'
computer which shuts down and just goes out of order
in *space odyssey 2001* while honestly it's the simple
things like the distant familiar image of clothes of
some stranger on a clothesline which saves our soul


proof 1:

And so maybe all it was all it was all it was
all you needed was just one kiss just one kiss
just all it was was all it was all it was all it was
was just one kiss all you needed was just one
kiss was just one kiss all it was all it was all
it was all it was all it was was all it was was
just one kiss what it was is what it was was
just one just one just one just one just one kiss
in the midst of the mist was just one kiss in the
middle of the mouth in the midst of the midnight
was just was one was just one was just one was
just one was one first last kiss to keep you adrift

proof 2:

The concept of love has been hyper-intellectualized
while it's absurd to think that it can in any way possibly
be objectified, as something that comes instinctively
straight from the gut and heart and mind, naturally
chemically and psycho-dynamically, while simultaneously
healing all the hurt and loss and pain and trauma, and all that
emotional and spiritual damage that feels like a whole other reality


proof 3:

And we find in the end he who played the role
of both king and ruler when his disguises are
removed very much that of a ridiculous buffoon
while he who was forced to be something of a
clever jester and deferential very much a man
of wisdom of philosophy and royalty the king's
daughter with her constant mind games and
games of seduction will always just remain
the king's daughter while the audience the
masses only capable of pathetically following
the plotline and what the actors have to offer
not by coincidence both slave and critic where
we find absurdly similarly ruled by both passion
and conviction and when all their disguises finally
come off pretty much helpless and desperate

as in the very end or denouement it's all
dostoevskian and a band of out-of-work
actors simply built and based on a whim


128

How we instantly recognize those distant shapes & forms
& configurations embedded in our primal & aesthetic
consciousness in brilliant transcendent pieces of art (also of
course it's important to travel to establish a simple foundation)

proof 1:

I keep on seeing on my computer all these advertisements
to travel cheaply to paris but what am i gonna do keep on
going back to the eiffel tower even though i sincerely loved
it as all i really want to do if i return again is take a flat again
in monmartre with those views at dusk through open curtains
and weep openly under the shower of a clawfoot tub and that's
the only way i am going to return to paris drained anonymous to
weep hysterically in a clawfoot tub in sacre-coeur with views at dusk


proof 2:

Sitting in the rainy window of my room
at *the jack london* eating one of those
chinese specials i love after getting
my weekly paycheck working all
day in the mountains of portland
call girl taking the elevator up
playing country-western after
spending all day flashing
the old men in alleys...


proof 3:

I wonder why in my old age i have this obsession
with going to vegas like some holy grail for glitz
and glamour, as honestly take absolutely no
pleasure in betting at all is it the warm desert?
is it the big breakfast buffets they supply you?
is it getting sauced around the pool? is it the views?
losing yourself fading away when the sun goes down
looking out from your grand panoramic window to the sacred
sierra nevada's end of the world blinking neon at last anonymous
alone like some holy forgotten protagonist stoned in a glossy postcard

proof 4:

That eternal glowing prism within a layer of glass
like the eternal echo of the ocean in a conch shell.
think of these images & forms when suffering & struggling
with the contradictions of the mortality of your own existence


anti-proof:

For the most part the part of 'tourist'
presents as desperate and pathetic
(empty and vacant) always looking
to greedily while ironically stingily
take something (stealing in plain
sight, blatant and obvious) with
very little to offer and experience
and if in fact really want to learn
anything about a particular culture
just stay out of 'the historic district'



129

"I'm a scared! i'm a scared!"
famous last words of the great one
gleason, jean genet and dostoevsky


proof 1:

Camus, jean-paul sartre...
does one really need their sanity
to prove they exist as have experienced
when i was most desperate and in crisis
these high-expressed emotions most keen
and lucid and then the ridiculous and ironic
sensation of a certain sense of disassociation
of it being of little significance and all irrelevant

it is in periods of transition when
i've had my greatest revelations


proof 2:

Almost every true philosopher or man of wisdom
is something of an undercover agent desperately
trying to solve the mysteries and contradictions
of human nature and the things that plague him
having gotten his start and origins from a certain
loss of innocence or even absurd false accusations
(a mistaken identity passionately fighting for his identity
and reputation) as this subconsciously and spiritually becomes
the narrative for his vigorous defense and intense argumentation


proof 3:

o my god some people bullshit and lie so much
they 'honestly' don't know the difference between
right and wrong, what's true and what's false; they
literally no longer have any sort of baseline and start
believing themselves which ironically becomes totally
unbelievable (delusional) 'absurd' and dangerous, and
advise you to stay as far away from them as possible if
don't want to lose complete direction and perspective


proof 4:

Those who live and thrive off expressions and body language
of smiles of sarcasm and whispering always found the most
pathetic in their ridiculous desperate efforts to try and
'distinguish' themselves through rather unmotivated
tactics and obvious hostile dynamics of a 'conformist'
they instantly give themselves away as a part of the masses
manufactured and about as convincing as a broken record

proof 5:

Why is it always the fuck-ups of society
who always make you question your
reality and identity? i don't know maybe
because there are just so many fuck-ups
and then it's like that experiment we did
in science class in high school with the
supersaturation point, and you drop in
just one more particle and it all falls out


non-proof 1

You know love when you're suddenly
able to take that deep long breath
that you never even knew existed
that you never knew you existed
when the whole world ceases
to exist when all that exists
is just her and you and all
the leftover  wine and chocolate
and sweet nothings and blues


non-proof 2

We treated our first love
like a sacred and holy
piece of art that cannot
be damaged or destroyed
by what times does to us


130

They seem to appreciate you so much more
when you walk down the aisle as if should
feel honored to be a part of their ridiculous
and responsible club but if they only knew
how much more you had to offer when

they used to ignore you and suffered
and were all by your lonesome…


counterproof 1:

Maybe in fact really not a "bad boy"
and he's just way more perceptive
and they're full of shit as comes
by no coincidence how makes it
just more convenient for them
to refer to him as a bad boy


counterproof 2:

All of my role models turned out to be the biggest assholes
and suppose it wasn't just by coincidence that they simply
played roles without soul (you find out in this life if done
enough living and through perseverance and a certain
amount of wisdom there's a fine line between the
scholar and salesman, even interchangeable) and how
ironically nowhere to be found when need them the most


counterproof 3:

Those overly polite and overly formal
always seem just a bit too passive-aggressive
for their own good with a clear agenda and eventually
in the long-run without hesitation gonna get something over on you


counterproof 4:

Who the hell even wannabe be on the straight & narrow?
they're all just really crooked anyway and so much
more prefer to find out what's happening inside
outside under over and around the mountain

counterproof 5:

Freedom in america is the illusion of the pristine
safe and secure suburbs with its perfectly surreal
forms and images keeping the immaculate illusion
alive by workaholics who will deprive themselves
of pleasure and try to competitively out-do and
one-up their neighbor while the ultimate rebellion
(due to classic clinical denial) with wives and
children who show no love for them to dream
and fantasize about growing and developing
daughters and other miserable wives and
whoever can hide the secret best and plays
the most convincing role of good family man


counterproof 6:

It's my theory when guys get married
they become a lot like charlie from
*charlie's angels* pathetically fawning
and flirting from a safe distance over
some artificial medium and mechanism
while you hear this pathetic perverted
voice from some unknown all-knowing
figure as they pretend to act mutually
interested and flattered between this
old man who plays the role of control
and power and symbolic seductive sirens
proud to be admired like demure daughters
who can do no wrong even be more persuasive


counterproof 7:

I'm sorry but the drag queen
when he lays there on his deathbed
did he not contribute far more to culture
and civilization than most businessmen?

counterproof 8:

Has anyone ever coiled in the fetal position
of their shrink's couch and when they woke
up thought i could have done this cheaper at
*the best western* to realize all of existence
is just pushing the snooze button for your
15 minutes of not wanting to be famous
and to be left alone and be a stranger


counterproof 9:

And so god pretty much mentioned to us poor wretches
and of course only paraphrasing fake it 'til you make it
while maybe i already did and not even aware of it

met a pretty young lonely french girl in montreal…


counterproof 10:

When we get older we make an effort
to reach our standard baseline for what we
perceive and dream is our sentimental vision for home


counterproof 11:

My wife got towed
with white flowers
in the drizzle after
she got hugged
from behind
in the arcade
by one of my
son's best
friend's
mothers
who wouldn't
let go of her

and the lady
in the hardware
store told her to
do a downward
dog which supposedly
is a yoga move to help her
find the core to her center
and returned home past
the overflowing muddy
brook in the tow truck
past the blood bank
butcher and barroom
with the white flowers
in the drizzle and put
them right in the vase
because she said they
made her feel alive


counterproof 12:

The punishment rarely fits the crime
while usually way too precise or punitive
or well thought out or obvious, or simply
reactive and impulsive and not thought
out at all, and who's to say what's really
a crime while "the sentence" just as absurd
considering existentially what life does to you


counterproof 13:

And so we got all these brilliant splendid ceremonies
for marriage and even funerals (and that's lovely and
and all well and good) but always find myself shocked
by how clueless and little people know (how impulsive
and all that acting-out and lack of communication)
when the conflicts and complexities of life hit them

counterproof 14:

Every so often couples will accuse each
other of stealing each other's mood cause
perhaps maybe that's all they have to hold onto


counterproof 15:

I have always gotten a kick out of the aloof people
as they always seem to be trying too hard to make a
statement while ironically find i instantly forget them
in their desperate efforts to try and attract attention
through pathetic means of an indifferent disposition


counterproof 16:

Reputation with its definition and traits and characteristics
when it comes down to the nitty-gritty is reserved for those
with an ulterior motive while a diluted form of morals and ethics
a whole heck of alot of imitation, manipulation, and taking advantage


counterproof 17:

That statement "pleasantly surprised"
what the hell does that really imply?


counterproof 18:

How dare they say such things like wouldn't want
to run into him in a dark alley like how the hell
they know would even want to run into them?

131

They have gotten very comfortable with (you in the role of)
all that crucifying and conveniently scapegoating but when
they finally find out you're a pretty nice and decent guy
"kills them" (as couldn't at all possibly be true and all
the things they did to you, putting their reality and identity
into instant question) and thus interestingly (not so much
so) predictably and paradoxically turn more hostile with
the machination and psychodynamic and natural defense-
mechanism of deflecting and denial and will even go so
far as to come up with a whole other new fabrication


proof 1

We fall in love with those
who break our hearts a little less
or those we deem may have the potential
to put all the shattered pieces together again


proof 2

Death, honestly how can it
really be much different than life
so why not just have a good time?

think i might've had a decent dream last night…


proof 3

At the end of one's life we look back not just
necessarily at those we cared about and loved
but also perhaps to that one individual who may
have treated us fairly, while in the scheme of things
represented some form of respect, consistency, beauty

proof 4

My favorite 'heroes' have always been the ones
misinterpreted misunderstood and underestimated
i guess maybe the real-life martyrs, all part of that
unfair and unjust character portrayal (inaccurate
label or form of stigmatization and criminalization)
which proves to be a part of the solitary 'absurd'
challenge they are forced to face on a daily
basis that may have in fact perversely given
them their courage (even their character) not
always necessarily living "happily ever after"

eg: take a look at such protagonists like old man goriot,
gregor samsa; actors like peter lore who always played
these lowlife sleazy minor characters, strange eccentric
sort of slurring petty thief hustlers, knowing he'll never
be a leading man or family man but there's something
really to be said about that 'cause he somehow seems
to accept this and just barely make it and get the most
out of it usually somewhere like out in some expatriate
dive right around the romanticized crime of northern
africa in undercover disguise swimming in his over-
sized white linen suit in a straw hat usually with some
kind of drinking problem just to help him get by
accepting his plight trying to get through this life

132

It is ironic how practically as much damage done
with all the things not said or done (in crisis) than
the original words and things from where it began

133

If the punchline only knew all the suffering
that went into the build-up of the riddle

trust me would choose to live a life
far more comfortable and simple



134

Too much 15 minutes of fame seems awfully lonely
hen glances at you sideways wanting a little privacy



135

In those transcendent romantic intimate relationships
they are always pleasantly fragmented, while having
the spirit of something of a free-fleeting stable foundation
like the image of a rainbow with its glowing colorful prisms
and no real necessary destination, just the keen beauty of that
spare simple image with no real beginning and no specific end


proof:

Women get you through the night
women get you through this life
when they get up in the middle
of the moonlight and then
return safely by your side
sidekicks to the long eternal sigh...


anti-proof:

A wife who can put up with and tolerate us
and even be a good sport to a certain
extent is a saint of sorts...

136

When you go back to a memory and that too
is imbued or based on sentiment, romance,
and escapism, there is apparently something
innately, instinctively, so significant, necessary
and meaningful about the dynamics of dream & fantasy


137

What is sublimation but everything
blossoming from a broken heart
like that rose in spanish harlem


138

Getting caught with your pants down
i'd like to get caught with my pants down
i've never been caught with my pants down
like a good ol' jack lemmon or clint eastwood film
in their haberdashers or ten-gallons when manhattan
was lit by a single lightbulb in the medicine cabinet
slow-dancing cheek to cheek with their loved ones
in winter overcoats with drinking problems at closing
time desperate alive and santa claus staggering home

when you really gave a damn about
them and plot twists and denouements

what happened to all those
real-life slapstick comedians?

139

Has the wife of a clown ever declared
out loud hold down the fort
gonna powder my nose?


140

-1

My wife catches me taking a whore
bath right in our kitchen sink caught
between cleaning & weeping & asks
"what are you doing?" i just simply
respond the only way i know how–
"just being myself" and continue over
to the freezer for the *chock-full o' nuts*
my gas and energy and the only thing
i know i can rely on for the remainder
of the day heading over to the tv to see
just another member of the trump cabinet
getting indicted on criminal charges and
thinking we gotta constantly believe all
their brainwash about a booming economy
while honestly i don't really know what
the fuck got anything to do with me?

Hx of kulture:

I was one of the flying wallendas who didn't make it
as really just didn't care or give a damn if you get
my drift about exceptionalism & showed absolutely
no aptitude or interest while watched my very highly
competitive obnoxious brothers & sisters doing their
backflips & single & double somersaults & tightrope
in mid-air while down there right down there without
my parents even being aware as just did not really care
about being acrobatic substituted it for a drug problem

nodding-out first from sniffing glue and then heroin with
a slight grin orgiastically watching the cow & cats & dogs
& hens & chickens & stolen furniture & methadone & medicine
& spoon boiled down dope in for the syringe jump over the moon

I always fantasized and wished as a kid
when they had one of those game shows
and they said you can take what's behind
door #1 door #2 or door #3 and they choose
the wrong one and like something from roman
times out pops some sort of wild lion who maims
and mutilates and rips them into a million pieces
i guess not taking that tour around the world some
set of living room furniture or shiny red sports car
leaving his body parts scattered all over the floor
and that blonde-haired bimbo in a sequined dress
with her ear to ear *dentyne* smile points down at
his remains and cuts to a commercial for *reese's
peanut butter cups* where they show some klutz
who just happens to be holding a bar of chocolate
running into another schmuck holding a jar of peanut
butter and bites into it and gives some great big idiot smile
like getting laid for the first time living happily ever after
putting off studying for your social studies homework
with a text book all wrapped up in a brown paper bag
where there's some grand explorer standing proudly
up on top of some precipice in the phase of manifest
destiny looking out over all the united states of america

Those tender dewdrops on the morning windowpane
of gleaming white sandstone hotel right in the middle
of the madness of real-life hustle & bustle tenderloin
district, san francisco groggy anonymous so far away
from home not knowing a living breathing soul solo
so low is the essence of the core to the empty vacant
suffering of the facts & falsehood of this fragile folk
lore we so prematurely like to call our time on earth

One day when i get
really old i expect
my wife to just

show up and
turn me off in
the dark glowing
tv room and that
will be all she wrote
next morning the black
& white muted film noir
gangsters in sharp suits
and hats still as always
taking care of business
strangely somehow
paying their respects

What i wish at my funeral:

baked brie
a pu-pu platter
chocolate baklava
slabs of pork
from pig roast
girl on rollerskates
from the disco era
serving pigs
in a blanket
in ten-gallon
with pink gun
in gold holster
down & out old
timers passed-out
at one of those
ol' time nostalgic
chinese restaurant bars
with exotic pastels of
pagodas & sailboats
floating through the
bumpadabumpa
of hong kong
soldiers &
drug dealers
shuffling in
& thieves
& slapstick

comedians
transfixed
with the
gigantic
goldfish
young lovers
with a whole
future ahead
of them with
great big grins
grabbing from
that bowl of
jelly mints
talking shit
contemplating
on the way home
with a good buzz
either from the
plum wine or
pork fried rice


0

Sometimes melancholia just gets a hold of you and you
don't know where it came from or what to do with it
but if you really dig deep enough do know exactly
where it came from and naturally just start thinking
about a year and a half ago how this moose got hit
on the highway during an impossible never ending
winter in the thick wilderness of one of those weird
and eccentric towns in the forest right by the exit near
the hospital and really feeling bad for it and somehow
on some human, sentimental level (always been this
way) relating to it as opposed to the natural perfunctory
reporting of it and seeming to just care about the statistics
or safety of the commuter, while if i was a state cop and
arrived on the scene probably would have put a convenient
bullet right in the brain of the human being who most likely
didn't give a damn about the conditions or terrain and just
leave this lowlife right on the side of the road for road kill
for the game warden (who usually plays games with semantics

or doesn't return phone calls) following the exact protocol they
tell you to and usually doesn't show up anyway till the next day


141

                \*

Yellow finch fly in from the morning mist of the forest…
thankfully your wife has already scrubbed down the floor
of the bathroom whose olfactory trigger allows you to just
naturally (forgive &) forget the nightmares you just had
and move on with the seasons and become a new man


      \*

The steam from the shower
seeps through the window
mixing with the crystal
dew still on the pumpkin
perched on the back porch


    \*

Sky-blue dragonfly
sidling up against
screen window

you got nothing left to offer
then buzzes back towards
the lake in the mountains

somehow giving the impression
completely aware sympathetic
and on the exact same level

*

There's a certain kind of whimsy
even slight sense of humor
watching the sun-lit leaves
fluttering on the trees
birds communicating
small talk on wire
the svelte minnows
winnowing from
top to bottom
the salamander just
hanging out in the
baking sun the stray
cat doing the same
on top a trash can
in the winter of brooklyn
moose coming down from mountain
and realize you have to do absolutely
nothing at all will always last forever

*

A light sunshower
falls on the rabbits
coming out from
the pachysandra

*

Alas bear comes
out of mountain
in the thunder

*

Butterfly when
you least expect it
and most desperate

*

The thick accent of crickets

*

One day like the caterpillar
crawling through my days
and the absurdity my life
has become i'm going to
suddenly spontaneously
spring open into a colorful
butterfly and just soar and
never be seen from again

*

Horses transported
in red caravans
in the lighting
and thunder

*

Midnight mountain rain
pouring down on the
sky-blue robins' egg

*

Evening's a very lonely business.
as long as there are fireflies
to help you to get by…


*

The best thing about dusk
is how quickly it turns to night



142

In this mock life
all i need and require
are the nightbirds warbling
and dying down in my garden


anti-proof:

Everything in my life which has been required
i look back on and meant absolutely nothing
at all but those things of spirit and spontaneity
(soul sentimental value) like first love the world


print 1

Watermelon trucks and chopped wood
come into town after all the rain comes
down in the mountain; homes have
a pattern to smell much sweeter
and riper after all the rain and you
take in all the deep scents of wood
pain and what life has done to you

there are very few people
you can say you were
truly able to rely on

puddles like a miracle
prove them all wrong


print 2

What is it about that slight coat of frost
on the roof of the barn that always
sets the soul a stirring fluttering


print 3

Iridescent crystal icicles on the chilly
magical lattices like sacred steeples


print 4

Leftover nightbirds flying through
the morning mist of mountains


print 5

O the fog which covers the morning & dawn
which gives it all its shape & form which
gives it a language of its own which
covers the blessed drooping silent
trees which covers the valley that
winds gracefully through dreaming
foothills feathering the slope of
awakening mountains which
covers the wild murmuring
mellifluous river which runs
& whispers through the heart
of the village beneath covered

bridges sleepy towns & sacred
tick-tock land of hours which
covers the clock towers & cattle
cathedrals & miraculous cornfields
all rolling flush against the horizon
to the core of the quiet great unknown
which covers all suffering & sadness
& madness & melancholy which makes me
feel more alive like the dewy grape on the vine


print 6

That great big ball of purply red sun rising
glowing and beaming over the autumnal
hills finally alas setting the imagination
flickering flaming and on fire once again



143

The roaring fire that just plops down by
the old deaf dog and couple growing old

great big window in the living room
always with a view of the backyard
growing larger building up in snow

birds returning from winter to your home
because they just got nowhere else to go

the woodpile just happy to be a woodpile

scarecrows in the back of red pickups

thunder tip-toeing across the mountain

stumbling over pumpkins

the town is budding

how tilling the soil smells exactly like
the sediment at the bottom of the lake
like kissing her for goodness sake

stream starts picking up speed heading
towards the setting sun of the mountain

the snickering nightbirds at your
window and you already passed-out
from what this life has done to you

morning dew from the garden
ripples through screen window
onto peppermint cactus in sill
giving off its sweet aroma

those gigantic scarlet damp leaves of maples
scattered in exact same area year after year

banister making itself smooth and warm
comfortable for all the crumbsnatchers
sliding down the long spine of its torso

the french classic country dining room table creaking
contracting & retracting due to the change of weather

the walking sticks and grandfather clocks seasonally
collecting dust slowly winding down in ticks & tocks

the blast of foghorns and train whistles semi-retired
but still with the need & desire to go through their
routines & rituals of bringing life to the town

nothing more comforting than rain coming
down in the mountains 4:32 in the morning

the smell of raindrops on verdant leaves
bleach and they're putting up letters
on the marquee in the morning

that ole time donut shop not sure if it's open or not
like some tarnished diamond in a treasure chest right

below some lone towering redwood rising to the heavens
lining that nostalgic crumbling avenue rolling on forever

1970's listening to rock & roll radio station in our bunk
barely coming in during summer camp in the berkshires
somewhere around that radiotower in the mountains

just the perfect amount of fog & mist
to help the husks of corn & squash
& pumpkins reach their climax

after the storm the wild apples
rising in bundles to the heavens

playing hide & go seek with jesus
on a misty morning in autumn

the frozen over lake which takes on pretty young ice skaters
and old timer ice fishermen with their drinking problems and
old money mansions paper factories and institutions in the hills

simply the pensive gurgle of swollen over purple-blue brooks
babbling whispering through pachysandra after all the rainfall

the rain which falls past the plantation shutters
finally drowning out all the idiots of civilization
the mad symphony of tree frogs in the swamp

the ping-pong chorus of toads croaking
back & forth in the lagoon at dusk

the crickets & cicadas doing their nightly rounds
then suddenly dying down for no particular reason

fireflies carrying neon flashing in
fly-by-night internal organs at night

the nihilistic sighing which guides
gets you through this melancholy life

144

Pies leftover
in the sill
in the drizzle

      what connects the memory
  to the olfactory trigger?

145

Have the acts in the three-ring circus
ever looked out at the audience and
said this is like a three-ring circus?

proof:

If we outlast them all
does that make us angels
or were they always just devils?

proof:

What else are they
gonna try to steal from you?
we spend our whole lives trying
to gain it back to barter the blues

146

All those things that broke you down
if you somehow manage to hold on
are the exact things that ground you
provide the foundation for insight
intuition, strength, and wisdom

anti-proof:

They train adults to become liars...
real-life telemarketers and supposedly
the more you contradict yourself and not
give a shit and live with it (to take advantage
of the client and manipulate language) this is
what it means to have charm and be a success
to tell those long drawn-out stories (with run-on
raconteur riddles and pithy punch lines) in the form
of absolutes and anecdotes to connect and sell the product

anti-proof:

When they grow up become so mature and formal
as if this is what they think it is to be a grownup
while you are not sure what they are thinking of
that proverb you never quite understood either
"i trust them about as far as i can throw them"

anti-proof:

Growing up with someone with clinical narcissism
you end up hearing about their history on a daily
basis, but if you are a kid don't know about these
overbearing manipulative traits and characteristics
and end up without being aware of it taking it out
on yourself (with constant guilt and conflict) and
self-destructive ways, like jesus hanging himself
on the cross not knowing how to reach out for help

anti-proof:

Life seems something of a strange surreal dream
but the people often so much more trivial and petty
constantly testing you and trying to get something
over on you, while those true-blue real-life dreams
derivations and representations of these conflicted
and confused, repressed, hurt and hostile feelings

we have every right to put in their place those
trying to play cruel brutal games with our fate


anti-proof:

They just drain you how they try to keep you feeling guilty
and angry while ironically don't have an ounce of integrity


anti-proof:

If people once had the integrity
and character to take responsibility
for their own actions as opposed to
the satire (and all that time put in and
invested for their built-in bullshit excuses)
or what the history of culture & civilization
is built on think what a better world we'd live in


anti-proof:

Attitude should work a little harder
in having a little less attitude or do i
have that backwards really doesn't matter


proof:

The wisdom i have gotten from strangers
(from real life thieves and hustlers on the road)
so much more than what'ya call one of those very
formal higher educations which was so full of shit
and contradictions has just made me so restless
and reactive and naturally act-out and hit the road
and find the true-blue soul through forms of escapism


proof:

Real diversity is experience (while what eventually comes
along with it is the ability to have empathy and compassion)

proof:

Coincidence rarely comes by coincidence
while usually from periods and reasons
far more deeper and accurate


proof:

The true man of wisdom (and intuition) is like the thief
who knows all your moves before you try to pull them


proof:

The true artist has always been something
of a fugitive on-the-run somewhere between
his intuition and what he's created and done

he in some way shape or form has
known this ever since he was young



147

Criminal always felt like a criminal
way before he became a criminal


proof 1

My god after experiencing the trauma of a
dysfunctional family unit one spends the rest
of their existence whether aware of it or not
trying to escape it or get out on good behavior

proof 2

More often than not the primal creature
does not appear to remember, yet also
profoundly more than likely not forget


proof 3

People will only tell you so much about themselves
while interestingly find myself disinterested in that as well


proof 4

Perfect metaphor for bureaucracy and authority
i ran into my mail lady and for some strange reason
felt the need to try and impress her or gain her approval
and told her we just put in a new mailbox because it got
all bent out of shape during the winter, while she very
casually, matter-of-factly responded that it didn't look
like it was the official height as didn't quite know how
to really respond to that and almost reacted like
a kid might getting disciplined explaining how
hard we worked on getting it into the ground
and guess in certain ways my old man was
right that they just don't stop or never quite
seem satisfied until you are six feet under…


proof 5

Trying to get on in this life seems very much like
when you pick up some film right from the middle
and don't know exactly what happened previously
with your instinctive ability to repress and deny and
compartmentalize to find how it all ends is very much
like how it all began and how sometimes those strange
and sudden experiences (plot twists and turns) of trauma
play such a profound role in unconsciously influencing
the mood and ambiance of this absurd tragic drama

proof 6

When we get older it becomes much lonelier
to travel for all the implications it has to our
mortality (everything in the past and future,
personal losses, and natural nostalgia) denial
becomes a little harder; the distance between
there and our perceived imagined sanctuary

proof 7

I find the closer i get to my mortality
the murder rate of what they do to you
in this life (how they wear you down with
their runarounds and constant bullshit excuses)
how much more i am able to relate to and appreciate
the true-blue conflicts and issues of those who seem to
have been through it too let's say like a humphrey bogart

you get to a certain point in your life
with the craziness of it all and knowing
what you're about where you develop
something of a code where you honestly
don't give a damn what happens anymore
and if you drop dead right there on the spot

proof 8

Doesn't it seem those days you were a bit more drunken in bars
how much easier it was to pick off people's silly straight roles?

proof 9

Those who question your sense of humor and just don't get it
in my estimation are the personification of 'the criminal' and far
more dangerous with their need for such proclamations and persecution

the humorless leave so much 'to be desired'…

proof 10

The real true-blue comedian stands alone
in the dust of his punchlines and mortality
trying for some reason to keep the masses
laughing and happy yet will still always return
tragically solitary alone to his profound suffering

proof 11

One becomes "famous" (which kerouac said is 'like an
old newspaper blowing down bleeker street') somehow
strangely surrounded by a whole new scene of strangers
and idiots who simultaneously worship, while due to
human nature try to steal every chance they can get
and to a certain extent (the public and critics) expect
you to be 'on your best behavior' (some sort of projected
caricature) and at the same time the pillar of morals and
ethics (to say 'life is stranger than fiction' would be an
understatement) but it was this necessary and desperate
rebellion which got them to this exact position with a certain
amount of introspection, insight, independent thinking and
persistence; courage is not just in one's conviction but also
fighting an absurd and unjust and cruel rigid system; so what
is one simply supposed to do now? bow their head and give in?
inextricably, put in constant raging conflict, thus in essence, all
one can really do is contemplate and reflect, pretty much ironically
the exact same cognitive dynamics that got them there in the first
place; everything comes full circle and comes back to haunt them
in a sort of ridiculous and distant, sentimental, maddening way...

proof 12

To me it came as no shock that jesus
got nailed to the cross, as that type of
betrayal and bullshit happens on a daily
basis and what the humans refer to as
their routine and ritual and daily activities
of their everyday functioning. what i find
even more shocking though was the apathetic

demeanor and instant change of allegiance
and convenient amnesia at however it worked
to their advantage after he represented and went
all out for them, and no one even thinking of
helping him get down from there. right after
this brutal and barbaric slaying and sacrifice
and slaughter the humans started organized
religion which presented almost as a rationalization
or intellectualization for all their guilt and conflict
from a very safe and secure distance; here come
the lawyers and life insurance salesmen, as our
dreams are something of a manifestation of the
'fight or flight syndrome' running away from
all the mean people and couldn't feel more alone.
the recording over the phone repeats itself over
and over again–"thank you for your patience...
a home depot representative will be with you
shortly" going into the 15$^{th}$ 16$^{th}$ 17$^{th}$ minute
while you hear a loud staticy version of
"everybody wants to rule the world..."


proof 13

They sometimes look at you so parasitic and hostile
as if you stole something from them and were some
sort of criminal or some leftover punch line to a false
rumor, but by this exact selfsame ridiculous dynamic
if they only knew how truly lost and delusional they were
like some insular, pathetic, petty microcosm of the masses

these people seem to thrive at weddings and
funerals and don't treat them much different


proof 14

They'll make certain claims about your personality
but know when you first got married used to send cards
out to them for every season even with good looking pictures
of your kid but when did you ever once receive a card from them?

and this is whom you wish to
so desperately gain approval?


proof 15

It's a perplexing thing about human nature
those deemed and given the reputation of
being the most honest with integrity when
it comes down to the nitty-gritty in real life
are so far from it and close to the opposite
while those constantly doubted and not trusted
interestingly, the ones who may very well be
the most loyal, reliable, and go all out for you


proof 16

Most people's judgments are simply projections
(an active form of transference and displacement
or one's 'superficial' or impulsive belief system on
to a representative individual) of past experiences
they feel included (made to feel a part of and keen
sense of belonging) or alienated (deliberately and
cruelly excluded with unresolved hurt and damage)


proof 17

People (through human nature) seem
determined to make other's lives miserable
why don't they teach us any of this in school
with classes on bob dylan, bukowski, baudelaire,
camus, nietzsche, wilhelm reich, la rochefoucald


proof 18

We feel the full scope and emotion (and depth) of loneliness
way after the horror and trauma of its instinctive experience

proof 19

Loneliness never ever really wears off
except when with a loved one which somehow
gives the impression of saving and rising above


proof 20

Those who habitually do things solely
at their own convenience have convinced
themselves (through some ridiculous form
of rationalization, as well as maladaptive
thinking of something grandiose or sacred,
even a bit delusional, pompous and pretentious)
of a certain type of significance (which has not
been earned) and by those selfsame dynamics
give themselves far more credit than they deserve


proof 21

Remember in middle school or high school
when you like made the exact same spelling
error or something similar in a second language
and the teacher made the effort to show genuine fairness
and sympathy and compassion and said i won't take off
or penalize you all those times because it just happened
to be the exact same faux-pas and wonder if we can find any
time in our later life where that ever went down or materialized?


proof 22

All these guys in their later life tell me how
they found jesus or love (like door to door
salesmen where i have absolutely no interest
in their product or what they have to offer)
and act and play the role of some sort of
messenger or martyr but if you only knew
their record and all the drama and lives

they've destroyed in the interim and
madness and mishegoss that got them
there makes me also want to down a beer


proof 23

Man is infamous for/giving out advice thinking
they're being so helpful and insightful and will
recommend and even swear by it (which you
wish they wouldn't) of specific chiropractors,
acupuncturists, behaviorists, physical therapists,
aroma, art, animal therapy while it's all some kind
of "big schmooze" and literally 'who you know'
for the kids like some distorted form of country
club nepotism for anger management, as all
the same delinquents in the same suburb
and school district (due to emotional,
psychological, and spiritual neglect)
ironically end up seeing the exact
same therapist for group therapy
(thus once more stigmatized and
humiliated) as if they are almost
creating their own country club
for the lost and forgotten yet
has it ever been thought of
or considered in providing
the most down to earth and
intuitive support and guidance
on how to find just for the short
while a little slice of happiness
or how to survive all the bullshit
of the maddening, erratic behavior
or mankind who rarely ever follow through
on any of their words, conviction, and promises?

proof 24

O my god! mon dieu! how one has to fight so hard to gain
their freedom, but the ironic twist and social and cultural
paradox when you get there (due to the pettiness of human
nature and the greed of ambition) seems futilely, absurdly
(ironically, illusory) as many hypocrisies and restrictions


proof 25

Man is so adept in acting-out and being angry
but does he ever once step back and reflect and
question why he's always full of rage and blaming?


proof 26

All those burnouts not as liberal
as you may very well think…


proof 27

Please take off
your door by the shoes, blues
zookeeper attacks zookeeper…


proof 28

Where is god and if not
who is watching my
fucked-up life while
hope they're enjoying
the hot-buttered popcorn
yiddish was created as a
secret dialogue to keep
away from the czar

"don't hock me in chinick…"

proof 29

Inferiority complex…is that one of those oxymorons?
just sayin' mean just asking you know what i'm sayin!


proof 30

What does it mean to be taken seriously
i never really wanted to be taken seriously
cause then you're sort of stuck with all those
very serious people who have a tendency to
take things way too seriously which includes
you and them and all of those other little things
which never really wanted to take too seriously


proof 31

Real humanity is trying to dig just a little bit deeper
with instinct and intuition and intellect and compassion


proof 32

God damn! doesn't life just sometimes seem
like an interminable neverending dress rehearsal
for a play you ain't even sure they're gonna 'put on?'

(you keep on getting promises
from producers and backers
who never return your calls)


proof 33

Don't think i ever was able to get raskolnikov
out of my system and used to read all that kind
of stuff whenever i'd runaway from home to my
aunt's home in the suburbs with green velvet
walls pristine immaculate tiles and mirrors

all over while used to really love to read
depressing shit like that to pick me up

think i did that as well for "nausea"
nietzsche freud wittgenstein spinoza


proof 34

Symbolism with all its triggers, curses, implications
is the shit that really fucks you up like a nightmare
turned inside-out trying to figure out the difference
and results between coincidence and fate and all
its hateful influences and obstacles while people
just don't seem to mind their own business
yet still somehow in some shape or form able
to stagger through this thing we call existence
while the surreal and slapstick (which usually
comes from a place pretty traumatic and tragic)
not always so humorous and a real fine line
between the dream and nightmare and such
terms like 'expectations' 'happily ever after'


proof 35

If i had it all over to do again
i'd do it all over again do it
all over again do it all over
again 'cause in fact really
did nothing wrong to begin
with in the first place (matter
of fact had the instincts and
intuition to pick up all their
bullshit) and had absolutely
nothing to do with good
or bad or right or wrong
or any one those predictable
obvious elements or morals
and ethics and still just waiting
to be picked up from the library

proof 36

At the end of life the writer has very little identity
to speak of yet more so all the characters he has
created while what proves to be far more important
than being "famous" is shaking the foundation a little
influencing changing the thought-pattern of the masses


proof 37

I think i have always been something
of a natural exhibitionist (not in its most
crude and vulgar sense) welcoming and
receptive, self-conscious and sensitive
to all forms of ignorance and indifference
one becomes a thief at a very young age…


proof 38

Romance (the chance or threat of it
however you wanna look at it) is about
the best one can hope for for this sad lot of humans


proof 39

The best thing about growing up
in those neighborhoods were all
those pleasant gossip and rumors
tinged with a little truth little false
hoods the old timers hanging out
at social clubs on the corner and
the daughters turning into real life
angels at dusk on the river the only
way able to get any sleep was with
an ole coffee can of iced tea before
hit the full moon futon on the floor

proof 40

On the internet whenever they show hotels
with their quota of token conference rooms
with their rows of chairs and tables and big
screen tv's (i suppose to impress the business
people) they always look like those great big
vast empty areas when astronauts took off
in those sci-fi films for the future and you
stop to think a little bit about it and wonder
and reflect is it really that much different
knowing the nature and element of the mass
mentality cookie-cutter conformist salesman?
whenever i see these configurations in the effort
to try and impress that type of guest i always
move on to the next as could never stand that
very cut-throat competitive classless population
who thrive off a certain mean-spirited soulless
alienation think they refer to them as climbers?

proof 41

The people and things that people choose
to be loyal (and faithful) to all for like the
sake of the company or country or cause
is the sign of a weak and ridiculous blind
follower as more times than not ironically
breaks and betrays all the core moral and
ethical values, principles, and rules (they
believe they are so nobly obeying and
swearing to) and never once even go
so far as to think or consider (which
is almost a crime in itself) to question
or ponder the clear contradictions and
hypocrisies of policy (often simply
adopted for convenient self-interested
and litigious placating reasons) and how
in fact in the long-run actually pathetically
ends up hurting and harming everyone all around

proof 42

There is an interesting phenomenological
and paradoxical pattern in human nature
that all those constant liars of existence
will make you experience the instant
psychodynamic of profoundly 'questioning
yourself' and how it does such severe damage
(even shatters) your identity (having manipulated
and taken advantage) making you feel like *you*
are the one who is the liar while in the long-run
'punishing' (yourself) being so hard on yourself


proof 43

All those people whose job it is (usually in administration)
to make assessments and evaluations and conclusions
trust me if you really get to know them and really knew
what went on behind closed doors; the backstabbing
and breaking of confidences and hypocrisies and
contradictions and cruel mean-spirited vulgar inside
jokes usually coming at the expense of their own
employees, ironically in fact the ones doing all
the tireless work in the trenches (while comes
natural as they feel privileged and entitled with
the other heads of departments and in the long-
run will face absolutely no natural consequences)
and paradoxically break practically every code of
morals and ethics and thus realize without hesitation
who the real violators and criminals (and thieves) are


proof 44

Almost every time i have tried to do the right
and responsible thing by seeking guidance or
support from let's say someone like a supervisor
or for that matter human resources i have found
myself more so instantly resistant and frustrated
as could tell right away did not have the instincts

or intuition or even humanity or street knowledge
to really help me out with my problem as ironically
triggered and exacerbated it by breaking all forms
of trust and confidence(s) and promises on a spiritual
and literal level and ended up becoming more the victim

proof 45

It's amazing the employees who are given
second, third, even fourth chances. they like
to refer to this dynamic as 'in-house' or 'intra-
department,' as there are those who are not even
given a first, while ironically have so much more
to offer with merit, skills, intuition, and experience

proof 46

We often give far too much credence and glamorize certain people
but if we ever once really made the effort to get to know those
others working in the trenches, as opposed to just the ones who
often ('make it a living') use the "con" art of nepotism (no real
experience or independent thinkers) way up in administration

proof 47

With that infamous fucked-up board of trustees who i wouldn't trust
as far as i can throw them and their insular, all-knowing exclusivity
who you ironically never ever really see, like some false gods, self-
congratulatory, usually more often than not, overcompensating due
to some form of previous unresolved guilt and conflict, and through
their self-entitled virtue and good deeds (these soulless cut-throats
or 'old money' retirees) looking to be perversely worshiped
(preserving reputations) while at the same time redeemed

proof 48

It's interesting as well as ironic and befuddling
how the hard-working employees never get to
meet or for that matter see the infamous board
of trustees who like false gods of nepotism make
all the final decisions and assert all their authority


proof 49

Likewise all those infamous boards (zoning, condo,
trustees, yeah you name them!) of false omniscience
(which seem more like something of sexless old money
than anything of quality or merit) who-you-know self-
absorbed forms of alienation (where in very subtle exclusive
ways of self-absorption always strangely comes back to be
about them) their constant functions and celebrations of quasi-
'virtue' and 'morals and ethics' overcompensating in the form
of archetypal philanthropic causes (but if you ever knew what
really went down in their nuclear family unit; the history of
emotional, psychological, and spiritual abuse playing diametrically
polar opposite roles in how they desire to be viewed in their culture
and psychosocial environment would sicken you) while once you
figure them out and get through their mandated prerequisite tribunal
of questioning just seem so obvious and full of nepotism (control freak
conventions of self-interest and attention-seeking) and lose instant
interest (and respect) in having to get their approval and consent in
becoming a subservient member of their punitive pusillanimous group


proof 50

Most people detest and loathe the white-collar criminal
and swindler not having so much to do with principle
but that they were able to keep the secret and pull
off the act better, and even deep down, resentful and
jealous as were able to thrive and make a living off it

proof 51

Even 'the anarchists' are full of shit (more often than
not a bunch of rich spoiled kids with enough downtime
who can afford it) and just as self-serving and self-
interested, manipulative, and take advantage (while
eventually find in the long-run not exactly so trustworthy)
as those supposed institutions (ironically becoming as much
'an industry') they claim to so vociferously be railing against

proof 52

The signs seem too clever and the people seem too well-dressed
at protests in america these days heck i even remember working
one of these really long grueling graveyard shifts at a bookstore
in soho in the sweltering summer and this spoiled girl showing
up early for some sort of strike or another with her sign at the
ready already with the little orange cones staked out and very
practically and proactively conveniently taking out her smart
phone (in the middle of the orange cones) and very casual
and comfortable ordering take-out (to that exact part of the
block) think it might have been something like a kale salad
with a smoothie and believe it or not protesting something
like the gentrification of the neighborhood a place she never
grew up to eventually look very good on her activist resume

proof 53

The history of man shows absolutely no behavioral pattern
(the effort or inclination) towards the desire or ability and
potential of intelligent and insightful communication
no wonder why with the history of civilization
so many battles and revolutions, while what
a brutal and brutish way towards resolution
and when they conquer and take over and
divide up new tracts of land and countries
doesn't seem like really a whole heck of
a lot ameliorated, learned, and resolved

as ironically and not by coincidence, new
governments more fanatical and authoritarian

148

We lead these ridiculous lives like curators of wax museums
with paint-by-number forests bleeding outside our window
and rubber cement smokestacks swirling over miraculous
industrial bridges right where they keep the out-of-work
jugglers and drug dealers and half-crazed ushers who
are really romantics and simply did not want to follow
in their fathers' footsteps as salesmen as feels like her
deception happened only yesterday, but amazingly you
moved on immediately, like a puppet finally at last with
out strings attached rowing down the ferocious swollen
rivers of spring through keen fluttering golden leaves
of the season flooding and nourishing the fields where
young virginal girls like saints in sundresses tilled and
the delinquents rode off on their bicycles at sundown.
they took down the corner diner the other day which
seemed something of a sin, but you being a survivor
will simply find a whole other way of being with a
brilliant bleak type of ambiance, somewhere between
the creaky town, cobblestone alleys, blinking, bleary-eyed
candelabras, boxcar diners, runaway raconteurs, labyrinths
and steeples set flush against the anatomy of the mountains

sound of faraway familiar trains bring you back
to life again and the seagulls have grown wiser


proof #1

What breaks your heart at a relatively young age
is when you discover practically everyone's a liar
(nothing makes you feel more alone and isolated)

and have to almost figure out who will offer
the most love and passion while bringing
about the least amount of damage

proof #2

Does anyone ever really shake off a best friend
or brother's jealousy and envy leading them to
do such cruel things as still so difficult to believe
(or conceive) anyone can be so malicious and mean
(justifying practically everything) to want to do such things


proof #3

That lazy cliche expression "at least you got your health"
always comes in periods of your greatest hell (which only
makes you feel more lonely and angry; really got nobody)
while couldn't care less whether you got your health or not

tomorrow's another day means nothing as well...


proof #4

The apathetic firing squad working second jobs
aim their arms right at you kneeling on the ground
from an eternal guilt and crime you still know
absolutely not what you did nor are guilty of


proof #5

Those who have deliberately emotionally neglected
a dear ole past friend who have shared many close
memories and experiences (and been there for them
in mind body spirit and soul) to a certain extent are
guilty of a 'crime against man' as when it comes
down to the nitty-gritty cannot be rationalized
or explained away with any of those convenient
pithy sayings from the fake and phony of bullshit
and betrayal who always have a built-in excuse
and never take any responsibility pathetically
pretending with their reverse-psychology
like self-righteously had some right to it

proof #6

Wow! there are some people
who have never once apologized
what fictional and absurd ridiculous lives!


proof #7

Too many men will choose to lie first
(if we can even say that much and go
through the process) than to tell the truth
as literally have no idea at the concept of
communication for purposes of clarification
and to resolve a conflict as appear to literally
have a cognitive disconnect, never taught it
(passed down from generation to generation)
or pure absurd male stubbornness and ignorance


proof #8

God anyone can be indifferent
takes absolutely no strength
or courage or creativity at all
i've seen more on a billboard!


proof #9

Those who always appear angry
are the opportunists who could
not quite fully take advantage


proof #10

Jealousy and envy is as obvious and predictable
as a letter of recommendation from your enemies

proof #11

I swear trying to survive marriage
is like working a 9-5 at some
costume shop trying on
different disguises
in a state of denial


proof #12

Sometimes seems the institution of marriage
certain partners only feel alive and they exist
if they bicker and quarrel and power-struggle
and care nothing necessarily about clarification
or communication like some kafkaesque hostage
crisis with constant demands never quite sure
what they want or will satisfy them in the end

which feels a lot like that ridiculous
repetitive description of what hell is

at least with those one-night stands
they seemed (and gave the impression
opened the imagination) they gave a damn


proof #13

People are just lonesome and suffer and that's a fact
and more times than not are not even aware of it
(as have just gotten so used to the emptiness)
and the only thing that can possibly heal or
cure it is the potential of (the concept of) love
or something romantic or gives the impression
(or fantasy or illusion) or resemblance that
someone might actually care or give a damn
about them which for the moment (with this sense
of 'eternal belonging') feels like the best feeling in the
world of being reborn without ever having existed before

proof #14

It is paramount to remember your past visions
of your dreams for the future; everything
in between lacks insight and intuition


proof #15

When one speaks of the spiritual concept
and configuration of intuition because it
empirically deals with natural instincts,
something both physiological while also
philosophical and metaphysical, and the
core essence of spirit it can never really
be used for purposes of self-interest or
to try and gain an advantage due to its
pure subliminal (other world, ethereal)
and absolute, contemplative nature


proof #16

Confidence is highly overrated…


proof #17

Almost everything that gets glamorized
you realize because in fact it did not
meet your needs or desires the first time


proof #18

Almost all forms of good judgment
(insightful and objective) stem and come
from pretty poor overwhelming circumstances

proof #19

On the nature of the spirit of inanimate objects
when you put just enough contemplation into it
or absolutely none at all when you think about it


proof #20

Practicality is the remains
of crisis and craziness…
a sort of reverse sublimation


proof #21

Some of those suburbs you lived in
where it was a struggle just to get out
of bed and go to bed you would be hard
pressed to prove the existential question
that you even existed or felt very much like
pre-columbus times of some long awful never
ending dragstrip stripmall with this ridiculous
desolate postmodern landscape where in fact
the world might as well of just been flat (its
dead ends and cul-de-sacs; a strange surreal
static seething forest behind that) while all
its inhabitants had fallen off way before that


proof #22

Culture and civilization eventually in the long-run
is a cross or fine line between the truth and lie
very sober-minded and those in desperate
need of sobriety, excess and idiocy
and the higher-than-holy and thief

proof #23

Even the radio dj's these days have become critics
wish they'd just shut their mouths and play the music


proof #24

Does not existence in retrospect
and the long-run just seem like
being woken up in the middle
of one of those lonely dreams?


proof #25

May heaven be like one of those good libraries
where they used to whisper and leave you alone
those lone brooks babbling through pachysandra


proof #26

The delinquent was really the good son…


proof #27

Your son tells you very modest and
humble about what he did in the pool
that day; how he finally jumped off the high
dive as he got inspired with his pal just standing
right there on the level below which motivated him
to just leap off and then casually happened to mention
how he thought this may have even felt more important
than graduating middle school and reflected about this
image a little and thought how can one really argue?

proof #28

Life humbles you while ironically
(psycho-dynamically) end up
spending the rest of it searching
for one true-blue humble individual


proof #29

The way white people (the snob
and slob) stare at you when you
walk into the barroom and pool
(they all look at you like you stole
something from them; a sign and
symptom of envy and jealousy and
live lives of such self-pity and petty
and with their preconceived notions
of reality with their insular and insecure
being of delusional and sweeping false
truths) i don't know could just never
be that way as always was so much
more interested and grateful in just
what maybe they had on the menu

the tourist is useless (aloof and arrogant
alienating the native, while ironically
desperately pathetically searching
for meaning and purpose)


proof #30

They know (not what they do not know...)
and either hide or blame to put on a show

proof #31

Eccentric's really not so much a gimmick or imitation
or obsessive need for attention-seeking but just trying
to get on in this life with all the suffering and struggling


proof #32

If you do not quit and give up on this existence
eventually you find it's all just like some grand card
trick with a couple secrets and quick moves figuring
out the bullshit of the schmooze behind the illusions


proof #33

Watch out! beware! the status-quo who have conveniently
because they felt comfortable labeling him as a 'bad boy'
 "can't keep himself out of trouble," the 'at risk' child
might very well have a heart of gold and be something
of a real-life martyr if give him the chance and opportunity
and might even in fact go all out for you when in real dire
need, while all those lovely good deed doing volunteers
(with their ulterior motives, driven, opportunistic, some-
times sexually frigid, or stemming from a guilty conscious
not always quite as welcoming as that image would want
to have you believe) coming from privileged communities
and a heck of a lot of advocating and false advertising


proof #34

College inspired me to drop out and give up on life
(with all its really soulless obnoxious spoiled brats
of nepotism and connections from the tri-state area)
and get into the real world and get experience and
really write, which i started to do with true-blue
passion and passing observations at midnight right
on my electronic taxi paper receipts for passengers
watching the constant state of flux (on so many levels)

and the madness of half-crazed insane humanity like
that flickering taper whose damaged soul told us all
about the fine line between the illusory image and
carnage of what really went down in the real world


proof #35

You know you've finally made it (not sure what the hell
that means) and are a real-life adult when contractors
(no pun intended) drive you up the wall and have a
constant attitude or infamously don't return calls
and have to advocate to death and be as sensitive
as possible (due to that very fragile male ego)

that it's all just 5/8$^{th}$'s of an inch short
feeling like some strange surreal subtle
grand metaphor for your time on earth


proof #36

Considering the psychological hx of
man's impulsive and erratic behavior
and character one might look at culture
and civilization as a certain kind of fool's
gold before & after the sacrifice & slaughter


proof #37

Technicolor finally colored in the beige 'flesh-colored'
scenes and faces with melodramatic shades; made
the deep shallow and vice-versa leaping right off
the deep end into the mysterious melancholia
manicured beauty and tragedy and drama of
suburbia with a behavioral pattern and plotline
and reality and self-fulfilling prophecy which
couldn't help but implode and turn self-destructive
everything which went on behind closed doors in late
50's early 60's shangrila life of leisure caucasia america

proof #38

Skylines have become too obvious
modern monochromatic hollow
neat & tidy in america

for example we used to really
know where we were when we were
in ol' new york & ol' san francisco…


proof #39

Anyone doing anything 'bout global warming?
people have been assassinated for far less
how the fly struggles everyday just to get
up my window to take his last breath
and of this i am far more sympathetic


proof #40

The hx of america…
after all the brainwash
and abuses of power
finally fighting back
against mccarthey
exclaiming–"sir do
have no decency!"
fragile falling like
humpty-dumpty
out of the hand
of citizen kane


proof #41

I view the president of the united states
of america as like one of those lounge
singers sitting at a piano whose job it
is to calm and assuage all the damaged

and broken down souls and those who
i think were some of the best at what
they did were barack obama, john f.
kennedy, dwight d. eisenhower, f.d.r.
and abraham lincoln as think spoke
the best and made the effort to
address all the concerns and
conflicts of the suffering status-
quo playing rounds and rounds
of cool jazz piano during some
pretty rough times while in between
having the ability and charm to comfort
them with compassion, sympathy, sense
of humor and fine flickering fireside chatter

said mayor laguardia during a major newspaper
strike actually read the funnies over the radio…


proof #42

Politics is like a bad cult with a souvenir shop
which sells manufactured tchotchkes that glorify
slaughter all in the name of patriotism and religion

a human resources department where
you know you know far more and got
far more experience than the interviewer

you're lucky if your neighbor or babysitter
or fellow worker ever return your books
you lent them on domestic animals and

artists and guide books to central america
while human nature precludes you got to
even ask them like a subway stuck under

ground during the sweltering summer having
forgotten you repeating over and over again–
"thank you for your patience…thank you for…"

proof #43

eg: if you only knew how the clean-cut
bible salesman and vacuum salesman
(who 'pray' on you) are pretty much

the exact same people trying to sell you
and take advantage of your fragile feelings
of self-loathing and low self-esteem and guilt

and feeling filthy offering and guaranteeing
you a life where you may once more feel happy
and clean (doing good deeds) virtuous and redeemed


proof #44

Don't know if i'm starting to become
a bit like my half-crazed mother-in-law
while for the first time ever this morning
found myself getting into neil diamond
as actually felt had a damn good spiritual
soulful voice and was crooning and belting
something about 'pack up the babies and
grab the old ladies…hallelujah' on the
oldies…not put a bullet in your brain
morning radio station; maybe tonight
for supper will have brisket and orzo


proof #45

Compare the absolute statements of
the child and adult of "let's pretend"
which tends to imply a whole heck
of a lot of harmless and hopeful
imagination and the free will and
volition towards an active kind
of escapism against the coy and
playing possum conviction of–
"i've heard" which is something

of perverse, random, false facts
skewed, distorted perception
whispers, gossip and rumor


proof #46

A child always proves us wrong when we are so sure
to absurdly logically try to question their imagination


proof #47

One of the best feelings when you found out
through a best friend of hers one of the cutest
most *beautifulest* girls in the grade below me
liked me and got me through all those awful
miserable workouts in lacrosse and heart
literally leaping out through my uniform
able to instantly shake off all my worries
and concerns in the bleak brutal blue dusk
of autumn think were playing bruce in the
locker room and able to feel every single
one of his heartfelt romantic passionate
words incredible how those sentiments
and emotions can just sort of somehow
stay with you even like 40 years later

fair to say how romance can save you…


proof #48

Most individuals or supposed groups or cultures
who like to self-promote or advertise or refer to
themselves as 'anarchists' suffer from some form
of previous emotional or spiritual abuse and have
severe damage and a cognitive disconnect from
the false morals and ethics (constant contradictions
and hypocrisies) of an impossible overbearing authority
figure who took advantage or was supposed to in some

shape or form take care of them (thus on an unconscious
or similar psychodynamic level lost all belief and trust
in those selfsame social systems) and for the most
part are in a continual state of flux, denial, or some
form of 'avoidance' without even being aware of it


proof #49

Looking back growing up the kids
deemed smart just seemed like
a bunch of kiss asses who were
overconfident with good study habits
while in retrospect i think the ones
i learned the most from just couldn't
seem to keep themselves out of trouble


proof #50

It has always been so much more easy
and more believable for me ironically
to take advice literally from someone
on-the-run looking over their shoulder
than one of those individuals very safe
and secure and stable who speak always in
antecdotes and very little about coping or survival


proof #51

The real true-blue rebel is one who
cannot ask for help and with courage
and conviction heads determined to his
destination trying to maintain his dream
and vision while taking on every obstacle
and challenge they throw in his direction

proof #52

Would it be so wrong to write an erotic
poem about all that lovely pussy pretty
plumes of blonde brunette red & peach
releasing delicate panties and exposing
its deep secrets seeming on fire some
times just smoldering after not having
been touched for awhile but like some
thief-explorer still can't help but
to be in a state of awe and admire
that fragile pot of gold at the end
of the rainbow the lost & found
holy grail and when you ain't
got it feels like days weeks
months years without mail
and when you do suddenly
spiritually let out of jail
wondering how the hell
you even got in there and
nothing seems more real


proof #53

These
daze
i feel
some
thing
like a
cross
between
a clown
& jesus
& pretty
much
end up
ironically
not by
coincidence

hysterical
which one
really not
sure nor
really think
makes much
of a difference
or for that matter
particularly relevant


proof #54

The natural proclamation
of–"what an idiot i am!"
are all those false accusations
is how she just couldn't save you
is how she couldn't make you happy
is one of those origami fortune
cookies you made as a kid
which opened and closed
with different options
to try and figure it all
out and make sense
and determine your future
is both a love & hate letter
that cannot be translated
where you cannot make
a distinction because
all comes from the
exact same passion
and desperation
is the
difference
between
denial
and one's
destination
is a confession
fallen on deaf ears
is a damaged vase

of a dozen dried-up
wilted wildflowers


proof #55

When i meet the moronic contractor
as they're all just a bunch of fucken
phonies and liars and never get back
to you with their omniscient estimates
(somewhere between ex-convicts
and wannabe false prophets)
gonna flip the table on him
and ask him if he can do real
downhome demo and remove
this sweatshirt and undershirt
i've been wearing for ages
can he smooth me out like
some piece of clay being
molded on the potter's wheel
and get me back to boyhood
when he rebuilds our patio
can he also build a sculpture
of that old timer stripped down
to his skeleton strumming guitar
by picasso during his blue period
can he remove all traces of all that
disgraceful bullshit which just builds
up in existence that just makes
you want to give up and quit
makes you sad and solemn
and second guess your identity
all of those proclamations and
broken promises with a mantle
full of mai-tai's and those fine
tiny bamboo umbrellas can he
make grape leaves and potato
salad and baklava and pick up
a 16 pack of *milwaukee's best*
at the *sunoco* on the corner right
around when the sun goes down?

proof #56

You want to be comfortable or close enough
with your partner cute as a button when she
gives a great big yawn and go what are you
catching flies and she instantly retorts being
from the bronx grabbing her crotch after your
nonstop kvetching and complaining have you
grown a vagina must be that time of the month

we met in our second year of internship at that
mental health clinic under the el on jerome avenue…


proof #57

Marriage is forgetting
a mood ring on the night
table of *the holiday inn*
but happy at least probably
that nice kind young french
housekeeper probably's got it
at the bottom of her blue pocket
grateful and glowing and knowing
what it's like to really suffer yet graceful
remaining classy and modest and humble
more than likely getting better use out of it

you're pissed cause you forgot to tip
the arabic bellboys who were real good guys
and your wife asks why does it matter so much
while for this exact reason impossible to explain why


proof #58

Best thing can be said
                         by a son–
     "mom don't ride dad so hard
       he needs to listen
to his music"

          as she pokes  
her head in  
    & all that's seen  
      is silhouetted figure  
              like some  
     phantom of the opera  
beethoven jesus  
         weeping  
            something  
                 they'll never get  
   but when you're good & gone  
hopefully one day respect


proof #59

On your deathbed you want  
you wife's last words to be  
"you made great barbecue  
chicken" and go off smiling


proof #60

I hope on judgment  
day i'm allowed  
to have a couple  
defense attorneys  
cause if they only  
knew what i had  
to deal with on  
a day by day  
basis…that  
ol' negro  
spiritual  
of "can i  
get a witness"

proof #61

It is in periods when we feel vulnerable, fragile, on the brink
(the need and desire) that we start to really connect
and believe the photos and pictures on our wall


proof #62

Man to a certain extent always
returning home from war to a
strange surreal town he cannot
quite relate to or make sense of


proof #63

The history of the world is the pain & suffering
& anguished expression of some ancient pharaoh
greek philosopher sorrowful slapstick tragic jew
from vaudeville throwing his hands up in the
air 'cause just had it & can't take it no mo'
old timer retired merchant marine sicilian
fading away reflective thoughtful in front
of brownstone all a cross between *what ya'
gonna do* & *what's matta' ya* the nonstop
invasion & violation of boundaries & borders
& sacrifice & slaughter all for the sake of
religion & culture; how many real-life wars
(which could have been avoided) with purges
murdering masses by the millions by megalomaniac
madmen of maladaptive thinking & a penchant for
manipulation all under the guise (those guys) of patriotism
having them share in the collective delusional mission
kids rebelling cause just get so sick of hearing the same
ol' bullshit lecture like broken records of parents repeating
themselves over & over & over again & due to this brow-
beating behavior becoming klutzes or self-destructive with
their own built-in private self-fulfilling prophecies without
even being aware of it often developing drug problems
(for purposes of instant escapism) not caring if they live

or die caught somewhere between the bar & connection
& repressing & eventual complete lack of communication
not treating their partners very well taking them for granted
with similar actions & traits & characteristics while hard
to fathom how any of them even made it or lasted this long

who's got the biggest destroyer in port...


proof #64

Superman got lied & betrayed & nailed to the cross
also with his heart ripped out by the girl he loved
& the corrupt cops & government & his lawyer &
agent after he went all out for them which now has
just become a tourist trap for aloof arrogant asshole
tourists taking the exact same smartphone shots with
their obnoxious spoiled brats who never shut the fuck
up or seem satisfied or grateful with those thematic
hotels called things like *atlantis...paradise...shangrila*
with their token waterslides & waterfalls & that whole
band of starving traveling actors from the dinner theater
swallowing fire & doing their melodramatic renditions
of *the king & i sound of music & jesus christ superstar*
while his tormented prefabricated image gets placed
on placemats & plates & playing cards & candy bars
t-shirts & snowglobes being sold in souvenir shops as
reenactments to capture the moment & remember him by


proof #65

Tourists take great pride in being exactly alike...


proof #66

All the tourist motels lie on the outskirts of town
while the pretty country girls with abusive boyfriends
work as front desk clerks, slaves to absentee aristocratic
owners and will go all out for them, who sense this and

subliminally take advantage of them just like the soulless
guests, thus in effect are the true-blue saints and martyrs


proof #67

Whenever supposed authorities are 'suspiciously'
stopping to check my id. to prove my identity
i always find something real absurd and ironic
and funny, like exactly what has been proven so
suddenly and what has specifically changed in order
to allow me to continue to move on (in my reality);
some from past histories of subjugation and being
brow-beaten will even formally thank them or give
that infamous 'sigh of relief' when strangely enough
these figures of authority (who abuse power and try
to confuse and make you cower through backwards
forms of bizarre lines of questioning, mean-spirited
interrogation and sadistic reverse-psychology) want
to try to desperately make you feel sorry and guilty


proof #68

People will try to break you down as swear
can't remember the last honorable man who
has kept their word and wonder why they
even make those absurd and predictable
offers in the first place as can tell by
the look on their face and what they
are saying or what they are not saying
are overcompensating, like insincere
cookie-cutter salesmen reading straight
off the script (fill in the blank) who live
to placate and will just naturally manipulate
and try to twist the truth (something they
apparently have never known unless some
form of incentive or natural consequences)
working to their advantage; why i have always
turned to lovers and traveling and the seasons

proof #69

When the melting snows come flowing down the mountain
it turns all the rivers raging and gives them real character
like the first hollywood silent home movies and pictures
from the safari, grace kelly's wedding (as she sincerely
knew how to wave and already seemed like royalty)
had nothing to do during the day in that insane
castle beneath the decadent palm trees, would
have maybe fared better to marry jimmy stewart
even james cagney; the ambulating of buster keaton
and curly, charlie chaplin in his downtime clowning
around at the hearst estate; brando and james dean
desperately falling to their knees, hitchcock falling
asleep with pained grin as all of civilization begins


proof #70

They don't make actors in america anymore
they're all action stars like in the advent
of the movie industry with silent films
and porn, only those seemed just a
bit more creative inspired and raw


proof #71

Has anyone ever been assassinated
at one of those alumni or board
of trustee banquets?


proof #72

Remember this class a classic schmuck or another
real aloof and arrogant asshole pretty sure was
in the field of advertising an acquaintance of my
mother up at one of their infamous get-togethers
like celebrating another one of those milestones
adults are so famous for some birthday anniversary
reunion of sorts and my dad asked me to tend bar

which for the most part was just pouring wine and
this guy just walks up to me (mr. phony baloney
multiple personality) looking down on me (for
some reason with such hostility most likely due
to some sort of insecure identity) treating me like
some second-class third-class citizen beneath him
deliberately making every effort to make the desperate
distinction with no eye contact (i guess to pathetically
try to assert his authority or class standing ironically
always the ones so classless this little man with an apparent
napoleonic complex) while making his demands then suddenly
my dad comes by to ask how things are going and can see the
look suddenly completely change on his face when discovers
i'm his son and then all of a sudden becomes this happy-go-
lucky quazi nice guy (either due to some kind of fear of
consequences or people just naturally finding out what
a real-life phony he really was) and starts treating me
like an equal although ironically doesn't know himself and he's
the one negative and so far from anything positive like i should
now be honored to be one of them (this cowardly little man)
and this is supposedly one of those with one of those 'developed
reputations' (and am able to figure out within a couple seconds)
one of those silly little see-through specimens who always seem
to conveniently rationalize it all as being one of those hard-war
king workaholics in the very competitive business world.
later on after a certain amount of forgiveness and choosing
my battles we made one of those classic gentleman mano-
a-mano bets on some ballgame for like 20 bucks and even
exchanged addresses and was agreed upon who ever lost
would make sure to get the 20 dollars over in the mail
(i guess touching on the principle of trust and honor and
responsibility and character). of course after this little man
in advertising lost never once saw any of my money (i guess
a part of that winning personality) while ridiculously at the time
and that phase of my life (is this what they refer to as paying
your dues?) used him for some required prerequisite idiotic
letter of recommendation using such patronizing parentifying
phrases like–"the youth these days" and "chance and opportunity"
and so-called "searching for direction" while funny, ironically
had seen and done more living and had more jobs and life and
death experiences and substantial intimate relationships than
this dishonest indifferent insensitive know-it-all recently

divorced asshole in sales and marketing (the epitome of
'false advertising') and 10 of his lives put together…


proof #73

What a weird bizarre paradoxical phenomenon
in america how they have this three month
grace probationary period when you first
get a job as if you got to prove yourself
in a place you don't even want a part of


proof #74

If i was to put together and add
all the different colorful reasons
i got fired from a whole wide
variety of positions would
not equal the real reason
why i did not even want
to originally take them


proof #75

Too often we reach conclusions
through necessary rationalization
when the truth just becomes too
much to bare and way too much
pain and phoniness out there way
too much injustice and unfairness

until we find it's really not so much anymore
even about truth or non-truth (just irrelevant
or a moot point) but more so as simple
as good and bad or right and wrong

proof #76

Why is it the little things and the little people
who we often seem to fixate and obsess about
that carry absolutely no clout as perhaps it's that
exact fact that they are such little things and little
people and that's what bothers us as such, really
not deserving of any kind of respect and thinking
that they got the props to carry any sort of clout
how we have a tendency eventually in the long
run (with what life does to you and wears you
out) to internalize all the constant external lies


proof #77

You know when i see these candidates all lined up
in their neat little rows at the podium i honestly am
just totally turned off (and often find myself turning
on like *national geographic* or a good ballgame like
chicago vs. st. louis as to me just feels far more reliable
or relatable) while never thought much of all those goody
goodies from the classroom who to me usually were just
out for self and never ever quite found them to be as good
or nice or kind or trusting as you'd think and always just
seemed see-through and full of it while the talking heads
a team of obvious movie critics are all going to comment
on how they performed or their stance (on healthcare and
immigration something we hear over and over and over
again like there are no other possible issues out there) and
how they defended themselves or how they struck back
(all actions and personality traits i could never really
ever stand about the human species) as for me i swear
i'd prefer to see people like a drag queen and zookeeper
and dominatrix and hustler and embalmer and radio star
and previous girlfriend and best friend i grew up with
from the neighborhood while to me all these images
and things feel just a bit more convincing and have
far more meaning and aesthetically believe in

proof #78

They talk about the population/percentage
of all these voters in the upcoming elections
well do they have one for the where's waldo
white suburban woman having gotten sick of
their know-it-all husbands now literally scouring
hustling the back streets of the village (you can
see them at the end of the shore, near the board
walk, train station, at the end of the dead end)
aimless, having lost faith, dull-eyed, dispirited
having given up on the institution of marriage
(wind-up strangers looking for payback and a
final dose of romance) not giving a shit anymore
and looking to pick up younger men; i've seen
plenty of them even been picked up by them as
a kid (of this i swear and promise and pledge
allegiance) while their desperate demographic
did and if you only really knew how much
this infamous 'silent majority' existed


proof #79

Half the time it's those schmucks who were supposed
to be providing the right guidance and support when
growing up who ironically were making one feel more
resentful and angrier (so out of touch and just babbling
some bullshit about themselves) coming up with such
lazy cliche inane expressions like–"don't sweat the
small stuff" "choose your battles" the classic "get
past it" or "don't let it ruffle your feathers" while
have to try to picture or imagine what the hell it
even meant to have your feathers ruffled and look-
ing back at your youth and adolescence can see why
was almost always in a constant persistent state of
revolt and without even realizing it a wise ass acting-
out and getting yourself into trouble with almost every
figure of authority (who most likely would come up
with some more idiotic psychobabble like–'he's just
reaching out for help' only making you feel ironically
more helpless and hostile) which deep down inside

probably knew had no respect for and in some way
shape or form felt would take advantage or betray
your trust so simply gonna beat them to the punch


proof #80

And so when the grownups get all grown up
and all you get are those grownup statements
such as ones 'reputation precludes...' wish
there was just something which precluded
this false truth like some sort of evidence
or proof of integrity and honesty and honor
as opposed to that little glossy photo with
that phony wink and nod smile (the ronald
mcdonald before & after makeover) meant to
patronize and placate the customer to pretend
'to go that extra mile' (to make their quota)
but in real life just find the repeated behavioral
pattern from the used car salesman to the president
of the united states of america to the secretary
to the supervisor to some sort of father figure
nowhere to be found and literally find yourself
once again in the red tape abuse cycle runaround


proof #81

Gigantic tankers full of pool water
rumble through suburbia; their own
version of deforestation replacing all
the romantic nocturnal creatures with
a bunch of obvious high school bullies
trying to pick up angelic babysitters...

fathers all a bunch of lying life insurance
salesmen (with their quota of children)
whose wives eyes went dead years ago

proof #82

The factory at the end of the rainbow
this country started going down hill
when doctors stopped making house
calls with cigarettes and highballs…


proof #83

If we are all just mere players
methinks life just a hell
of a lot of stage fright


proof #84

Sidekick in need of a sidekick
and then becomes the true prince

the masses are simply buffoons
trying to get their kicks...

the decadent daughters
have just become too rich


proof #85

'The martyr' will always be hollow
no matter how many things in his
life he has done heroic and humble
while for this exact selfsame reason
been underestimated, misinterpreted


proof #86

One cannot help but to feel a bit situationally-depressed
when constantly surrounded by all the betrayers of bullshit…
funny it's the honest people you end up having a hard time trusting

proof #87

There is trust and belief in strangers.
in my life i have found loyalty in them
in those moments and interludes and elements
and images especially taking trains and ferries
from ancient exotic cities all the way out to the
mediterannean living in real poverty-stricken ghettos
and feeling more safe and less danger and at home
and welcome (something that they never tell you
about those cultures) sitting all day in the window
of diners and seeing my extended family of hustlers
and drug dealers and homeless hoteliers and artists
who once gave exhibitions at *the gugghenheim* and
*whitney* in that lady truck driver who literally gave
me the coat off her back looking out for me when
she thought i was shivering in the deep dark hills
of portland, oregon in the contemplative brilliant
beauty and constantly changing keen detail of the
seasons in those brief relationships with women
which i swear seemed to last an eternity and gave
me more insight and wisdom and a sense of being
while at that time in a reflexive way almost seemed
to save me i have found trust and belief in strangers


proof #88

Interesting all those hustlers and winos
and dealers and connections i once knew
who i can practically remember all their
names or made-up nicknames sometimes
with a very surreal and cartoonish quality
at times extremely serious and righteous
like presidents of the united states but
that whole lot of fellow coworkers or
colleagues (of the cubicle) i swear
true can't remember a single one

proof #89

I woke up from a dream
as if coming out of a deep
coma and had a sudden and
lucid vision and revelation
the essence of existence
was just like vaudeville
made up of all these surreal
balzac dostoevskian characters
of which our experiences
and phases of growth
and development
are all just really strangers
which we become familiar
and intimate with who take
on roles from how much
we choose to believe or
resist (from past trauma and
damage) the contemporary
mores and functioning
of civilization and our
psychosocial environment


proof #90

I am the answer
to all the multiple
choice questions
none of the above
the deflated wise
man put back
in the barn
held back
for not
applying
myself
leaves
scattered
all around

the above
ground
pool


proof #91

You sometimes wonder in marriage the point and purpose
or difference between policy and practice with how they drain
and wear you down, while all you're trying to do, all you've ever
tried to do, is reach some peaceful resolution, as they love to bicker
and just bring up futile incidences from the past and go straight for the
jugular going absolutely nowhere, while curious if camp david might
possibly have any availability if no one's using it in the off-season
and i'll bring my *mad* subscription and baudelaire's prose poems
plus an extra jug of sangria which been saving for just the right
occasion when i'm losing it and feel got nothing left to live for

maybe they'll be pictures of kissinger, sadat,
begin just trying to get away from it all...


proof #92

When the explanation at the end of a *wonder woman* episode
seems more plausible more sincere and sympathetic and
makes more sense than a husband and wife going at it
with all that nonstop bickering and just feel you need
those safe & secure bullet proof bracelets to fend off
her unwarranted attacks and just once would love that
truth lasso to toss around her and rope her in hopefully
just once sink in that you just don't care or give a damn
to argue anymore and that all you care about is her and the
family and marriage and when you're done with the madness
of it all like some catatonic dummy all unraveled and dead to
the world walk down the hall to your dark office to try and book
a hotel down in orlando, florida for the magical kingdom i suppose
that proverbial pot of gold at the end of the rainbow somewhere
between heaven and hell in the sunshine state i imagine
to get all enlightened and to eternally glow with a view
of the pool an instant panacea to cure the blues...

proof #93

In looking for a place to stay
      they seem to rate the rooms
with the criteria & symbols
         if they have wifi & a pool
& parking & restaurant
        & think i got 3 out of 4
of them in my existence
       & all i need is a pool
to keep me content
        also too seems
to not hurt to have
         one of those convenience
shops with pringles & lip balm
          & razors & harlequins
those ritzy luxurious palms
           without the coconuts
(for insurance reasons
            as we live in a suing culture)
but didn't that used
      to be the best part?


proof #94

The lounge act found nodding-out in the elevator
after his set happy to have made a difference
and his audience just a little less stressed
perhaps even able, for the time being, just
to forget all the little things in life that plague
them heading to his perfectly, pristine, pre-
packaged timeshare (in the stars) without
a thing moved out of place set-up straight-
up in the airport hotel (his own personal
version of shangrila or somehow living
a delusional safe & secure life of leisure)
even a picture-perfect-picture of him in sequins
with a pasted-on smile in the postcard carousel
(the concierge, a father he never had, the bellboy
a son, and front desk clerks make him feel like
he can do no wrong) hoping one of these days

to be discovered, while his own personal
absurd, distorted form of being reborn


proof #95

They seem to do all these repeats of idiot sitcoms in america
well how about *fantasy island* with tattoo and mr. rourke?
real-life contemporary dummy-ventriloquists like socrates
passing on his knowledge and wisdom to plato; during
the day like some half-crazed exhibitionist you peek
through your blinds to the bluebird in the branches


proof #96

Women when you first meet them
(if you are listening close enough)
will tell you practically everything
about themselves; all the trauma
and damage done to them in their
past, while don't only want you to
be their savior but may also come
close to sacrificing you for all the
hurt and pain and shame they feel
they've experienced and been inflicted
on them, cheated and given no chance


proof #97

People like to keep things safely stored
in their imagination while once they cross over
to reality not always quite as accurate to how they pictured it


proof #98

In retrospect, arrested stage of development not necessarily
always so bad if can be receptive and aware of it and can
somehow try to sublimate and do something positive and

creative from that stagnant, abusive, and traumatic phase
and period (and baseline) of damage and might even
simultaneously heal and grow a bit from that emotional
spiritual and psychological scar tissue like the dynamic
(and function) of language and dreaming really not
being so far apart in character and consciousness


proof #99

The real problem with all these gimmicks & contraptions
all these smartphones in the hands of the young, is i've
seen them roam clueless through the cities of culture
& civilization (with no sense, common sense, and their
senses cut-off) in real-life, real-time action & adventure
(the thing that satire is made of) oblivious, negligible
listless and lost with heads down to the sidewalk


proof #100

Too many hip renovations have been
done to the warehouses and cobblestone
of the slums while all the aloof and arrogant
white people from publishing & advertising
move in knowing nothing about its history

(not giving a damn about those
who live there which to me in my
opinion feels a little bit like a sin)

they only want the units which seem
turn-of-the-century, poverty-stricken
with the lopsided floorboards because
prefer that poor industrial look and lends
to the atmosphere while have something
to talk about with their millionaire down
and out starving artist acquaintances

proof #101

I don't know...white people to me often seem like these yuppies from hell or those fake liberals...pretty much the exact same people...one just decided to go right one decided to go left


proof #102

People who don't always tell the truth *in fact* ironically often come off as the biggest liars


proof #103

A shame how those rich kids from the suburbs abandon their friends for no particular reason as if they never even existed don't seem very much like kids even seems a little bit a sin


proof #104

I'm not sure what turns me off more those acting indifferent or those being too pushy, both in my opinion, having real questions in identity (not much of an upbringing)


proof #105

People like to always casually talk about other's hardships; some really fucked-up shit to make their own lives seem a little less miserable and a little less pathetic


proof #106

All our lives we just search for that futile tiny piece of territory; of privacy and silence and

solace and kindness (that won't rape and violate
and harass us) but seems around every single corner
are hit by just another sort of obstacle and challenge
set to make our lives miserable wondering the true
and false differences and realizing there's such a
fine line having a hard time making the distinction
between our rights and dreams and nightmares and
all those petty little motherfuckers who just don't
seem to give a damn out for their own self-interest
or straight-up suffering and pain and frustration and
constant inane repetition of all of our bad luck and
how much patience do we actually have left questioning
our time on earth and even our fate which in the end some
times just feels cursed no longer blessed wondering what
the hell we did to deserve this and eventually just turn
towards our postage stamp lawn gardening somewhere
between candide and don carleone for a little (damage)
control and peace of mind and quiet and what's left of
the torn heart and soul or most necessary futile fragile
delicate details of the woebegone everchanging seasons


proof #107

Loneliness along with profound forms of being
done wrong and injustice(s) is what truly tests
our faith, mortality, and our time on earth...


proof #108

We often don't know how lonely we are
even when we're right in the middle of it
(we reserve that for all the anger, frustration,
injustice and bullshit of everyday existence)
and only shows up several years later in our
dreams roaming through the burnt-out buildings
of the bleak desolate backstreets, trying to find
a way of getting back home (which also too is
an illusion of sorts knowing in truth how much
it tormented us and was the original cause to
why we took off) having absolutely no idea why

this continues to persist (to haunt) and why we
even deserve this? nightmares are like the gift
that keeps on stealing, running away with no
clear destiny; a house of mirrors we're
desperately trying to escape from and
wake up somewhere right around the
dawn, looking up to god, the stars,
something or someone, as that
usually for the most part helps
us out right on the spot...


proof #109

Everyone i thought i once loved
became a thief in one form or another


proof #110

We wait for the criminal to keep us company
in many ways to rescue and restore our sanity
to steal back everything that was originally taken

almost becoming a reenactment to the petty crime of living...


proof #111

I don't know waking up in the middle of the night
been so tough on myself these days look inside
the refrigerator and imagine my profile on a loaf
of rye the sticker inside reads *1-800 4 my home* in
case of break down also *1-800 le foyer* in french
as we're right on the border while an interview
with sophia loren on the movie channel and used
to be so stunning and gorgeous and exotic catch
sophia loren suddenly picking her nose for me i've
always been most intrigued in what is said between
the interviewer and interviewee and the casual banter
right after the commercial before they start speaking

again as feel like that's so much more profound and
relevant as opposed to what's supposedly revealed
and exposed in front of the camera like my italian aunt
who once fondled me when i was a teenager when we
came to visit them in columbus, ohio the very earnest
voluptuous weather girl like the portrait of mona lisa
with boyfriend problems or swingers arguing sexless
audience imagining their raw naked rawshack bodies
through dusty venetian blinds at night their silhouettes
climbing in and out of the shower before their useless
jobs memories of cross-country skiing with my sister
through the deep woods on winter vacation leaping
off burning rafts beneath the sweltering mountains
without an ounce of fat on my boyhood body in my
cut-off blue jeans the smell of fresh clean white t's
coming straight out the wrapper like clothes from
the chinese laundry all neatly tied with twine in their
brown parcel all the symbolic creatures in my night
mares finally getting redeemed guzzling cold milk
and seltzer by the light of the refrigerator like some
anthony quinn sophia loren fellini film by the shore

can't get that smith's song out of my head...


proof #112

Parable:

the coo-coo clock repairman sticks his head
deep down the hollow hole while humming–
"what do we have here?" and you thinking
what else in your life can possibly go wrong
and now we got a coo-coo who refuses to
come out of his home and sing us his song
only making us feel that much more alone
or some apparent coo-coo who has literally
flown the coup and left us with empty nest
syndrome so what do we do now? should
we write a manager or one of those so-
called supervisors or the owner straight
up who have all proven not to get back

to us and what would we say? the coo-
coo you sent us is lazy and broken and
out-of-order and totally irresponsible and
simply acting-out or acting-in however you
want to put it and just decided to suddenly
stop cooing for reasons we are not sure of
and refusing to come out his hole i don't
know maybe due to some sort of passive-
resistance or social phobia or should we
just give a call to the return department
who will ironically mechanically tell us
we are being recorded and thank us once
again for our patience and never pick up
the phone or just wrap him all up and send
him back to where he came from which is
of course *amazon* and ask for another one
who has already asked us like every other
self-serving survey poll to rate our transaction
with them and it's all so fragile and fucked
up cause all you've ever done all you ever
known since you were a young boy coming
straight from the heart is to provide friends
and acquaintances and literal strangers
on the road unconditional love and support
while look at your computer screen thinking
it says–"are you in need of a free spirit?" then
look just a little bit closer and it really reads–
"are you in need of a tax accountant?" and
you think of that brilliant biggie line–"i got
lawyers watching lawyers" and likewise
just don't know who to trust anymore?


proof #113

Ibid: you now know why people just become total fucken
drunks or decide to give up and be noble and just wake up
one morning and put a bullet in their brain where with
useless ceremonies they never ever really even straight
up liked or cared about in the first place anyway 'cause
never really seemed to be about them like birthdays (might
as well be president's day who got assassinated and betrayed

and now giving great discounts off *chevrolets*) the only one
who wishes them it is sam stamps from the used car lot because
a while back you were put in their system but ironically never
return any your e-mails or phone calls and in this soulless social
media b-day message say once again–"please feel free if ever..."
which has become kafkaesque and dostoevskian even throw
in camus' "myth of sisyphus" or perhaps pass it on to one of
those late-great classic ol' time slapstick comedians like chaplin or
buster keaton who all died (for you) very lonely tragic forgotten men


proof #114

Lawnmowing guys show up at their own convenience who recently
complained that you didn't answer your doorbell when were busy
and didn't even hear it and somehow was my obligation because
they forgot to bring their equipment and wanted to borrow yours
and due to the absurd nature of man whereas literally having
absolutely no idea how to communicate, neither them nor their
boss, are punitively increasing their rates and going to charge us
more because they now claim they have to weed whack more as
if the climate or nature of the lay of the land has suddenly changed
so drastically (within a week) and are frustrated with their alpha-
male anger because never once learned to speak to the human beings
and now someone is going to have to pay dearly for it, and you think
how pathetic and brutish and barbarbic with the pattern of man's basic
misinterpretations and miscommunication, a microcosm of the hx of
civilization to how most wars began due to this petty and histrionic
type of behavior; how even the great jonathan swift wrote in his
political satire "gulliver's travels" how the great battle began
based on bickering about what side you crack the egg on

Won't mention as well a thing about how they seem to impulsively
misperceive 'class' differences (their inherent jealousy providing
them the instant and ignorant justification and distorted thought
pattern and even arrogant judgments to always have this parasitic
behavior of always seeming to blame and be naturally hostile and
resentful, and ironically how much more humble and 'down to earth'
you are than them) and have absolutely no idea how much more you've
seen than them; how much harder you once had it and had absolutely
no one to turn to and lived in so many more gruesome and seriously

dangerous 'life and death' situations and how many more jobs i swear
under the eyes of god and my son's beating heart, a matter of fact that
exact job and never once would it ever cross my mind or consciousness
to complain as was just grateful at the end of the day (for a cold beer
in a warm shower) at the end of the work week for the money i got
under the table to pay the landlord my weekly rent at that welfare
hotel with blood donated and a view of the whole wide world
bounding in and out picking up their holiday gifts at the blinking
department store across the block at dusk and had just enough to
make one content to treat myself to chinese and a bottle of wine


proof #115

Half of this got writ while hanging over the precipice
where's savannah? the capitol of america? idaho? miss-
spending long woebegone days wasted dazed staring out
a lunch booth in *woolworth's* at some real-life strange half-
crazed parade displaced where everyone seemed to have a
place somewhere between the midwest and western shore
not knowing a living breathing soul with long rambling
undulating *little rascal* hills at a stopover in cheyenne...
saw it all, reno, on-the-run gleaming through the fleeting
evening window heading out to california and determined
one day to return which i did and lived a whole year at the
end of the tracks; solitary starving a former ghost of myself
returned home a better man as swear the dust from the desert
became my five o'clock shadow, like some long-lost sort
of saint-fugitive of destiny and damage, as what was
that they said again about that which doesn't kill you?


149

All those insults is what made me is what didn't make me
is what made me rise up above all that mediocrity like all
the shadowy smoke swirling from the smokestack factories
of a lower east side winter's evening strolling along the east
river a stalker of the truth and reality in my peacoat with
absolutely nothing to fall back on which was something
of a strange, perverse, existential, and spiritual feeling

fleeting, contemplating (anonymity such a sentimental
liberating feeling with no real end and no true beginning)
never giving up knowing there was really nothing to give
up on and if i just hung on long enough the essence to the core
of intuition, experience, and wisdom whose secrets could only be
fathomed in the subtle nuances of the changing patterns of the seasons


proof:

The only thing i really truly miss about the big city
was taking those long romantic strolls in the winter
up lexington developing a close and intimate rapport
with the mannequins and felt so much more familiar
from a distance whose scenarios always seemed
to have so much more to offer and just living
in that moment an anonymous stranger feeling
i was able to fantasize or escape and meant
the world and had so much more to offer
than the cruel and mean-spirited humans
who left so much to be desired and never
seemed to be particularly consistent or
kind or compassionate and when i got
back home to my solitary flat in the
lower east side to wash it all away
would warm up with a shower
and my mind always seemed
proportionally more keen
aware open and willing
to live than to die


150

After all the suffering all the sadness all the madness
all the depression all the isolation all the repetition
what's left but to become famous really a remainder
an addendum sartre bailed genet out of prison cuz
he felt he really had something to offer rimbaud
the raconteur says he remembers when he was
born and how he crawled across his ma's bed
nietzsche claimed to be born a very old man

proof 1

The most 'famous man' in the world
after all the suffering and struggle
does not recognize his reflection
in the moonlit puddle; fate of
the absurd and the archetypal
hero who's persevered through
all the doubters and all the devils


proof 2

Has anyone ever said
this is exactly how
i didn't picture it?


proof 3

I view our lives something like one of those
good ol' time poloroids where we used to
just press a button and anxiously eagerly
wait for that picture to come into focus
while hoping the image will be as clear
and lucid as possible; sometimes we'd
even wave it in the air thinking that might
help to speed up the process realizing that
life is really just a series of surreal moments
and reflections of strange absurd expectations


proof 4

People who know little something about tennis
people who know little something about paris
people who know little something about traveling
people who know little something about the imagination
people who know little something about the mediterannean
people who know little something about meditating
the palm trees and mermaids and things that save you

people who know little something about the silence of starfish
seagull's outburst and subliminal sacred smell of suntan lotion
people who know little something about the cadence of the ocean
its mumbling murmur and hypnotic rhythms which put you under
and helps you to instantly forget about all the hysteria of existence

proof 5

Out of respect for women like gertrude & alice b.

i love the fact that she'd been keeping secrets
    about sunflowers
i love the fact that she'd been keeping an eye
    on the sunflowers
i love the fact that she saw the beginning buds
    a couple days ago
i love the fact that she saw the sunflower about
    to sprout a day ago
i love the fact that she saw the first sunflower
    just pop open & grow
i love the fact that that sunflower planted
    new thoughts in my head something
    which had felt dead for so long
i love the fact that the first sunflower
    opened today & didn't tell me
i love the fact that she didn't tell me
    anything about the sunflower
    opening kind of hurt me but
    in fact you know not really
i love the fact that did not really
    hurt me the first sunflower opening
i love the fact that the sunflower opening
    provided a certain type of shelter & healing
i love the fact that the sunflower opening
    seemed in a strange way to finally
    put an end to all pain & suffering
i love the fact all suffering
    seemed to end due to
    the first sunflower opening
i love the fact that that sunflower
    opened in a sea of unopened sunflowers

i love the fact that in fact we have
    something to look forward to
    a whole track of sunflowers
    cracked open smack-dab
    against the side of the barn
i love the fact when it does it will
    all look like some strange surreal
    skyline against the apocalyptic dawn
    a place you & i are from having survived it all
i love the fact that i love the fact that i love the fact
    that there are no facts & in fact just gonna be a
    whole patch of sunflowers! sunflowers! sunflowers!

hey, what do you want for supper?


proof 6

I liken life to like some long slow woebegone
buster keaton movie falling asleep in the pews
of the cathedral in reno, waking up suddenly
married, hearing over the oldies radio station
at lunchtime–"participate, rollerskate!" thinking
wow feels like just yesterday (some strange
surreal dream) and knowing in many ways
it was, while our time on earth like some
ridiculous bizarre coincidence or
fine line between fate and time


proof 7

We both laugh and cry at our fate
for the 'strange absurdity' of its whimsy
and only take solace (in our imagination)
in the opposite elements and traits of beauty

proof 8

One should not feel sorry
for oneself when trying
to get on in this existence
but does not hurt every so
often to reflect and reminisce

that brilliant stretch of darkness
right before the sun rises...


proof 9

If man could only do a better impression of a bird on a wire
silent sensitive and solitary reflective and contemplative
all by his lonesome and then just vanish into thin air


proof 10

The manic 'desperation' of man with false images & forms
(in the slow-death silence & solitude) of suburbia and the
compulsive need and desire to try and maintain a sense
of homogeneous harmony (stability and consistency...
what a strange vague half-crazed criteria to shoot for)
with absolutely no change ('of being') in what
delusionally believes might make him happy


proof 11

The jealous and petty always busy
being hateful do not have the ability
to be grateful when in fact you could
have gone all out for them which is
all good and neither 'here nor there'

proof 12

If it's all about who you know
i don't want to know no one


proof 13

Philosophy's point of view of point of view
of point of view of point of view to realize
after they steal everything from you there's
just no point (to all those things we view)
trying to extract just a little piece of truth
from all forms (and illusions) of non-truth
like all that spirit coming from the blues


proof 14

Tricky thing about wisdom
is trying to combine all that
remembering all that forgetting


proof 15

Leaders are always making promises they don't keep
and the ones they do have very little to do with me
or meaning and relevancy to my everyday reality


proof 16

There is not enough pie in the bakery
to throw in the faces of all
those phony politicians

proof 17

Those who run the neglectful or abusive
dysfunctional family unit is like a corrupt
president and his cabinet with their scheisty
fucked-up fragmented lines of communication
(as extended family becomes their constituents)
and due to their constant abuse of power and
conflicts of interest will get processed and
(miss)interpreted in a flip-flop of morals
and ethics of who's good and who's bad
with their make-believe martyr and savior
or those of true honesty and integrity who
conveniently become an enemy of the people


proof 18

As such politics like family dysfunction seems to
all be about perception with the idiot masses making
the assessment (on character and behavior) pathetically
lazy in their judgments projecting their own losses and
shortcoming weaknesses looking for some substitute
savior while so lacking in experience and intuition


proof 19

Does it not seem like almost every recent
modern day presidency is like some punchline
(not particularly funny) for the theater of the absurd
where the straight men are dishing out the one-liners?

funny men forgotten ending up looking straight as arrows


proof 20

I think i really wouldn't mind politics so much if it wasn't
so damn political, like some horrible family dysfunction,
parasitic and vengeful, like dating some borderline woman

who one day makes you her savior and the next the cause
to all her problems; human nature at its worst, more specific
human behavior and character without the humanity and all
that backstabbing and betraying, feeling like almost every
shakespeare drama which ended in violence and tragedy
(all starting from some secret sheisty letter or whisper
from stage f/right; to know they're all goddamn lies
triggering and bringing you right back to all of that
mean-spirited bickering and fighting from high school
which tried to tear and terrorize and rip out your heart)
to know hamlet's castle not so much different or so far
from trump's white house when you consider all those
fucked-up dynamics and the natural leaking of top secret
confidential information to ruin and get at and damage
reputations, obsessively thriving off gossip and
rumors with little to no code of morals or ethics

rosencrantz & guildenstern the fall guys seeing 3-5...


proof 21

Traditions & customs i admire, black men
casually hanging out in barbers, sitting back
'conversating' in chairs, rapping a taste, cracking
up and getting it all off their chest; if only countries
and governments might consider being a little like this


proof 22

The idiocy in man's ridiculous desperate efforts
to convince himself with his obsessive need (and rigid
rituals and routines) to establish his illusory reputation


proof 23

The reputation of those who speak of reputations
is usually pretty lacking searching for direction

proof 24

Never put your judgment into those deemed
to be 'of good judgment' as will eventually
find in the long-run for this exact reason
strangely enough paradoxically the rules
appear to never apply to them while
there is a fine line between truth
and image perception and form


proof 25

The pursuit of perfection leaves one obsessing
(temporarily happy but never really contented)
in the absurd stagnant state of pursuing perfection


proof 26

There is a stark dichotomy and contradiction
in those deemed and given the reputation of
supposedly being so magnanimous and kind
and compassionate, as more times than not
ironically has to fully just be on their own
set of terms (or have all the control) while
seem awfully stingy by nature, opinionated
rigid and rather critical and punitive if
delusionally believing not resembling
all those so-called standards of their
pre-packaged advertised morals and
ethics which they now interestingly
(not quite as modest and humble)
appear to thrive off and take advantage


proof 27

At the family get-together (this applies to holidays
and weddings and funerals all pretty much inter-
changeable) it is very important to look something

like 'a success' whatever that happens to look like
and how it presents or some distinct sense of 'being'
or that you're constantly busy and being productive
perhaps like some well put-together backyard in the
suburbs with a newly-stained varnished all-weather
deck (and explain every minute detail in the process)
but strangely enough when it really comes down to it
all the kids are missing-in-action and taken off 'cause
they just couldn't take it anymore while at one of these
infamous family get-togethers very specific statements
are made about having a certain amount of employees
'working under me' (which provides instant self-esteem
and less insecurity) and even will quote exact figures or
quote racist riddles (as generational) and that warm feeling
of privilege and entitlement with a certain sense of comradery
and belonging while even the wannabe self-serving liberals
will giggle to be a part of things (or perhaps proactively
strategically not to be eventually the token scapegoat alien
hated and roasted) the coquettish cousins with crushes on
each other all symptoms of puberty (testing out their identity
and ability to seduce and attract one another) desperately
trying out their clever charm (really doing no harm) and
passion and impulsivity and imagination clinically over
compensating showing how much in fact they mean
to each other in a meaningless world which does not
seem to pay them any mind or ignores and feel small
(shaking off that self-loathing) and when the relatives
take off down the proverbial road after all performances
and so-called roles (of a real-life archetypal quality)
finally feeling a bit giddy with the world off their
shoulders through all those tollbooths over all those
bridges will start in with the natural gossip and rumors
(of how they did; of what they looked like and how they
appeared) each feeling a little bit better little less miserable
little less guilt and conflicted without all those taboo secrets
finding it so hard keep in and to live with even maybe the
sensation of a little bit forgotten while a little more forgiven

proof 28

Kafka's cockroach was hemingway's bull turned inside-out
somewhere between waking reality and the subconscious (the
difference and fine line between internalizing and externalizing)
having a difficult time making the distinction between both
forms of reality, only to eventually find out in the long-run
none of that really matters (as both thought-patterns pretty
much interchangeable) while in the end all turns dostoevskian
with severe and profound episodes of fixating and brooding


proof 29

It is by no coincidence that people end up taking
their lives over what others might perceive to be
pretty minor shit, but it's all that little shit that
just keeps on building and building and building
until they've just finally fucken had it realizing
it's all just that goddamn repetition and constant
tedium which gets under their skin (and drains the
hell out of them) and just ain't gonna get much better


proof 30

If only patience really got tested
by people and things worth it...
most people are just complacent
(with their convenient and built-in
excuses) and rarely follow through
on any of their words or promises


proof 31

Where are the good triggers to take you back
through the garden to know missing
in action not always a problem

proof 32

My support system i swear has always been
about as supportive and stable as one of those
fragile hot-air balloons getting blown all over
the place by some great out of control gust
of wind never exactly sure where i'm
heading which became something of
my absurd fate and long-lost destiny


proof 33

We are all on this lonesome journey
going absolutely nowhere while our
dreams and nightmares tell us so

well as long as we got the crows…


proof 34

In the end as long as you got those memories
and moments of the one you think you loved
and may have in fact even loved you back


proof 35

First love allows you to instantly 'forgive and forget'
a kind of rebirth and redemption from all that shit
which shouldn't have even started to begin with

consider this surreal existential example…

I.

My first love shows up to my door; this gorgeous German
girl named Andrea from several decades ago asking me if
I can somehow help to locate myself showing me a photo
probing me if I can recognize who I was (a romantic
teenager) not knowing I used to be this handsome
glowing, passionate, self-loathing Jew, brooding
and blue, curious, inquisitive in a fisherman's sweater
(her not knowing my heritage keeping it secret being
innocently self-conscious, all too aware of previous
historical carnage and conflicts, not wanting to chance it;
not wanting to lose her, starting to fall in love with her, making
it all that much more intriguing and intrinsically complicated)

II.

Just home from college during the holidays, spending
hours contemplating and wandering through the snowy
suburbs, isolated, melancholy in the strange silent solitude
of the seasons whose stillness and placidity (in an ethereal,
fictional way) seemed to separate one phase of my reality
from the other (from those once selfsame forms and images
of everyday functioning to the sudden spontaneity of a surreal
love and fantasy) and if time stood still so did these intense
feelings (of beauty); nothing could possibly feel more lovely
or lonely, this fragile feeling of falling madly for this radiant
stranger (now finding myself an enamored fugitive with
meaning and purpose, who finally at last held the key to
the kingdom; the secret to the grand inside riddle they felt
the need to compulsively, cruelly keep from you, between
someone I spiritually loved while on-the-run from all those
obvious, oppressive things of culture meant to mold and
manipulate me) spending days vacillating between her
presence and trepidation of the eternal timeless universe;
the core essence of quintessential quietude of our time
on earth, strolling over soft stone bridges above surging
swollen rivers of winter frothing in firmament, roaming
past crackling, frozen, babbling brooks, winding through
the whispering woods whose distant echoes and murmurs
sifting through the powdered pachysandra took on a sense

of redemption and forgiveness (even revelation) developing
its own silent, sacred language of transcendent stimulation
(whose brooding and rumination turned to a pleasant
sublimation, illuminated) dissecting the intimate, tender
details of nature, amplifying, and opening the senses

### III.

Other people's fireplaces welcoming and taking me in; the rin-tin-tin
drip-drip-drip magical rivulets of glistening water having melted and
now streaming on that one warm holy day, feeling like I could hear
the whole universe morphing, meditating, opening and closing like
some sacred stamen of a flower, flowing down the gutters from the
shutters of the village; the minutes, the hours of the clocktower and
cathedrals and funeral homes and barrooms and alleys; a hometown
draped in shadows, whose spirit now felt transient and foreign, solemn,
missing-in-action, mercurial and mystical; the mists of the silhouetted
train station blanketed in halos of lamp-lit snow, while finally at last
a deep, keen feeling, reflective and ruminating of a new, in-depth,
burgeoning, spiritual substance and meaning of past, poverty-stricken
scenes passing my dream-like window, not just in its final destination
but in the glowing presence of the journey; a crumbling kingdom
regenerated from the ashes of kindness and compassion, a kind
of object-permanence of fleeting and fragile nostalgia (while there
was a deep-seated, subliminal reason why I turned to the seasons
and turned to such influences like Bob Dylan's romantic, country
"Nashville Skyline" Jimmy Stewart in "It's A Wonderful Life" and
the brilliant, tormented Montgomery Clift falling in love, falling in
a dramatic heap of rags on the platform at some foreign train station)
the tumbling flakes of snow suddenly showing up out of nowhere,
falling like a miracle from the heavens, slowly, gradually gathering
and building up on the delicate eyelashes of all those sad, poor,
pouting horses lined up in a row with slow, woebegone heads
lowered from head to tail, still graceful, modest, mournful and
tearful across from *The Plaza* right in front of the park, feeling
like the only one in the world who made eye contact and really
gave a damn, looking beatdown, depressed, down on their luck
of which I always felt without even being aware of it akin, so
sympathetic, dreaming of shooting all those abusive, soulless
lawn jockeys, aloof and arrogant right through their tourist
top hats, while them all going on one final trot and mad

dash for freedom; the chattering teeth of the wild wicked
wind whipping against my iridescent, glowing, crystal
lattice, having spent a whole tragic, absurd existence

IV.

Whether real or imagined seeking that one, simple, elusive, illusory
sanctuary with opaque, stainless steel, tarnished fool's gold skylines
materializing from my mind through the shattered branches of
mythological, collapsible, pick-up stick forests, all burnt down
by mischievous boys with imagination and magnifying glasses;
those dangling, miraculous icicles like long precious daggers,
casting shadows and prisms of light from clattering chandeliers
in holy and haunted castles; the tender twinkle of twilight slightly
creeping through bleak and beautiful, solitary, sighing windowpanes
welcoming stray winds from the wild, mystical, mysterious outside
mixed with mollifying blasts of heat from the rhythm and beat of
the radiator, whose cacophonous symphony seemed to say everything
would be alright; the slight creaking of trees laden with snow bending
in the breeze, like likewise hearing an antique country dining room
table contracting whose fissures got narrower and wider due to the
subtle change of weather; all those different forms of sacred silences

V.

With girls like this anything seemed possible like some blissful fable
able to instantly shake off all those pathetic, petty problems in life
which might plague, even petrify us, struck with a sudden, keen
knowledge and insightful wisdom, able to instantly rise above
all that rhetoric and bullshit meant to inflict hurt and pain and
damage, having absolutely no need to react, a matter of fact
thriving and seeing through all the drama and acts of such
weak and insecure identities and egos (Bukowski said–
'people are not good to each other') with the natural
sensation and phenomenon of hearing ourselves for
the first time breathe aloud, something we had been
holding in for so damn long, and maybe all it really
came down to in the long-run was the sentimental
nostalgia and ephemeral rituals of staring into each
others eyes all night long (making midnight angels

on strangers' front lawns) the flickering shadows
of candles inside warm, toasty pubs, it just being
our song, our brand of beer, helping to quell all
anxiety and stress and fear, looking back at it as
some queer, romantic panacea never experienced
before or brilliant bittersweet memory somewhere
between a good and bad buzz when your song comes
up later on over the radio, realizing life is just about
that sole, magical moment, a mood you're in, some-
where between hope and fear, lust and love, caring
nothing at all about making the distinction and ditching
and escaping and taking off with that sudden, fleeting
feeling of freedom and liberation from a damaged
history of persistent, overbearing, psychological
subjugation as far as it'd take me never returning

### VI.

When she many years later showed me a photo of myself
as this thoughtful, sensitive, reflective, young adult, asking
me if I recognized myself I just very mechanically replied,
literally and philosophically that I did not, as I felt that secret,
soulful part of my sentimental, palpitating spirit start to creep
up from deep within and flare up once again, and when she took
off started to go into something of an emotional, uncontrollable,
trembling, hysterical panic ironically very similar to when she
had originally left me in the first place for reasons and circum-
stances beyond my control due to a domineering father and
submissive, enabling mother (along with guilt and conflict)
making it very difficult and virtuallyimpossible to break from
(due to these selfsame feelings of 'a guilty conflicted soul'
that I was not 'deserving of it' and constantly internalizing
that 'I was wrong') or what Freud alluded to in those cogent
psycho-dynamics of profound triangulation if one has not taken
the proper, necessary steps towards self-reflection or individuation
'not solely only dating your partner' but having to take on as well
the burden and responsibility of multiple members, leaving one
to experience that overwhelming phenomenon and sensation
and exact feeling and emotion of what it means to be keenly
and 'strangely deserted,' acutely alienated and abandoned;
in fact the microcosm and machinations of the conflicts and

complexities of what true love is, while the simple motion of
putting my head down on the pillow never felt quite so pure
or beautiful, having entered the 'sweet dreams' of living,
shrugging off all that pain and suffering and becoming
the real-life personification of that proverb of what it
feels in essence to be the perverse dynamic of 'forgotten
and forgiven' (devoid of 'being') and all those ridiculous
elements and things (of personality and identity) preceding
this. One should even consider the effects of first love on the
human condition and 'mature stages of growth and development'
with its physiological and psychological, kinetic energy and
'natural spirit' (its liberation and enlightenment 'of the senses')
intimate and intellectual maturation (willingness to make a connect-
ion and give of oneself), self-actualization, motivation and positive
cognitive and behavioral independence from the everyday, required
routines and rituals of the methodical, functioning and futile masses


proof 36

"If you only knew" one of the truest
most modest and humble, unsung
declarations in the english language


proof 37

It's crazy shit when you first met
they practically revealed everything
to you as if you were there to figure
everything out and solve all of their
problems and then marriage comes
along and it's like some long dark
secret asking them if there's anything
you can help them with knowing deep
down inside there really isn't as just
want her to be happy something that
has evaded you your whole existence

proof 38

Lovely whimsical weird motels on the sea
even stranger those bed & breakfasts run by
what seemed like widows or women whose
men just walked out on them and acted all
cheery more so miserable and melancholic
(often hostile and passive-aggressive) and
with your young bride to be with all this
heavy silence and solitude seemed something
like the amplification of one's mortality while
wondering how long i would realistically be
able to keep up this absurd charade in reality?


proof 39

He died in a darkened room with the shutters closed in naples
the muffled sound of merchants and street urchins fading into
the early evening with just the sound of u2 "it's a beautiful day"
murmuring on the tv screen reminding him of his anonymity
sole solitary being figuring better than almost any of the
other options and a pretty decent way to meet his maker

no one could possibly know the true-blue loneliness and
emptiness after a breakup (watching the pathetic vaudeville
actors in sequins in a whole other language dramatically cracking
one-liners laughing; seemed like the perfect metaphor for this reality
and state of being) ironically with that feeling of constantly sinking
taking a ferry through the desolate evening from naples to sicily...


proof 40

I know this sounds out there but don't really care
yet think i would have liked to have made a calender
for every single one of my past naked girlfriends with
their half-crazed seductive psychotic smiles and when
ever i'm feeling real down in the dumps and driven mad
by marriage can just look up at their glossy profiles like
those pagodas or bridges on chinese take-out calenders

and can instantly escape and explore all my options as
the mind and memories and imagination have a tendency
to conveniently make it look like it's all coming up roses
even though you know how loco they really made you…


proof 41

I love like 15, 20, 30, 40, 50,
100 years into marriage wives have a
tendency to ask all those hypothetical
questions like–"what if i hadn't been here?"

but you are here! you are  here!


proof 42

Blowing out
the candle
is both
the beginning
and end of the
ridiculous prayer


proof 43

There is a strange kind of vacant empty loneliness
when traveling even when constantly surrounded
by silence and beauty like when you fall in love
with her and constantly around her and start sleeping
over at each other's places (maybe a trigger to some
sort of separation-anxiety) perversely touching
on the delicate and brutal raw core of mortality

proof 44

All real sports & weather (bumpadabumpa traffic)
international news happens through the venetian
blinds of your lonesome motel room where you
sluggishly move in the brutal quiet silence of
the universe a real sort of zen-buddhist blues
of solitude like some life insurance salesman
at a convention or low-level thief of mistaken
identity trying desperately to steal it back while
all of these things (rituals and routines of time
and human interest, modes of functioning
and everyday reality) just appear absurd and
irrelevant with a languid lizard camouflaged
in the lush parking lot minding his business


proof 45

That strange eccentric town having become depressed
and rundown, if look close enough, perversely very much
keeps most of its old charm, societal customs and norms
intact; the details of its colorful, vibrant cycle of seasons
its concrete memories and moments (that leftover crumbling
movie theater and boxcar diner beneath the mountains; 'the
freak' with a cognitive-delay never leaving the corner always
looking confused and conflicted, or that family generation after
generation with its mysterious, deep dark secrets usually stemming
from something pretty abusive, tragic, or traumatic, having a hard
time making the distinction between myth and magic, truth and
taboo and where it all started and ended) matter of fact all for
the exact fact has sentimentally, nostalgically become lost
and forgotten, developed something of an everlasting
spirit in the romantic, collective unconscious


proof 46

We become enamored with artifacts, mosaics, fossils, cave paintings,
and ruins because they transcend all suffering and sorrow of the ages;
because they provide a necessary foundation (in such desperate)

need of) to persist and outlast us, and even brings about a certain amount of strength and energy we profoundly feel that we're losing, taken, and stolen (from our being) on a daily basis


proof 47

Almost all those things good and stable
come from something spiritual
primitive and wild…


proof 48

Know yourself like the northern star
whose constant orb throbbing in the dark
glows & sputters making you feel alive
know yourself like the northern star
which instinctively intuitively
makes you feel at one
know yourself like the northern star
as all your life they'll try
to deny who you are
know yourself like the northern star
as all they try to do
is constantly rob
know yourself like the northern star
as may seem so far but trust me
far closer than you can ever imagine
know yourself like the northern star
like some prayer or mantra
that cannot be forgotten
know yourself like the northern star
like some penetrating spirit
that cannot be described
know yourself like the northern star
where they cannot move you
however hard they try
know yourself like the northern star
where they cannot rattle you
wherever you are

know yourself like the northern star
like some long-lost pal
way before any this started
know yourself like the northern star
constant flashing like neon in the dark
& no longer doubt or question who you are
know yourself like the northern star
as is the heart & soul transcendent
glowing way below all that's scarred
know yourself like the northern star
as is reflection redemption & what
it means to suddenly be reborn
know yourself like the northern star
as trust me will never ever
again feel lost or alone
know yourself like the northern star


proof 49

We struggle and suffer and travel all this way
to try and reach our illusory destiny in this
strange half-crazed glossy postcard life

hopefully in the end there might
just be a good place to find decent chinese
and wash it all down with a fine bottle of wine


proof 50

When you find often are just fighting
some futile battle in a war that ended
some time ago which is some scholar
(brooding, reflecting through no fault
of his own way beyond his control)
strolling through the skulls & bones
of sand & stone; of fossils & facts
& folklore & can only in the long
run turn towards the source &
soul of the sad solemn shore

proof 51

And in the end all you see are the portosans
in the fog being transported on the back of
pickups to the carnival on the boardwalk

to know in fact the real hero or martyr
faced the world all alone and did it all
on his own and the exact opposite

in mind body spirit and soul
of everything they thought
and claimed he was...


151

In the end we become
something like warped
sun-scorched skeletons
of driftwood washed
up along the ocean

while upon second thought
that image doesn't really
sound all that depressing.

Joseph Reich is a social worker who lives with his wife and fourteen-year old son in the high-up mountains of Vermont.

He has been published in a wide variety of eclectic literary journals both here and abroad, been nominated seven times for The Pushcart Prize, and has written over twenty books of poetry and cultural studies.

He wholeheartedly agrees with Voltaire and Neil Young that man needs a maid, and still trying to make his way through *Finnegan's Wake*.

www.ingramcontent.com/pod-product-compliance
Lightning Source LLC
Chambersburg PA
CBHW030849170426
43193CB00009BA/547